Higher Reality Therapy

Nine Pathways to Inner Peace

First published by O Books, 2010
O Books is an imprint of John Hunt Publishing Ltd., The Bothy, Deershot Lodge, Park Lane, Ropley,
Hants, SO24 0BE, UK
office1@o-books.net
www.o-books.net

Distribution in:	South Africa
	Stephan Phillips (pty) Ltd
UK and Europe	Email: orders@stephanphillips.com
Orca Book Services	Tel: 27 21 4489839 Telefax: 27 21 4479879
orders@orcabookservices.co.uk	
Tel: 01202 665432 Fax: 01202 666219	Text copyright Anthony Falikowski 2008
Int. code (44)	
	Design: Stuart Davies
USA and Canada	
NBN	ISBN: 978 1 84694 257 0
custserv@nbnbooks.com	
Tel: 1 800 462 6420 Fax: 1 800 338 4550	All rights reserved. Except for brief quotations
	in critical articles or reviews, no part of this
Australia and New Zealand	book may be reproduced in any manner without
Brumby Books	prior written permission from the publishers.
sales@brumbybooks.com.au	
Tel: 61 3 9761 5535 Fax: 61 3 9761 7095	The rights of Anthony Falikowski as author have
	been asserted in accordance with the
Far East (offices in Singapore, Thailand,	Copyright, Designs and Patents Act 1988.
Hong Kong, Taiwan)	
Pansing Distribution Pte Ltd	
kemal@pansing.com	A CIP catalogue record for this book is available
Tel: 65 6319 9939 Fax: 65 6462 5761	from the British Library.

Printed by Digital Book Print

Higher Reality Therapy

Nine Pathways to Inner Peace

Anthony Falikowski

BOOKS

Winchester, UK
Washington, USA

CONTENTS

Dedicated With Love To My Family

Preface

Higher Reality Therapy: Nine Pathways to Inner Peace is an intelligent, but accessible book designed to relieve psychological suffering through new and innovative therapeutic applications of philosophy and metaphysical psychology. Entirely unique in its eclectic approach, this project constitutes a trip *back to the future.*

Higher Reality Therapy combines ancient and more recent philosophical traditions, both Eastern and Western, with modern psychology and newly emerging forms of spiritual practice. It offers a fruitful alternative to people who have not been helped by conventional psychotherapy. It also offers an alternative to those who feel alienated from organized religions, finding no respite for their troubled minds in dogma or ritual. People who are suffering from chronic or diffuse psychological malaise, but who are not yet ready to seek out professional treatment, will benefit by this book as well.

What is offered is a program of spiritual self-healing. At the level of personality, improved psychological hygiene is the objective. Taking steps to achieve greater peace of mind is the process.

Higher Reality Therapy comprises four parts. In the first part, the problem of psychological suffering is introduced. By questioning people's common sense assumptions about stimulus-response psychology, and by demonstrating how reality is constructed by the mind, the point is made what we are all largely architects of our own misery. That's the bad news. The good news is that by changing our way of thinking, we can change our perceptions of reality and hence our emotional and psychological well-being. We can also come to remember our true identities in spirit.

Part one explains how our faulty ways of seeing life evolved as we all became separated from our Essential Being – what some call the Higher Self. It is by remembering our true identities, by becoming more aware of our Essence that we heal ourselves. Awareness is curative.

In part two of the book, we explore nine different ways in which people become psychologically separated from their essential nature in early childhood experiences. Each way develops into an alternative worldview which eventually crystallizes into a specific character type. These types are given numbers as well as names for ease of identification (e.g., Type Eight: The Powerful Maverick). Each character type is described in terms of how *"lost essence"* occurred, what *worldviews and compensating ego strategies* developed in response to lost essence, what the *healthy and unhealthy manifestations* of each type are, and what *shadow elements* need to be dealt with. Concluding the discussions for each of the types is a section entitled, *Therapeutic Recommendations for Promoting Psychological Hygiene and Finding Inner Peace.* To help readers know which recommendations are most appropriate for them, a *Character Type Self-Diagnostic* is provided in the Appendix for them to complete. Reading the more detailed character type descriptions in the chapters will help to verify anyone's type.

In part three, a number of general over-arching therapeutic recommendations are provided for all of the types. It is in this section that the value of understanding and forgiveness is under-scored. By coming to recognize how we all fall prey to the defensive distortions of the ego-personality in our efforts to cope with psychological suffering, it becomes easier to see ourselves in others. As we do, we learn to forgive them. In the process, we are then better able to forgive ourselves. Ideas in this section are largely inspired by *A Course in Miracles.*

In part four of the book, the major advantages of *Higher Reality Therapy* come to light. Philosophical and psycho-spiritual insights drawn from the preceding character analyses are used to point out the limitations of William Glasser's conventional Reality Therapy, a therapeutic modality now used by 75,000 practitioners worldwide. It is shown how Glasser's theory and practice of psychotherapy are little more than a reflection of his own Type Eight psychological preferences. What becomes apparent is that my own innovative approach allows for breadth, depth, and spiritual growth in ways that conventional Reality Therapy simply doesn't – and in fact can't – given its assumptions. What also becomes apparent is that conventional Reality Therapy's lack of spiritual insight causes therapists using it to perpetuate the very problems they seek to alleviate in their clients – which is clearly a matter of extremely serious concern.

If you are a therapist interested in the spiritual dimensions of life, someone looking for greater psychological insight to promote better psychological-hygiene, a person on a spiritual quest, or just an individual striving to reduce stress and anxiety for greater peace of mind, then *Higher Reality Therapy* is for you.

By way of closing here, I wish to acknowledge all those people whose valued ideas and teachings contributed to the development of this book. Over the years, I have attended many workshops, seminars and conference sessions provided by enneagram teachers such as Don Riso, Russ Hudson, Jerry Wagner, and Helen Palmer. They all have enlightened me on ego function and spiritual psychodynamics. Their influence on my work is evident throughout this book. Sandra Maitri, Claudio Naranjo, A.H. Almaas, and Richard Rohr are other enneagram teachers from whose works I've also benefited.

With respect to the other major inspiration for this book, Ken

Wapnick at The Foundation for Inner Peace in Temecula, California has made *A Course in Miracles* understandable and accessible to me. My past twenty year study of *The Course* would have been far less productive without insights provided by Ken in his own books, seminars and instructional materials. He is a gifted teacher and for his contributions I am truly grateful.

I also wish to thank the countless people who have shown interest in my unorthodox and rather unusual intellectual pursuits, especially my students and academic colleagues at Sheridan College. Observing the transformational benefits they have derived from ideas and insights discussed in this book tells me I'm on the right track.

Of course, there's no way to personally thank intellectual immortals like Freud, Jung, Nietzsche, Sartre, Piaget, Kant, Plato, Socrates, Buddha, Chuang Tzu, the Stoics, the Epicureans, and all the spiritual mystics who have played a role in my thinking and in the writing of this book. Inclusion of their genius will have to suffice as an expression of my gratitude.

It's my pleasure to be their messenger boy!

A.F.

Part One

INTRODUCTION

THERAPEUTIC PHILOSOPHY FOR THE TROUBLED MIND

Vain is the word of the philosopher which does not heal any suffering of man.
Epicurus

Suffering I teach - and the way out of suffering.
The Buddha

Centuries ago the venerable Buddha concluded that life is suffering. We suffer as we age and decay. We suffer with illness. We suffer in the process of death and dying and we suffer because of our attachments to people and things in the world. We constantly worry over the possibility that what we want, or seemingly need so desperately, will be unavailable or lost to us.

We experience anxiety over the impermanence of things and thus, over the possibility that what we have achieved will be short-lived or forgotten.

Still further, we are fearful that we will be separated from those things which make life worth living and without which there's no point in continuing on. And if not fearful about the possibility of future separation, we often experience unpleasantness in the present moment. We are frequently bored and frustrated or angry and outraged at the world.

Though surely we all have our moments of happiness, joy, and excitement in our lives, there is always the sub-conscious

5

realization that the good times cannot last forever. Mental pain is just around the corner and we know it.

Now, if the suffering addressed by the Buddha were pathological, we might take some solace in the notion that those of us in psychological pain could simply visit a mental health practitioner and receive counseling. Perhaps a little pharmaceutical pick-me-up like Prozac could get us through the difficult times. The problem is that suffering is not an occasional occurrence, but a large part of the human condition. It is not an exceptional dysfunction but for most of us an ever enduring state of mind.

The good news from Buddha is that he claims to have discovered the source of this suffering. It stems from craving. He argues that what we need to do is stop this craving by breaking our attachments to worldly possessions. By doing so we could alleviate much of our self-caused anguish. To the extent that this is true, Buddhism is not only a religion, but also a form of therapeutic philosophy for the suffering soul. Not only does Buddhism attempt to diagnose the central problem of the human condition and identify the problem's source; it also offers a course of treatment to heal the troubled mind.

This treatment is found in the Noble Eightfold Path whereby one works to achieve wisdom, moral correctness, and mental concentration.

Since the life and times of Buddha, many Western philosophers have also addressed the problem of human suffering. Especially impressive are the writings of the ancient Stoics such as Marcus Aurelius, Epictetus, and Seneca. In line with Buddha's admonition that we should not cling to transitory objects, Marcus Aurelius advocates a similar notion of psychological detachment.

In his *Meditations* he insisted that: "*...things do not touch the soul, for they are external and remain immovable; but our perturbations come only from the opinion which is within.*" He believed, like Buddha, that the mind could be retrained to think in ways that could greatly reduce our psychological disturbances.

Still more recently, existential thinkers such as Søren Kierkegaard, Rollo, May and Viktor Frankl have tried to understand and deal with psychological issues of anxiety, meaninglessness, and guilt. Frankl, for instance, contends that meaning can be found in any circumstances, indeed in *all* circumstances, no matter how difficult, no matter how painful, and regardless of how challenging.

In 1981, Gerd. B. Achenbach founded the German Association for Philosophical Practice. He has made efforts to help people sort out the difficulties in their life predicaments. In New York City, Lou Marinoff has established the American Philosophical Practitioner's Association which offers philosophers training in philosophical counseling and consultation. More and more, philosophers are descending from the ivory towers to help people deal with their moral and existential dilemmas by applying ancient wisdom to modern life, rationality to the problems of living.

Inspired by present day philosophical practitioners, and all those ancient thinkers who have brought us messages of hope throughout history, I plan to present a discussion that is both therapeutic and existential. I will present you with a transformational, psycho-spiritual philosophy constituting a form of *higher reality therapy*, understood in a very broad sense.

My ultimate aim is to help you find greater peace of mind in philosophical wisdom. This is not my wisdom, but the accumulated wisdom of the ages. The outcomes to be achieved are not by my design, but are the proven centuries-old results of incorporating philosophical insights into everyday life. My humble task is simply to act as the messenger boy for some of the intellectual immortals who have come before. By synthesizing their insightful ideas and by helping you to integrate them into your own life, I will enable you to find direction and hope in a

7

world filled with insanity and despair. My intention is to accompany you down a path where you can expect to find greater psychological freedom from anxiety and a release from the kind of *troubled mind* which has enslaved and tortured you up until now, the troubled mind that prompted you to pick up this book in the first place.

My claim that philosophical wisdom can be psychologically therapeutic is not without foundation. I know from personal experience that the sweet wisdom of philosophy has had positive transformational consequences for me both spiritually and psychologically. Also, for close to three decades I have had the privilege of teaching philosophy to thousands of college students, countless many of whom have shared with me the personal benefits of seeking wisdom, understanding, and truth. It has been their reactions and expressed desire for more that gives me confidence that philosophy heals or at least ministers in worthwhile ways to the existential pains of living.

History reveals the benefits of applying philosophical wisdom to everyday life. Alexander the Great sought the philosophical counsel of Aristotle to help him with his decision-making. Queen Christina of Sweden enlisted the services of René Descartes as a personal tutor, while the Earl of Shaftesbury called upon philosopher John Locke for advice. So, not only my personal and professional experience, but historical record as well bears out the fact that philosophy has a special directive and illuminating function in the *Sturm und Drang* of day to day reality. May it serve that function in a concrete and meaningful way for you.

In the pages that follow, we will first examine the ontological status of things that psychologically upset you. So often we see our personal frustrations, worries, fears, and negative emotions such as anger as a response to people and events in the external world. The idea that there exists a cause-and-effect relationship between a situation or event, say, and the "inevitable" emotional reaction it produces will be challenged. Misguided thinking on this point is what often causes people to feel like helpless victims. If my problems originate in the external world and I have no control over that world, then it would appear that I am inevitably destined to suffer. Insights to follow will question such thinking and further feelings of personal empowerment. Anticipate with gladness how the restrictive chains of *victimhood* will soon be cut allowing you greater freedom and possibility in your life.

After coming to see that there exists an alternative to what common sense stimulus-response psychology can explain, we will begin to explore the numerous misguided and irrational thought systems that often serve to make people architects of their own misery. You see, unhappiness is to a large extent an inside job, not solely the product of external forces. People of different personality types have their own perverse systems of existential logic which display an internal coherence and consistency, perhaps, but which in the end inevitably undermine psychological health.

In the detailed philosophical psychoanalysis which will be provided shortly, we will uncover patterns of thinking and psychological worldviews which are dysfunctional and a serious threat to emotional health and well-being. In the process of this revelation, you will come to see how philosophy, and a deeply penetrating analysis of the psychologistics of the human mind, can indeed serve a hygienic function. What we are engaging in here is a higher reality therapy.

Philosophy ministers to the human spirit. In matters of mind, it brings peace where there was conflict, truth where illusion once reigned. Illusion, like conflict, leaves us in psychological bondage; the truth sets us free. Thus, our aim is to remove illusion and mis-perception in our lives. This will bring a greater degree of peace. While we may never find ultimate Truth, we can at least work toward removing some of the obstacles that stand in the way of its achievement.

A point of clarification is probably in order here for the benefit of anyone who is a mental health practitioner or is otherwise aware of psychological counseling methods. What is being proposed in this book is not conventional *Reality Therapy*, the technique originally developed by William Glasser in 1965 and now based on a what he calls "Choice Theory" psychology. What's to follow is also not just an improvement or further development of the same process. In conventional Reality Therapy, Glasser first has clients identify their wants. Then he has them describe the things they do, say, and feel physically and emotionally in relation to those wants. Third, he facilitates client evaluations of their total behavior. He encourages them to ask whether their current actions are helping or hindering them in terms of satisfying their stated wants. If their current behavior is not helping, he gets them to plan for success by engaging in alternative courses of action. For Glasser, by getting what you want, basic human needs are met. These basic needs include: survival, power, fun, freedom, care and belonging. According to Glasser, to the degree that one's basic needs are met, to the same extent one is in effective control of one's life.

The ultimate aim of Reality Therapy is therefore to help people change and take more responsible, effective control of their lives by doing those things that will enable them to satisfy their basic needs. In a nutshell, this is the process of conventional Reality Therapy.

Now, I fully agree with Glasser about responsible living. However, many of the basic philosophical assumptions providing the foundation for conventional Reality Therapy will be indirectly challenged and criticized in what follows. Specifics regarding my theoretical concerns with Glasser's model, and his employment of psychotherapeutic techniques, will be discussed more directly at the end of the book where I distinguish in greater detail the differences between an emerging field of philosophical counseling, of which Higher Reality Therapy forms a part, and traditional psychotherapy.

This discussion will probably have greater interest for readers in the academic and professional communities than for the layperson – hence its positioning at the end. For now, my aim is not to engage in any debate of methodologies or fine theoretical distinctions, but to promote psycho-hygiene and to pre-empt the need for professional psychological intervention in the first place.

As the saying goes, an ounce of prevention is worth a pound of cure.

Well, if *Higher Reality Therapy* is not an action-based technique designed to get your basic needs met, then what is it about? In answer, it can be said that Higher Reality Therapy entails a kind of philosophical psychoanalysis required to achieve one of its primary goals, namely, psychological liberation. More than just a rational inspection and evaluation of one's overt behavior, it also involves a close inspection of the internal workings of our mind; and still further, a reconsideration of our basic sense of self.

This sort of depth analysis is foreign to choice theory psychology. In ways to be illustrated later, it also calls into question the unconditional value of want satisfaction in the first place.

Suppose, for example, that what you want is unethical or what you want is precisely that which would hurt you most, but you and your therapist don't realize it. And further suppose, hypothetically, that who you *really* are has nothing to do with your self-concept.

Let's say that your self-perception is a delusion – how unfortunate. Could you imagine if your wants and self-esteem were based on a delusory self-definition, that what you took pride in didn't exist or at least was a distortion of what you truly are? Now just imagine that this delusion is not hypothetical, but real; that you really do *not* know who you are, but *are* deceived about your true identity. Depending on where you are in your journey of life, you may indeed be deluded. You may seriously require some form of spiritual psychotherapy to uncover the truth about yourself.

It's time to take Socrates seriously and "Know thyself." In the pages to come you will be invited to reexamine the concept of self on which you base your life. You may be surprised to find out that you are not what or who you consider yourself to be.

Equally illuminating will be the realization that you are seldom upset for the reasons you think and that what you want is sometimes exactly what you don't need – that what you want is precisely what would hurt you the most, but like an infant child, you don't know it.

Seek not your Self in symbols. There can be no concept that can stand for what you are.
A Course in Miracles

Before we begin full-tilt, a preliminary caution is in order here. The journey to philosophical enlightenment is not always an easy road. Unpleasant revelations must sometimes be accepted. Strongly held assumptions may have to be altered or completely abandoned. Perhaps commitments are forced to change, while perceptions of reality may have to be consciously reconstructed to conform to new values and beliefs.

The existential rebirth that philosophical wisdom offers is not without pain, much like childbirth itself. On a positive note, many mothers who have experienced the pain of childbirth, find joy in the wonder that new life brings. Joy and wonder are what you, the philosophical newborn, can expect to find at the moment of rebirth. The warm glow is peace of mind.

Writing on the necessity of dealing with the dark side of ourselves before finding peace, the ancient Chinese philosopher Chuang Tzu tells us the following story:

> There was a man
> who was so disturbed
> by the sight of his own shadow
> and so displeased with his own footsteps
> that he determined to get rid of both.
> The method he hit upon was to run away from them.
> So he got up and ran.
> But every time he put his foot down
> there was another step,
> while his shadow kept up with him
> without the slightest difficulty.
> He attributed his failure
> to the fact that he was not running fast enough.
> So he ran faster and faster, without stopping,
> until he finally dropped dead.
> He failed to realize that if he merely stepped into the shade,
> his shadow would vanish,
> and if he sat down and stayed still, there would be no more
>   footsteps.[1]

Unfortunately, too many of us are satisfied with the illusions of the ego. We have created selves that we think we can improve with just a few minor adjustments - and so we run. We believe that with a few character-chiropractic manipulations we can relieve our mental pain, become psychologically realigned and happy. We're simply too invested in ourselves to go beyond that. One could call this willful blindness – a refusal to see how misguided and deluded we are.

If we are mistaken about who we really are and what is wrong at the core of our being, no minor personality adjustment will suffice. What is called for is radical psychic surgery. Such a serious measure will allow for the possibility of a new way of being in the world. It's worth a try, isn't it? The old ways certainly have not worked. Your life is living testimony to this fact.

We move about the earth with unprecedented speed, but we do not know, and have not thought, where we are going, or whether we shall find any happiness there for our harassed souls.
Will Durant

CHAPTER ONE

THE MISTAKES OF COMMON-SENSE PSYCHOLOGY

*Men are disturbed not by things, but by the view which
they take of them.*
Epictetus

*You have paid very dearly for your illusions and nothing
you have paid for brought you peace.*
A Course in Miracles

Before we begin to unmask our true identities, it is first necessary
to examine common-sense psychology and demonstrate how it
contributes to our misperceptions about ourselves and the
world. Once we do that, we will explore the essence of human
nature or the nature of the Higher Self. From there, we will be
also able to better appreciate the various illusions of the Lower
Ego-Self. It should prove sadly amusing to see how creative
human beings can be in their distortions of reality.

In our efforts to uncover the basic mistakes of common-sense
psychology, let us first ponder for a moment the kinds of things
people often say to one another in conversation. No doubt
you've heard this one: "My boss drives me crazy." Maybe it's
your spouse who is driving you insane. Perhaps it's your
children. Do you ever become angry and frustrated when
commuting to and from your place of employment? Have you
ever screamed at someone from the security of your car
something like: "Idiot! Where did you get your license? In a

Cracker Jack box?" In other words, have you been a "victim" of road rage? Does the traffic "make" you go ballistic? Do people "make" you mad? If not, maybe you've been stressed over an impending deadline, saying something like: "God, I hate it when people make such unreasonable demands!" Do external expectations placed upon you "make" you upset, worried or otherwise disturbed? Have you ever said sulkily: "I'm so depressed." Did your failure to get the desired grade, job or promotion "lead" to your depression?

If you answered, "Yes" to any of these questions, then you have implicitly accepted a stimulus-response model of psychology with respect to your emotional state. More than likely you believe that other people, things, and events serve as the causal factors which produce your feelings. This must be the case. After all, you wouldn't willingly choose to drive yourself mad, would you? No rational person would want to do this.

The stimulus-response model is not limited to negative emotions as the examples above might suggest. It can just as easily be used to explain positive affect as well. You might be happy as a "result" of the attractive person in the room smiling at you, thinking he or she "made" you feel this way. You might jump for joy "in response to" the news that you just won the lottery. Or you could get excited "because" your favorite team just made the play-offs. Their victory "gave rise" to the excitement you feel.

Sometimes, the stimulus-response model is presupposed in our explanations to others when we try to account for why we are, the way we are. We might say, for example: "I act this way because this is how I was raised." or "I believe this because this is what I was taught." In other words, our early childhood upbringing "made" us or "caused" us to be who we are today. We thereby assume we are simply "products" of our environment. Whatever values, ideals or beliefs we have, someone else put them there. Such thinking is consistent with the writings of philosopher John Locke, who used the notion of a blank slate or *tabula rasa* to describe the nature of human mind at birth.

He wrote:

> Let us then suppose the mind to be as we say, white paper, void of all characters, without any ideas: How comes it to be furnished? Whence comes it by that vast store which the busy and boundless fancy of man has painted on it with an almost endless variety? Whence has it all the *materials* of reason and knowledge? To this I answer, in one word, from *experience*. In that all our knowledge is founded; and from that it ultimately derives itself.[1]

Picking up on Locke's notion that the mind is a *tabula rasa* at birth, J.B.Watson (1878-1958), a founding father of contemporary behavioristic psychology further postulated that human beings are simply a product of their environment, and that their behavior is nothing more than a product of conditioning.

To underscore the notion that the external world shapes and moulds us to become who we are he writes the following:

> Give me a dozen healthy infants, well-formed, and my own specified world to bring them up in and I'll guarantee to take any one at random and train him to become any kind of specialist I might select – doctor, lawyer, artist, merchant-chief, and yes even beggar-man and thief, regardless of his talents, penchants, abilities, vocations, and race of his ancestors.[2]

There's a certain perverse comfort from buying into the empiricist account of mind and human behavior. This comfort is purchased at the expense of freedom, however. If I'm just a passive organism, completely a product of the environment, then

I cannot reasonably be held responsible for my actions. In fact, criminals often plead for lesser sentences given their unfortunate or otherwise tragic childhood circumstances. Since the criminal could not control those circumstances and because it's assumed that these circumstances somehow led to the crime in question, or at least were a contributing causal determinant, then upbringing should constitute a mitigating factor in the minds of those doling out the punishment.

While this form of reasoning has some *prima facie* cogency, the force of the argument evaporates when we consider that not everyone from exactly the same set of circumstances engages in the same kinds of social behavior or even criminal behaviors.

For example, two children may come from the same broken home. One child swears never to get married in order to avoid the grief of his parents and the toll exacted on the children at home. By contrast, the other child vows to marry as soon as possible in order to have some semblance of a normal life with happy parent-child relations. Here we have two children, from the same broken home, but with different emotional and behavioral outcomes. One child is embittered; the other is optimistic. The first child might say their attitudes toward marriage were formed in childhood. The second child might say the same; yet, the mind-sets and resulting behaviors would be opposite.

Ultimately, what each child does in this case turns out in the end to be a matter of free choice. In a moment we'll come to understand how this is possible. No one stimulus circumstance (e.g., a broken home) necessarily leads to any one behavioral or emotional response (e.g., embittered bachelorhood or vengeful criminality). Other factors come into play.

Taken to the extreme, attempted escapes from responsibility have led to heinous crimes. In 2007, at Virginia Tech University in the United States, Cho Seung-Hui killed 32 students and accepted no blame for his actions before taking his own life. As he pointed out in a self-created video, others were to blame. "They were forcing" him to do what had to be done. It was "their" fault. Others "made" him do what he did. He was simply a victim of circumstance. His actual words were: *You forced me into a corner and gave me only one option. The decision was yours.*

Clearly, attempted escapes from responsibility, coupled with paranoid delusional thinking, make for a lethal and insane combination. Though most people are not delusional in any severely dysfunctional paranoid way, efforts to escape account-ability for one's actions still often lead to serious and sometimes devastating consequences in people's personal lives.

At a bare minimum, refusals to accept personal responsibility are often perceived as signs of immaturity. Furthermore, as we often witness, human communications often degenerate into screaming matches of blame and recrimination. No sense of well-being ever came from playing the blame-game.

When individuals are unable to accept responsibility at the personal level, they often carry over that tendency into their broader dealings with people, whether those dealings be familial, institutional, corporate, governmental or international. This tendency can have catastrophic global consequences which, in the end, are a product of personal failings. For instance, a failure by political leaders to accept responsibility probably never achieved peaceful resolution of any international conflict. In the Middle East conflict, we witness how revenge has been elevated to the level of virtue; the enemy is almost always to blame, whether it be Iran, Iraq, Israel, Al-Qaeda, the Palestinians, England or the United States. Frequent attacks on either side of the conflict must be made in the name of self-defense. Such attacks may cause "collateral damage" (a euphemism for killing women and children non-combatants) but as some would argue, it is unfortunately a necessary price to pay when one protecting oneself or one's interests. Such thinking begs the question whether fear and nationalistic paranoia have transmuted into global insanity. Innocent women and children must be killed in the national interest, our leaders tell us.

There's an eerie parallel, I suggest, between the murderous paranoid schizophrenia of Cho Seung-Hui and the rationalized deliberate killing of innocents in the name of freedom and democracy, or even worse, in the name of God, Allah, or the State. I wonder whether God would sanction such killing? Does killing in the name of God really make one a hero, martyr or saint, or does it simply reflect the thinking of a delusional murderer? Many in the West mock the suicide bomber in the Middle East who is "brainwashed" into thinking that by killing himself and innocent others, he will guarantee himself a seat in heaven. Relatively lesser concern is voiced when a U.S. president views himself as a defender of the faith and agent for God's work on earth.

To the neutral observer, there appears to be a gross inconsistency in perceptions of faith-based killing. For now, let's say God only knows. What does seem certain is that blaming your enemy and making efforts to kill that enemy are not likely to create enduring peaceful results. If individuals won't accept responsibility at a personal level, it's unlikely that they will at a national or international level. A half-century of war in the Middle East proves my point. For the moment, however, let's leave any discussion of global psychotherapy necessary for world peace until another time. Here, we are preoccupied with our slightly more modest goal of existential enlightenment! Before we start with changing the hearts and minds of the world, we'll work on changing our own first.

He who cannot change the fabric of his thought will never be able to change reality.
Anwar Sadat, Assassinated President of Egypt

I mentioned earlier that personal escapes from responsibility are purchased at the expense of freedom. The sales transaction cannot actually go through, however. As Jean-Paul Sartre, the philosopher who coined the term, "existentialism" points out, we are all *condemned to be free*.

There are no excuses to be made. Whatever you think, feel, or do is a matter of choice – your choice.

Still not convinced? Still adamant that others are responsible for making you mad, glad or sad? Then why is it that a rude insult emotionally devastates one person, but leaves another untouched? It is not the insult *per se* that determines the result, but the value and meaning that someone attaches to it. If an insult originates in a person for whom you have the greatest admiration and respect, then you are quite likely to be hurt by it. By contrast, if it comes from someone you deem to be a loser, and a person for whom you have only condescending disdain, then you are left untouched, repeating in your mind the child's refrain: *Sticks and stones can break my bones, but words will never hurt me!*

In this reaction, you implicitly recognize that your emotional response to the insult is in your command, not the verbal attacker's. The value you place on the insult determines your response. The value judgment is a matter of choice. Because people place different values on the same stimulus events (e.g., insults), no one stimulus event can be said to cause the emotional or psychological response to it. Thus, to blame another for your feelings is an attempted escape from freedom – one which in the end is futile.

Human beings are psychologically free whether they like it or not. Nobody else is to blame for how we feel. Between any stimulus and response is the individual who interprets and evaluates the comment, thing, event or situation, etc., that presents itself. The individual doing the interpreting is you.

21

It is sometimes extremely difficult to accept ownership for our feelings, especially when others have done terrible things to us. Let's suppose, heaven forbid, that you are a victim of child abuse, either physical or sexual. And let's say you are enraged at the perpetrator of the abuse. Some would say that you are justifiably angry at your abuser and that it's no wonder you feel the way you do; the abuser has emotionally scarred you for life, or so some would believe. It's true that this line of thinking very probably represents the norm and would seem to be reasonable, given the circumstances. However, the anger and emotional scarring is still not a causally necessary outcome of the abuse.

Terrible events in our lives can be overcome by granting pardon to those who would hurt us. For instance, Pope John Paul II harbored no anger or vengefulness, but sought understanding when he went to the jail cell of his would-be assassin to let him know that he was forgiven for attempting to take the Pontiff's life. He didn't want his assassin to live in any sort of emotional pain.

No doubt the best religious illustration of healing pardon is Jesus of Nazareth. Like Socrates, Jesus was charged with a crime for his teachings - in this case promoting the gospel of love. For his efforts, Jesus was condemned to die. Was he angry with his accusers? Did he wish them damned to hell for unjustifiably crucifying him? We know from history that the answer to these questions is No. We can imagine Jesus looking up into the heavens when he said in his last dying breadths, *Father, forgive them; for they know not what they do.* The chosen emotional response of a man being wrongly accused and condemned to death was compassion and love. On behalf of those who tortured and killed him, he advocated that they be pardoned. By comparison to this dramatic example, what petty injustice, personal insult, or violent confrontation "justifies" your angry vengefulness? Does finding closure mean getting payback? Is

22

much of your day spent plotting revenge in your imagination? Is hurting someone in return the road to peace of mind? Would Jesus agree? If not, perhaps it's time to choose again the next time you perceive yourself to be victimized.

Experiment with forgiveness and see what happens; it may be the key to the peace of mind which until now has eluded you. You can, of course, choose to remain justifiably angry for the rest of your life. Many people do. Or, you can choose to feel the healing calm which comes by letting go of recently earned, or not yet forgotten ancient hatreds. The choice you make in response to the ill-will directed at you will have lasting consequences - many of them for you. Be careful to make the correct decision. Your psychological health depends on it. But above all, recognize that how you feel is ultimately a freely determined choice which hinges on how you wish to interpret the events in your life. Decisions made in your mind will control the kind of life you will find.

If you are pained by any external thing, it is not the thing that disturbs you, but your judgment about it. And, it is in your power to wipe out this judgment now.

Marcus Aurelius,
Roman Stoic philosopher

Love your enemies, bless them that curse you, do good to them that hate you, and pray for them that use and persecute you.

Jesus of Nazareth

One contemporary psychological counseling technique which picks up on the notions of 'free choice' and 'interpretation' is Albert Ellis's Rational-Emotive Behavior Therapy. Ellis would agree with the existentialist that people can exercise significant control over their emotional experiences, that they are largely responsible for how they feel. He also accepts the stoic notion that interpretations of negative life-events and circumstances play a major role in determining whether or not we are in any way stressed or pained. Like Marcus Aurelius, Ellis takes the position that "judgment" comes between what happens to us and how we respond emotionally and ultimately, behaviorally.

By consciously changing our judgments, then, we can thereby alter the responses to external stimuli over which we may or may not have control. Emotional and behavioral reactions are not necessarily automatic. We are not like Pavlovian dogs simply reacting to bells and other stimuli which impinge upon us. For example, we are not conditioned or determined to pick up the phone every time it rings. If we judge that we are too busy, then we'll let the call go to our voice messaging service. Or, if our call display function indicates who the caller is, we may judge the call as unimportant and thus decide not to take it. Late at night, we may stop for red traffic-lights out of habit, even when no other traffic is around. This is not because we are forced to do so by way of conditioning. Had we been in a rush to get to the hospital, we might have decided to run the red light, judging it was more important to get medical attention than to obey a traffic law, especially when nobody else besides ourselves would be affected either way by our violating it.

Interpretations determine responses, not stimuli alone. To illustrate this point, Ellis provides us with what he dubs the 'A-B-C Model'. He uses it to explain emotional responses to what some people would take to be stressful events. In the figures that follow, you can see how common sense stimulus-response thinking about stress differs from the A-B-C Model which recognizes the important role played by cognitive appraisal.

In Ellis's model, the "A" stands for activating event. Think of it as the stimulus, that which is *potentially* stressful, say. The "B" represents the belief about the activating event. Now depending on what beliefs are attached to "A" different consequences are possible. Obviously, "C" is used to indicate the consequence or response to the activating event. Whatever "C" outcome we experience is influenced by our beliefs about what just happened, what was just said, and so on. Thus, by changing our beliefs, we can change our emotions. By changing our emotions, and thinking differently about our life circumstances, we can more easily alter our behaviors.

In this way, my thoughts, emotions and behaviors are inextricably linked, holistically combined, and ultimately mine. They are not everyone else's fault, rather, they are my personal responsibility. You might be reluctant to accept this burden of responsibility; but with it comes freedom. With this one decision to own your feelings, pilgrim, you can be free – free at last! It's really that simple.

The problem is that simplicity is difficult for twisted minds! What logical contortions will you need to continuously rationalize your behavior as other people's fault? Will such false testimony ever truly prove your innocence providing the peace of mind you so desperately seek?

Rest now, finally realizing that your feelings and attitudes belong to you. What happens may not be what you want, indeed what happens may even be horrific, but how you choose to respond is entirely within your control. In this knowledge, there is self-empowerment. In this insight is discovered the stoic dignity of self-possession. Be assured that greater calm can now accompany you in your daily travels. You walk free, responsible and dignified. Out of the shadows of victimhood, you are rescued and comforted by the recognition that *external things touch not the soul, not in the slightest degree.*

Men are not disturbed by things, but by the view they take of them.
   Epictetus

Figure 1
Common Sense Stimulus - Response Model of Human Psychology

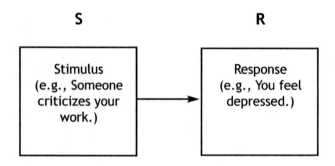

Figure 2
Albert Ellis' A-B-C Model of Emotional Response to Stimulus-Stressor

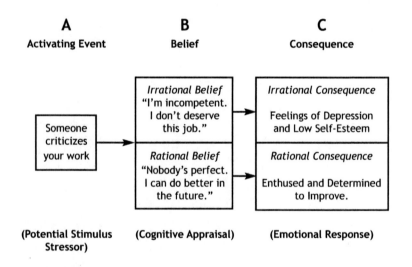

So far, we have learned that the first basic mistake of common-sense psychology revolves around the assumption that stimulus events cause feelings or behaviors in some kind of simple, direct linear fashion. We have seen that, in truth, there's an intermediary cognitive element which comes between – an element which determines what, if any, effect a particular stimulus will have. Different beliefs and value judgments will lead to different responses. Insofar as people ultimately have the ability to choose their own values, much more is self-determined than is generally assumed. We're in more control than unreflective awareness would have us believe.

A second problem with common-sense psychology stems from questionable assumptions regarding the stimulus itself. These assumptions deal with the nature of the "stimulus" or "stimulus events" that we perceive in the external world.

To illustrate what is meant here: Let's suppose that a young man named Lance is the captain of the high school football team. He is rich, good looking, obviously athletic, and admired by all the girls in the school. Virtually every female student in the school would die for a chance to date Lance. There could be no greater pleasure than to be seen with the Captain in his shiny Porsche driving down Main Street on the way to the beach. Now, one day early in September, a new girl to the school, Becky, enters Math class. She is drop-dead gorgeous, dressed to kill, and immediately captures Lance's attention. She takes up her position at the back of the class and for days doesn't speak a word to anyone, including Lance. She promptly arrives just moments before class is scheduled to start and leaves the second it ends. More than once she has brushed by Lance in her comings and goings without a word or even the slightest glance at him. It's as if Lance does not exist. She appears to completely ignore him. Lance, of course, is not accustomed to such treatment. No girl has ever just ignored him the way Becky has. Lance is "Mr Popular" and he knows it. So what's up with Becky?

Finally, Lance concludes that she is nothing more than a condescending stuck-up bitch who ticks him off. *"What's her problem?"* he asks himself. One evening, while having dinner with his family, Lance finds himself in a foul mood. When asked by his parents "What's wrong?" he responds by saying that he was brushed off by a girl who thinks she's too good for him. He continues by complaining how she upset him with her aloof and condescending behavior.

Now in this case, we have a stimulus event, as it were: Becky's condescending and aloof behavior. We also have the response: Lance's upset and foul mood. With this example, it would seem that common-sense psychology is able to clearly explain Lance's negative emotions. Becky's behavior served as the stimulus that "caused" the upset emotional response.

The problem is that the "stimulus-event" as perceived by Lance, does not actually exist in reality and never did. There was, in fact, no condescending and aloof behavior whatsoever. That was all in Lance's mind. You see, before arriving, Becky lived her entire life on an isolated farm miles away from the smallest town. Moving as she just did to a large town to attend high school was like going off to New York City to live alone, both friendless and afraid. In efforts to cope with her anxiety about starting out in a new school, Becky went to a number of exclusive boutiques to buy some expensive big city clothes. She didn't want to stick out as a country bumpkin. She believed that if she dressed well, she wouldn't be noticed. Further, because of her country accent, she was afraid to speak for fear of being embarrassed among her peers. The selected strategy to mask her background, as well as her fearful shyness, was to hide out at the back of the class. In light of this, it is clear that Lance responded to what was *not* there. The behavior of the "condescending stuck-up bitch" was nothing more than an attempt by a shy and fearful young women to fit into a new and terrifying situation.

Hence Lance totally misread the situation and Becky's intentions. He responded to a phantom stimulus, one of his own making. The whole experience of Becky was little more than a self-created negative hallucination stemming from Lance's own insecurities about himself.

The example of Becky and Lance points to something extremely important, namely that the people, events and situations we perceive in the external world are constructed by us, the knowing subject, the individual having the perception. "Stimulus-objects" do not have an entirely independent existence. They are not simply "out there" on their own. They are not ontologically independent.

Whatever Becky became, she became as an object of knowledge for Lance. Lance thought he knew what she was like. The person he saw and the person he knew, however, clearly had something to do with the involvement of his own active mind. As we've shown in our example, Lance made Becky into something she clearly was not. Of course, Becky did indeed present Lance with the withdrawn silence, the fancy clothes, the prompt departures, the diverted eyes, and so on. It was Lance, however, who configured these stimulus variables and constructed them into his own object of scorn.

This was done in Lance's cognitive unconscious. Lance, and people generally, construct reality so quickly and automatically that the entire process of object construction goes unnoticed. Some socialites who value friendship, for instance, could have taken the same stimulus variables as Lance and constructed a loner in their minds. Still other people could have been impressed or intimidated by Becky's quiet demeanor, seeing her as a beautiful sex-object or a scary person who is not-to-be-messed-with.

What Lance needs to understand is that he is responding to a false reality of his own making. When he looks at Becky, he sees not her, but his own insecurities projected outwardly. As will be explained and illustrated more later on, *perception is projection*, a projection of one's state of mind on what appears to be an independent world. To change one's mind is therefore to change the world as one experiences it. And you thought changing the world was impossible!

You maker of a world that is not so, take rest and comfort in another world where peace abides.

A Course in Miracles

The idea that the mind helps in the construction of reality and in the formation of objects of knowledge is one that is central to Immanuel Kant's epistemology. Kant was a Prussian philosopher who lived from 1724-1804. He is regarded by many to be the most important thinker in the Western Intellectual Tradition after Plato and Aristotle. On the basis of his own rational investigations, he concluded that the empiricists were wrong. Objects perceived in the external world do not just imprint themselves, as fully constituted objects, on the blank slate of the human mind. He also took exception with the notion that knowledge of the world is somehow innate, totally independent of experience.

This position was too extreme on the opposite side of empiricism. What Kant concluded is that: *There can be no doubt that all our knowledge begins with experience...But though all our knowledge begins with experience, it does not follow that it all arises out of experience.*[3]

The knowing subject brings to any experience structural elements of perception and categories of understanding which enable the knowing subject to form objects of knowledge. So, a potato chip for instance, is simply not all out there as an object of experience. Its sensory properties – crispy, thin, salty, yellow and greasy – are combined by the faculties of sensibility and understanding to make what becomes a fully constituted potato chip. The mind gives unity and substance to it. We are able to see a potato chip, as a potato chip, not as a scattered array of sensations.

Likewise, going back to Becky and Lance for a moment, Becky presented a number of sensory stimuli to Lance on the occasion of his experience of her. Remember her clothes, diverted eyes, and so on. How these stimuli were arranged, assembled, interpreted and unified, however, came from Lance's mind. He brought something to this occasion of his own experience. He contributed something to the construction of her as an object of scorn. Thus, Lance's reality involved an interaction of elements; a process of synthesis and unification. Quite likely Lance brought to his experience of Becky past impressions and interactions with well-dressed, beautiful women who either didn't notice him or deliberately ignored him. It is quite possible that Lance interpreted Becky's actions by including them under what he already knew about "stuck-up bitches" from past experience. This concept or idea represents a form of understanding which Lances apparently now uses to make sense of the world.

This underscores the notion again that the world is not simply out there, as an independent entity. As the Kantian influenced cognitive-developmental psychologist Jean Piaget has pointed out, "...no form of knowledge, not even perceptual knowledge, constitutes a simple copy of reality, because it always includes a process of assimilation to previous structures." [4]

If Piaget is correct, then to a very large extent the world you see, like Lance's, is a reflection of your past. New experiences are assimilated under previous structures of understanding which you have formed in your mind without knowing it.

In case you're having difficulty understanding this whole cognitive business of constructing reality and the objects of knowledge within it, it might be helpful to glance at the four frames below (see Figure 3). What do you see in each? Have a good look at each one before reading on ...

Now, that you've had a chance to look at each frame, reflect on what just happened. Did you notice how 'your mind's eye' kept scanning the various

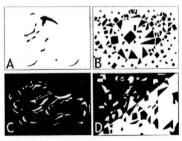

Figure 3

fragmentary pieces in each frame? You brought to this experience prior forms of perception, knowledge and understanding. Using them, did you sense how you were consciously trying to "make" an object of experience in each of the frames? You may in fact have been successful, maybe not.

To use Piagetian language, you may have been able to assimilate the sensory data to previous structures, namely concepts or cognitive schemata you had already learned and now use to organize reality. You may also have made mistakes like our friend Lance. For instance, many people looking at Frame B see a chicken or turkey. Actually, there's a teapot. Having provided you with this particular mental construct, can you now see what you could not before? Does the teapot suddenly jump out at you in an obvious way, even though before it was hidden in the manifold of random shapes? If so, you should now understand how sensory data can be assembled and unified by the forms and categories provided by the mind.

To appreciate this process a little better, try to see the 'person-riding-a-bike' in Frame A. Also look for 'three shoes' in Frame C. Frame D contains a 'water faucet'. As you do this, notice the significant activity involved in the experience of seeing the various objects, as unified objects of your experience.

What's interesting to ponder in this context is the fact that not all peoples in all civilizations have the same concepts as we do. Suppose that in a particular society, say, there was no running water, no taps or faucets and hence, no words for them. Would a person from that society see a tap or faucet in Frame D – obviously not. The same visual stimulus fragments would be presented, but the observer's mind could not organize them in the same way, lacking the concepts we possess in our minds. Similar would be the situation wherein a culture knew nothing of shoes and had no concept of shoes. A person from that culture could not possibly see shoes in Frame C. Our "Shoeless Joe" might have seen the snout of a crocodile instead.

A profound insight stemming from this discussion of mental object-construction returns us to the notion of responsibility. Not only are we responsible for our feelings and actions; but to a very large extent we are responsible for what we perceive. Yes, what we see in the world is in large part determined by us. We can in fact choose to see reality differently. *We* decide whether the glass is half empty or half-full. We can choose to see a "jerk" or a "child" or "God."

Our preference will be our perception. Further, we can reflect on our inherited, or otherwise unconsciously developed, ideas and cognitive schemata that we have previously used to construct our version of reality and make value judgments on them.

We can consciously alter and revise them or simply discard the unacceptable ones from our minds, refusing to use them any longer. We can self-consciously censor our perceptions. We don't have to bound by them or be influenced by them if we don't want. To illustrate: whether or not anyone sees the world in terms of inferior peoples is a personal choice for which we are responsible. We can also make efforts to learn new ideas, entertain new concepts and develop new forms of understanding to help us structure the world in different ways than before. Again, this is a choice.

With new cognitions comes a new world order. If we introduce Shoeless-Joe to shoes and the concept of 'shoe' he can now see what was previously invisible or unintelligible to him.

If your previous ways of viewing reality in terms of guilt, shame and imperfection, for example, have made goodness and truth invisible to you and have left you miserable and unful-filled, then it's time to re-organize and retrain your mind. When you make the necessary psychological adjustments inside, the world will surprisingly change outside. Your "new mind's eye" will verify this claim in terms of your refreshed experience of life.

Welcome to a new dawn. Let optimism and gladness begin to fill your consciousness. There *is* a better way. Don't pull a Lance causing yourself pain by your own distortions of reality; commit to seeing the truth and eventually you will. Viewing the world through the cognitive filter of your own psychological defensiveness is guaranteed to cause you misery.

Think about what happened to our friend Lance. All the money and social status in the world couldn't buy him happiness or peace of mind. Without knowing it, Lance was the architect of his own upset, though sadly he wished to blame innocent Becky. Let us not take any kind of perverse pleasure in blaming Lance, however. He is not himself guilty of anything, he is only deceived by his own ignorance. He requires gentle instruction, not the harsh punishment of public ridicule.

Analogously, so do you; so do I. Let's just commit ourselves now to washing away the dirt of defensive distortion from our eyes so that we can begin to see more clearly. There is exquisite beauty to behold just behind the apparent evil and ugliness of the world before which you stand witness. Be patient to find out how this can be so.

The world we see that seems so insane is the result of a belief system that is not working. To perceive the world differently, we must be willing to change our belief system, let the past slip away, expand our sense of now, and dissolve the fear in our minds.
William James

CHAPTER TWO

PERSONALITY VERSUS ESSENCE

"I cannot live with myself any longer." This was the thought that
kept repeating itself in my mind. Then suddenly I became aware
of what a peculiar thought it was."Am I one or two? If I cannot
live with myself, there must be two of me: the 'I' and the 'self'
that 'I' cannot live with."
"Maybe," I thought, "only one of them is real."
Eckhart Tolle

Research in cognitive-developmental psychology suggests that when a child is born, its experience is quite different from that of the adult.[1]

William James has described it as a "buzzing, booming confusion." Imagine a two dimensional blur with garbled sounds and a myriad of other indistinguishable olfactory and tactile sensations. In the beginning, the child has no sense of self. It doesn't see others, *as others*, distinct and separate from itself.

This world is a world without objects, a world without space and time. There are no dimensions, no moments which come before and after, just immediate undifferentiated experience, what some might call *pure being*. This is probably why we don't have memories of our first days and months of life. There is no 'self' to have the experience to be remembered. Once a defined sense of self begins to emerge, then memories become possible. There is someone, a self, to have them and remember them. An implication of this is that selfhood is the product of a gradual psychological construction, not an endowment or something pre-programmed in us.

Given that it is possible to exist without a sense of self, as the infant example illustrates, it is interesting to ponder what it means to be 'human' outside of any self-concept. What could human nature possibly be without selfhood? In other words, what is the essence of the human being – that which is most fundamental, prior to, and independent of, any notion of psychological self or ego-identity? And how does personality relate to this essential nature and how does it form around it? The answer to the last question will be discussed later. As for 'essence,' we'll try to make some sense of it now.

Discussing essence poses a logical problem. Typical explanations we give for things and events in the world use, or at least presuppose, concepts like space, time, object, number, and/or other scientific notions like cause-and-effect, laws of motion, and so on. The problem stems from the fact that pure being – the sort the infant must experience – doesn't appear to be made up of identifiable physical shapes and substances. Objects are not present or absent, here or there. They are not created and then destroyed.

In the infant child's world, they don't even exist. There is no time, no space, no substance, no causality when it comes to essential reality. All the language we use to describe and explain phenomena in the world hinges on such concepts, however. So, we're trying to get at something with the child that words can't explain. We can't view essence through a microscope. Neither can we touch it or weigh it or sample it by direct taste.

Essence transcends sensory experience. It is beyond the space-time continuum. Because it cannot be seen or heard, it escapes our attention. Being out of sight, it is out of mind. The "existence" of essence is not something many people ever acknowledge or recognize. The fact that we can't see it or hold it doesn't necessarily mean essence doesn't exist, however. We can't see or hold microwaves and radio waves either, yet they exist. The fact is that all of reality is not immediately and totally accessible by conventional sensory channels.

This is not to diminish the importance of sensory experience, but simply to point out that there exist elements of a greater reality beyond the physical plane.

The notion that there are two realities – one sensible and one supra-sensible – has led some to describe the former as lower and the latter as higher. The whole notion of a 'higher reality' might strike the spiritually uninitiated as questionable at best.

Attachment to the physical, material world and a firm commitment to scientific rationality make talk about alternative realities sound like a bunch of hocus-pocus nonsense, something not worthy of serious discussion. I'm not here to rationally convince you otherwise.

If you're a materialist and scientifically minded, the only proof you would accept would have to be empirically verifiable anyway. Such a proof requirement would already predetermine what the acceptable conclusions would have to be in advance. Alternative metaphysical and ontological realities would be precluded from discussion before any could even begin.

At the risk of sounding irrational, I invite you to temporarily put aside your proof requirements and suspend judgment. You can go back to your scientific rationality later, if you still wish. For now, at least entertain the possibility that there may be an 'essential realm of experience' which may have its behavioral, emotional, physical, and other psychological manifestations, but which cannot be entirely explained by them or reduced in terms of them.

This invitation is not entirely insane folly, for indeed, it is inspired by centuries of religious tradition and mystical experience. Even Plato, the supreme rationalist himself, claimed that empirical knowledge was a lower, inferior form of knowing. According to him, sensory-based empirical knowledge only gives one knowledge of mere appearances. It is direct and immediate experience of non-material "forms," as he calls them, in the *realm of forms*, which provide truth about a higher reality. Things in the world constitute only imperfect approximations of perfect forms found in that realm.

A triangle I draw on the board, for instance, is only a rough approximation of the form 'triangle.' No matter how hard I try, whatever triangle I produce will have its flaws and imperfections. Further, specific triangles on blackboards or in books can come in and out of existence; the form never changes. Its ontological status is independent of any one worldly existing triangle. Important to understand is that the direct apprehension of the forms, 'Goodness' being the highest, is not achieved by logic and rationality; neither was it to be arrived at by scientific investigation.

To say an irrational leap of faith is required is perhaps a little misleading. What is required, for Plato, is immediate awareness, an awareness of what is unchanging and eternal. Empirical and scientific methods of understanding cannot capture what this unchanging and eternal something is. Infinity and eternity don't make good objects of scientific investigation. They exist in another dimension of experience.

On this note, I'm reminded of a story about St. Thomas Aquinas, a medieval philosopher-theologian. Aquinas, as you may know, was a priest and is today considered a Doctor of the Roman Catholic Church. He was a prolific writer having written more than 60 works in a lifespan of less than 50 years. His writings have been considered profoundly important in the teachings and doctrine of the Catholic faith. One day, while celebrating Mass, Aquinas claims to have had a mystical revelation of God, a direct and immediate experience of the Divine. Subsequent to this he concluded, "All that I have written seems to me like straw compared to what has now been revealed to me."

A major work of his, the *Summa Theologica,* then in the process of being written, was never completed. Human language apparently could not express what union with the Divine revealed. What was expressible in language was not worth finishing.

Now, if God is Good, as I was taught as a youngster in Catholic Catechism class, then it intrigues me to think that Plato's 'Goodness' might be Aquinas' God, in a different form – no Platonic pun intended! Both thinkers point to something ineffable, yet ultimate and essential to higher reality. Knowledge of God and knowledge of Platonic Goodness are both based on direct, immediate awareness. As mentioned, this dimension of experience is not for science or logic to explain, but for the mind to know. This direct apprehension of the mind can be understood as a type of mental or spiritual discernment.

The Holy Spirit has the power to change the whole foundation of the world you see to something else; a basis not insane, on which a sane perception can be based, another world perceived.

A Course in Miracles

But it is written, Eye hath not seen, nor ear heard, neither have entered into the heart of man the things which God hath prepared for them that love him.....But the natural man receiveth not the things of the Spirit of God; for they are foolishness unto him: neither can he know them, because they are spiritually discerned.

1 Corinthians 2:9 and 2:14

Knowing that Plato and St Thomas Aquinas had mystical encounters with other-worldly or supra-sensible dimensions of experience gives us some confidence that we're on the right track with respect to what we are trying to identify. Certainly, neither could be considered an irrational fool; in fact, it's by their supreme rationality that they both have come to be distinguished historically as intellectual giants. Yet, this in itself, is not much help in our efforts to understand essence.

So, let's go back to the infant child and its experience of the world, at least as we understand it through cognitive-developmental research.

One thing that can be concluded from the child's "buzzing, booming confusion" is that there is no separation of figure and ground. There are no boundaries distinguishing one thing from another, things are not even perceived. If separation is impossible, since singular objects do not exist to be separated from other singular objects, then experience of human essence must be characterized by a state of *non-dualistic oneness*. Consequently, essence is not spatial. It is not something three-dimensional.

Another conclusion we can draw about essence is that it's *timeless*. In a world without objects, things do not appear and then disappear. They do not come in and out of existence. They do not come 'before' and leave 'after'. They do not begin and end. In an experience without objects, there can be no enduring quality to them, since they don't exist in the first place, at least in the infant's mind.

So, we don't have newer and older things, things that have lasted longer, things that prematurely end, things that are running out of time, things that gain or lose fashion depending on the season or year. There is no duration; deadlines don't exist; the time clock doesn't run out; nothing commences or ceases, and there is no impending or upcoming anything. Nothing exists that could "come up" in the first place. Essential reality is not only spaceless, but timeless.

A third conclusion following from the notion that essence is both timeless and spaceless is that it is something which cannot be explained in terms of cause-and-effect relations. Causal explanations presuppose close proximity of objects and events in time and space.

When we take pain medication and shortly after the pain disappears, we conclude that the medication relieved the pain. The medication "caused" the pain to go away. The fact that the pain relief came soon after taking the medication allows us to make the causal inference. But with no space and time in the infant's world, spatial and/or temporal contiguity is impossible.

Therefore, essence transcends any reality which operates in a cause-and-effect dimension. Clearly, this poses problems for scientific rationality and any efforts by it to understand what stands outside of its paradigm of explanation, namely, essence.

Our conclusions about objects, space, and time also logically imply that the empirical 'Self' – the self with a name, an ego-identity, a history, and a location – does not belong to essence either. The reason is that selfhood would require object-relations.

The child would have to perceive itself as an object differentiated from other objects like moms and dads. This it cannot do at the beginning of life because its experience is non-dualistic.

Second, the Self, as object, to be seen and understood as such, would have to exist in time. From one moment to the next, the child would have to perceive itself as the same person, not a new person each and every moment. But without objects, and hence, without a psychological, empirical ego-identity, there can be no time. How could there be, since nobody exists to experience it, to synthesize one moment of time with the next.

The radical implication of this is that personality falls outside the boundaries of essence. Personality is all about individual history: childhood, adolescence and adulthood. It is understood in terms of developmental progress. Second, personality involves object-relations. We talk about children "bonding" with parents, caretakers and others. We refer to people as gregarious or extroverted. We describe people's personalities as friendly or withdrawn.

In each of these cases "self-other" object-relations are assumed in a reality characterized by dualism and separation – things not belonging to undifferentiated pure being.

Oddly, then, it makes sense to say, "I am not really myself."

More accurately stated, "In essence, I am not my personality."

The individual in the process of ego development actually has imbibed his personality from the environment, and now he is the personality. The enemy of the essence is no more only the environment. The greatest adversary now is one's own personality.

A.H. Almaas

The suggestion that you are not your personality can be seriously disturbing. You might ask yourself, "Well, if I'm not myself, then what am I?" Presumably, in essence, I'm not a physical body. My pure being is also non-temporal. It has no causal effect upon anything else external and nothing else external affects it. I can't see it, touch it, hear it, smell it or taste it directly – yet this is me? This is more me than my personality? Even if so, why should I choose essence over personality? At least personality is familiar to me; essence is a stranger and it makes no guarantees I can understand. Is there some sort of spiritual fine print I can't see and the implications of which I will regret?

The elusiveness of essence has already been established. Understanding what essence cannot be, it appears perhaps that all that's left is some kind of vacuum or dark void. Why would anyone willingly choose to thrust themselves down a black hole? Why not continue to side with personality?

In answer to these questions and concerns, let it first be said that the 'void', so called, is not a frightening dark hole. Spiritual leaders, mystics and gurus down through the ages, whether they be Hindu, Buddhist or Christian, for example, have sought this 'emptiness' and encouraged others to find it too through such things as meditative practice, prayer, or structured exercises designed to retrain the mind to perceive reality differently.

As they know first hand, once one's personality or ego-identity is shed, one enters into an immaculately empty space. In this sublime space is experienced an inner sense of expansiveness. This open space is boundless, clear and crisp. The experience is not like some kind of rational intuition, heartfelt emotion, or physical sensation, though there may be correlates of such things in the person experiencing essence. A.H. Almaas, from whom much has been learned on this matter, has described essence as pure consciousness and luminosity as the beginning of it.

It is enlightenment beyond reason, beyond feeling, and is not limited in any way by the body. It is not an intellectual insight; it is not a feeling of happiness, nor is it a biological reaction. Yet, he claims that it remains an actual and palpable ontological presence reflected in our aliveness, strength, peacefulness, compassion, awareness, love and joy.

Such elements rush in to fill the emptiness left by the departed ego. The experienced presence of such things is what allows for description of what essence is all about. For example, essence can have an emotional effect. One can feel warm and gentle in the experience of essence, but in the same way that 'hardness' is not the diamond, but a quality of it, similarly, warmth and gentleness are not essence, but manifestations of it.

With respect to physically felt sensations, Almaas allows essence to be experienced and felt physically, but clearly he takes the position that it is not a bodily response either. Again, to reason by analogy, we can "feel" our stomachs, but the feeling is not the stomach itself.

On the subject of intellectual insights and how they differ from essence, Almaas tells us that the two are distinguished insofar as the an insight is an *event*, whereas essence is a *presence.* An insight is an experience of understanding a specific truth, while, by contrast, essence is what might be called an embodied presence, an ontological actuality. Almaas does not dismiss the value of insights, however, for they give us liberating information of how our minds, emotions and personalities function. Insights can thereby lead us to essence. But, according to Almaas, though insights can be powerful and exhilarating, they are not essence in themselves.

Essence is more beautiful, more magnificent, and more meaningful. Essence is the only thing which will completely *quench our hearts,* as he puts it. Essence is the only thing that will be our peace of mind. Essence is miraculous and its characteristics are "sheer delightful magic." Nonetheless, we can still use insights, emotions and bodily signals as traces of evidence for the existence of that which we cannot see with the naked eye.

To learn more about essence we must learn to experience "presence" and forget trying to find it as an object outside. When we are completely and totally present to the moment, and to ourselves, experiences are heightened. This heightened experience is not essence, since essence is non-dualistic, but it reflects our state of being. What follows from 'presence' is an exceptional high definition clarity and vividness in our perceptions of the world - perceptions once blurred by the filter screens of the ego.

Colors may display an other-worldly exquisite quality. Sounds may gain texture and resonance in ways never before heard. Taste buds can come alive as the simplest food suddenly becomes a communion banquet. Snowflakes become nature's work of art. When one is completely present and totally absorbed by one's surroundings, there's a feeling of merging with the objects that are being experienced. For instance, an individual might feel "one" with nature or "one" with the music being enjoyed. In the latter case, the person is not listening to the music; he or she *is* the music.

On this note, (sorry for being 'punny' again) I sometimes wonder whether this is why iPods, headphones, and earpieces are so popular. By removing almost the entire physical space between the sound-source and the playing of music in one's head, there's created an experience of being virtually "inside" the music. Different instruments and voices can be heard at different "locations" in the emptiness of the mind. Colorful patterns and visual images may even be produced. Such experience can be sheer delightful magic. To the extent that the notion of music playing in your head captures the "oneness" that is so hard to describe in normal language, and insofar as it is intensely beautiful, you can now better understand how giving up personality is not necessarily a sacrifice in the end. It is actually a very inviting and illuminating experience.

Before finally making the decision to side with either essence or the personality, let us not forget our friend Lance. His insecure personality created a false reality in which he lived and to which he chose to respond negatively. His personality made for him an illusory living hell, at least in his relations with Becky. He was not really upset at Becky for the reasons he thought and the real reasons for his upset were invisible to him.

Can you be so sure that your version of reality is any less twisted or distorted by your own psychological defensiveness? Have you made your own hell here on earth? Can you deny the fact that you are often anxious, worried, fearful, regretful, and guilt-laden, and, at other times, apprehensive, vengeful, angry, depressed or nervously preoccupied? Is this the emotional basket of rotten fruit personality offers you which you so desperately wish to hold on to? Given that you are responsible for your feelings and that you choose your own emotions, are you insane? Remember, nobody else makes you feel the way you do. Feelings are a personal choice. Besides, are those rare and fleeting moments of happiness and jubilation, which come with your infrequent occasions of success and material acquisition, enough to commit you to the ego?

Have you forgotten the Buddha's message concerning such worldly honors and trinkets of amusement? Deep down, don't you share the Buddha's insight that happiness based on earthly delights cannot last, that suffering will soon follow? With no previously known alternative, it's understandable how you might have chosen a temporary, and thus illusory, bliss over no bliss at all.

Be glad in the knowledge that there is a better way. This alternative path provides a direct experience of all you've ever *really* wanted – reunion with your essence, what some would call your Source, others God. It reveals to you who you really are absent of conditioning and the defensive, intrusive distortions of the ego.

As Almaas says, "The more the individual is grounded in the embodied experience of essence, the more accurate his perceptions and the less it is influenced by the subjective mentality of his personality."

Don't you wish to know the truth? The truth has a liberating function. Liberation is what awaits you when you abandon personality. You no longer need to define yourself, improve your self-image, build your self-esteem, impress yourself, or exert yourself upon others. Neither do you don't need to impress the world or defend yourself against it. Finally, peace of mind is within reach. Don't be like the young boy scout from Newfoundland who, when asked what he missed most about home when away on a camping trip in Alberta, answered, "... the flies and the fog!"

This is what he grew up with and this is what he knew. This was what he was attached to and what gave him a sense of psychological place. For your own sake, don't identify with the flies and the fog offered to you by the ego. Essence offers you so much more. Why be satisfied with the crumbs on the floor when the banquet dinner table is prepared for you with delicacies you could never have imagined?

Essence is the real person, the real and true self. The personality is called false because it is attempting to take the place of essence...the personality and the ego identity develop to fill the void resulting from the loss of essence in childhood. So, it is really an imposter, trying to pretend it is the real thing.

A. H. Almaas

I sought for many things, and found despair. Now do I seek but one, for in that one is all I need, and only what I need. All that I sought before I needed not, and did not even want. My only need I did not recognize. But now I see that I need only truth. In that all needs are satisfied, all cravings end, all hopes are finally fulfilled and dreams are gone. Now have I everything that I could need. Now have I everything that I could want. An now at last I find myself at peace.

A Course in Miracles

To help you appreciate what a self without psychological identity is like, perhaps a little mind experiment is in order.

I want you to first read the following instructions and then carry them out. Start by closing your eyes... Next, imagine that there's a little red ping-pong ball hovering in front of your face... Become aware of that ball... Now, bring that ball inside your head... Put it behind and between your eyes in the darkness of your mind... Be aware of the ball... Examine it and observe it... Yet again, situate the ball in front of your face and become aware of it as you did before...Finally, bring the ball inside your mind... See it from every vantage point... Be aware of what you see...

Now, don't read any further for the moment and carry out the mental experiment as directed for about 1 or 2 minutes....

Now that you've completed the task, I would like you to conduct the same experiment a second time, only on this occasion when you focus your awareness on the ball, ask yourself at the end: *Who or what is it, exactly, that is aware that I am aware?* There is your focused attention on the ball, but *who or what* is focusing on your focused attention? Is this the ghost in the machine? The soul? Or pure being? Does this awareness have a name? Does it have a color? How about size and shape? How much does awareness weigh? What does it smell like? When was it born? Did it ever have a beginning? Can you tell me about its history? Will it ever cease to exist? Can you locate the boundary between your initial 'awareness-of-the-ball' and your 'awareness-*of*-your-awareness-of-the-ball'?

The point of the exercise just completed was to help you experience something about yourself which maybe you've never noticed before. Your "awareness of awareness" is probably closer to who you really are, to your essential higher self, than is your personality.

Notice that it does not share the usual characteristics of your ego-identity, yet still is palpably real and existing. It appears to be something like self-conscious awareness. In contrast to the lower psychological self that walks and talks, the 'higher self' does not display the same kinds of empirically observable actions. It's present, but unobservable with the physical eye.

This consciousness apparently is able to see and observe, yet it does so with the "mind's eye," not through the body's physical optical lens. Eckhart Tolle labels this awareness of awareness the "witnessing presence." As he points out, behind all of your thoughts and emotions, as well as your reactions to the world is "the silent watcher."

As you will discover later, the silent watcher in you will be called upon to help you catch yourself in the act of being yourself - your personality self, that is. When you make your personality the object of your own observations, detachment from your ego-identifications becomes possible. You can come to see that, "I am not myself," and that "I am not limited and confined by the boundaries of my personality."

On the subject of self-conscious awareness, Tolle makes the following recommendation:

Be present as the watcher of your mind – of your thoughts and emotions as well as your reactions in various situations. Be at least as interested in your reactions as in the situation or person that causes you to react. Notice also how often your attention is in the past or future. Don't judge or analyze what you observe. Watch the thought, feel the emotion, observe the reaction. Don't make a personal problem out of them. You will then feel something more powerful than any of those things that you observe: the still, observing presence behind the content of our mind, the silent watcher.[2]

Awareness is Curative.
Lama Surya Das

CHAPTER THREE

GENESIS AND PROJECTIONS OF EGO-PERSONALITY

You have no enemy except yourself, and you are enemy indeed to him because you do not know him as yourself.
A Course in Miracles

Before delving into the illusions of the ego-personality in detail, it is insightful to consider how it arose in the first place.

An interesting parallel can be drawn between the Biblical account of the Creation story in Genesis and the emergence of ego or personality in human beings. In the beginning, Adam and Eve were together with God in the Garden of Eden. They were united and in a state of heavenly bliss.

So too with the newborn infant; there is no real differentiation between self and mother, even though the two are not in fact the same person, they are so closely connected they may feel 'as one'.

Further, as we know from the Biblical story, Adam and Eve were naked in the Garden, but they felt no shame. They were content and happy in their natural condition. So is the newborn baby and young child in a state of innocent bliss from birth.

Of course, as we learn, Eve is tempted by the devil to eat from the Tree of Knowledge of Good and Evil. She eventually succumbs to her temptation and gives the apple to Adam who partakes of this fruit of knowledge as well. In this act, we see that both Adam and Eve want something that they do not have. They perceive themselves as lacking or deficient in knowledge and so they disobey God. This is what the Church terms their "original sin".

With children, a time eventually comes in their psychological development when they realize that all their needs cannot be immediately and fully satisfied. All is not well in the Garden, so to speak. They want more or they want it immediately and the world is not giving them what they want, whether it be warmth, security, attention, or whatever else. They discover that the world does not revolve around them 24-hours a day, seven days a week. With time, there comes the perception that something is "missing". There is a deficiency that now exists in their awareness.

What accompanies this perceived deficiency is the gradual formation of the ego-personality. Something is "wrong" and the ego emerges to deal with the situation. Like Adam and Eve, the ego will take action to compensate for this deficiency.

Now, once Adam and Eve have eaten of the apple from the forbidden tree, they become self-conscious – in both senses of the word – and they now feel their nakedness to be shameful, covering themselves with fig leaves. Guilty of disobeying their Maker and fearful of the imagined impending results, they hide in the Garden. When confronted by God about his wrongdoing, Adam quickly blamed Eve for what he had done. Adam claimed it was Eve's fault. Eve is quick to blame the serpent. So, in the beginning was born the "blame-game" predicated on Adam and Eve's fear of God, their perceived deficiency, their new-found sense of shame, as well as the projection of guilt onto someone or something else.

As for the still cognitively undeveloped child, with its ego in early formation, frustrations and blocked wants are internalized. The child lacks understanding of how the world works, doesn't understand what's wrong, and at some level it believe that it has done something to deserve this treatment. And so the child intro-jects these unpleasant occurrences as personal guilt.

Unconsciously, there's the underlying fear "I did something wrong" or "It's all my fault." Such thinking can be illustrated by the cognitively egocentric child whose parents divorce, and who all the while blames himself for the failed marriage, not appreciating his own innocence in the matter. Generally speaking, this perception of guilt in early life eventually leads any little person who feels burdened by a sense of shame, and is fearful of their more powerful parents, to blame siblings and friends. We often hear children scream in their own self-defense, "*They* made me do it!"

Pleased with its own strategy, the budding ego eventually goes on to blame classmates and teachers, and later neighbors, society, the system or anything else for its shortcomings, and it does so for an entire lifetime. Personal failings, inadequacies, or any other insecurities, which might arise, cannot be taken to heart and so must be projected externally in order to maintain one's sanity. So the world is to blame, not me.

We're reminded here of Cho Seung-Hui at Virginia Tech University who blamed others for his murders. We're also reminded of our friend Lance. In his mind he did not feel mad because he was consciously insecure about himself, but because Becky was stuck-up. She was to blame. As we already know, Lance was blaming a false reality created by projections of his own defensive personality. Illusions of the ego are born and insanity is allowed to reign.

Our metaphor for the ego is completed as Adam and Eve are banished from the Garden of Eden, each blaming the other or the serpent for their disobedient actions and their resulting suffering.

So too is the child forced to leave the comfort of the "merged presence" with its God-like mother to struggle for a lifetime blaming the world in its unconscious efforts to hide the internalized insane belief that it lacks worth.

"I am guilty and shameful from birth." "I was born with original sin." "I am damaged goods."

"No, this cannot be," says the ego, coming to the emotional rescue of the personality. "You are the innocent victim of unjustified indifference, maltreatment, and attack."

"But don't worry," says the ego, "I will protect you from the dangerous enemies which lurk around every corner. They are to blame, not you."

As a result of all this painful fear, guilt and shame, a human yearning for a lost sense of innocence arises – a return to the womb, perhaps, or maybe a reunification with our ultimate Source which is Heaven. There, all wants were once satisfied, all needs were met, and no deficiencies existed in time. In the beginning, we already had everything we wanted and we already were whatever it was we wished to be. There was no place to go and nothing more to become.

In my own family, my daughter tells me of her "Bubble Wand" experience captured on video-tape, which she claims was a life altering moment in the development of her own personality. This bubble wand experience constituted her *ego genesis*. It was around her second birthday when, during a twin-club party, my daughter dropped the "bubble-wand" being used to create bubbles into the bottle which contained the soapy water. At the time this occurred, I was filming to capture her on tape. What I didn't realize was how frustrated she was on finding out that she couldn't reach the bubble wand in the bottle with her tiny fingers. Also, I couldn't have imagined how hurt she felt because daddy was doing nothing but laughing at her while he filmed her frustrating moment.

Personally, I was pleasantly preoccupied watching and filming my little baby just playfully being a child. I wanted to record this moment so that we could both enjoy it later on in life. Without any intent in doing so, I caused my daughter a great deal of pain in this whole episode. In her tiny little heart, she felt abandoned and alone. Her daddy was not helping her in her serious moment of need. "Why is he just standing there, laughing at me from a distance, when I need him so much now?" "Why doesn't he understand the frustration and discomfort he is causing me by his inaction?" "Why am I being victimized like this? "Nobody understands me and I hurt."

In such thoughts a retreat to the ego began. A defensive posture toward the world started to be formed. A need to defend and look after oneself gave rise and a cold world was born. My daughter shares with me the fact that as far as she remembers, this moment set the psychological dynamics of her personality in motion. Childhood innocence was lost in an instant and separation from the "Father" became a *fait accomplis*. We were literally in the garden, but now more separate and apart than I could imagine.

Of course, I had no intention of hurting my daughter. In fact, I thought she looked so cute, I didn't wish to lose this moment forever, so I taped it. Nonetheless, my very young daughter did have an immediate need. She certainly couldn't know or understand what I was doing, she just wanted me to rescue her bubble wand, but I didn't come to her help. She was hurt at the core of her being.

She was spiritually wounded. This sad experience is typical of what's replicated in everyone's life. It doesn't matter how effective or well-intentioned your parents or caretakers were. It doesn't matter how much you love them or how much they love you. It also doesn't matter how trivial or insignificant your hurt appears to others – because it matters to you. No doubt you can identify one or more defining moments of your life when suddenly you felt helpless and alone.

Take some time and think of one moment right now... Someone didn't understand you. Someone in your early life hurt you by their insensitivity, inattentiveness or indifference to your wants. Worse still, they may have victimized you physically, sexually or emotionally. Whatever the source of your original spiritual wound, your current personality reflects the unconsciously chosen strategies you now use years after to deal with this world of separation and pain. Everyone has an ego and everyone has a painful story that could make you cry.

Projections of the Ego-Personality

Going back now for a moment, we learned in Chapter Two that there are two realities: higher and lower. Lower reality is the home of the ego, our empirical self, our personality. Lower reality is the world of perception, of change, of things that begin and end in time. In this dualistic reality, birth and death are real, so too are scarcity, loss, and separation.

In lower reality, one perceives opposites and opposing wills. People are hurt and disappointed, expectations are not met, and there's always the uncertainty of tomorrow. Between people, there is perpetual conflict, fear of attack, projected blame, judgment, the need to retaliate in self-defense, not to mention all the anxiety and depression associated with disturbances of the mind. To many, this world seems to be the only real one. No wonder some describe life as *hell*. Yet, it is the one to which they are attached and from which they simply refuse to let go. Strangely, it takes great courage to abandon this hell and accept a better alternative. Some people never do.

Helping us to understand the temporary and illusory nature of this lower reality so that we might some day give it up, Buddha is quoted as saying:

Regard this fleeing world like this:
Like stars fading and vanishing at dawn,
like bubbles on a fast moving stream,
like morning dewdrops evaporating on blades of grass,
like a candle flickering in a strong wind,
echoes, mirages, and phantoms, hallucinations,
and like a dream.
"The Eight Similies of Illusion,"*From the Prajna Paramita Sutras*

Buddha's comparison of life on earth as a dream is useful in our efforts to detach from it. Take last night's dream, for instance. Perhaps it seemed very real at the time, especially if it was one of those vivid nightmares that we all have on occasion. But where is it now? It has vanished, gone. So too is yesterday. Where is *it* now? What happened to *it*? Where were you yesterday? What were you doing? What did you experience? Where is that experience now? Evaporated somewhere out in the universe? Probably not.

It is still in your memory, more likely. But where is your memory, if not in your mind? Could it be that the world you actually experienced yesterday was itself little more than a hallucination or a fabrication of your mind? Was your experience of reality ever outside your mind? And just think, if your mind is separate and distinct from everyone else's mind, did everyone else experience the same reality that you did yesterday? Is everyone experiencing the same world you are experiencing right now, today?

In other words, is there only one *objective* reality for everyone to see? Or, is physical, temporal reality all just made up in your mind? Just a temporary illusion about to disappear like yesterday?

Our earlier example of Lance and Becky illustrates what *A Course in Miracles* teaches on the matter of mind and material reality:

> *The world we see merely reflects our own internal frame of reference*
> *– the dominant ideas, wishes and emotions in our minds. "Projection*
> *makes perception." We look inside first, decide the kind of world we*
> *want to see and then project that world outside, making it the truth*
> *as we see it. We make it true by our interpretations of what it is we*
> *are seeing. If we are using perception to justify our own mistakes –*
> *our anger, our impulses to attack, our lack of love in whatever form*
> *it may take – we will see a world of evil, destruction, malice, envy*

*and despair... We have distorted the world by our twisted defenses,
and are therefore seeing what is not there.*

We learn from *A Course in Miracles* that however reality appears
to the ego-personality or knowing subject, it is actually a product
of interpretation and a projection of one's wishes, fears, and
ideas. In other words, when we look at the world, we are
witnessing our state of our mind projected outwardly.

From this observation comes mother's wisdom: *What you see
in others and don't like about them is precisely what you fear and don't
like about yourself.* This reflection can be sobering, especially the
next time you are about to judge and criticize another person for
something they said or did. You may simply be attacking
yourself in projected disguise!

*If you hate a person, you hate something in him that is part of yourself.
What isn't part of ourselves doesn't disturb us.*
    Herman Hesse

The notion that reality is a projection is an idea that is very
similar to one held by philosopher Immanuel Kant. He
concluded: "Mind is the law-giver to Nature." For him, our
minds are not passive recipients of sights and sounds, or
uninvolved observers of different events and states of affairs.

As we learned earlier with the random-figure experiential
exercise, our minds provide the order and structure of the world
we perceive. (As we discovered before, one can't see 'shoes' if
one doesn't know what a shoe is or has never learned about
shoes.)

Our past ideas, conceptual understandings, beliefs, wishes,
and values give shape to what we see and know in life.
Sensations may appear to flow from the external world, but it is
our mind which organizes them, interprets them, and gives them
meaning. The world thus conforms to the mind, not the other

way around. Hence, *perception involves a process of projection, a projection of our past learning.*

Every present moment is greeted by our unconscious cognitive-developmental history.

What's unfortunate about our ego-projections onto reality is that they result in perceptual distortions. The distorted projections of the ego come in many forms. They become crystallized into different character type ego-identities or personalities which, in Kantian fashion, then cognitively construct different psychological worldviews.

While it appears that all human beings are genetically determined to eventually experience the physical world in terms of subject-object duality, time, space, and cause-and-effect relations, beyond that, people have very different perceptions of personal and social reality. They construct such things differently. But for any individual, the perception of his or her 'world' mistakenly serves as proof to the observing-ego that what *it* sees, in particular, is objectively true. *Just look.*

No wonder seeing is believing. The world one sees is a construction of one's mind. What the person observes in the world is regarded as conclusive evidence for his or her specific claims about the world. The problem is that this so-called 'evidence' is simply the product of the mind's distorted projections. The perception of 'objective fact' may be little more than a subjectively twisted reality.

For example, from Lance's psychological perspective, Becky was indeed stuck-up. The actual truth, however, is far different from Lance's ego-distorted version of her. His interpretations of her behavior were unfair. His negative evaluation of her was in fact, based on his own fears and insecurities. Maybe he wasn't as popular, good-looking and desirable as he believed? "This can't be so," said Lance's defensive ego, which rushed in to repress the thought in his unconscious mind. "Clearly, she must be a bitch.

It's not in your imagination Lance," said the ego "... anyone can see you're right about her. *Just look* at how she is acting!" Poor Lance.

It is clear that people have different life experiences and that physically and emotionally, not everybody is identical. Yet, personalities are not entirely unique to the individual either. Actually, anyone's ego-personality is just a typical example of one of the many characters or psychological archetypes which students of human nature throughout history have already identified, with greater or lesser accuracy.

Hippocrates, for instance, described four basic character types in terms of temperamental dispositions: phlegmatic, choleric, melancholic and sanguine.

Plato provided us with a typology of corrupt characters using political sounding labels: democratic, oligarchic, tyrannical, and timarchic. The ideal character was embodied in the philosopher king.

Sigmund Freud spoke of the "oral, anal, and phallic personality types". Eric Fromm outlined the features of the "productive and unproductive character".

Carl Jung presented us with his theoretical notion of psychological types, labeling them in terms of their introverted or extroverted tendencies, as well as by their preferred ways of taking in information about the world and making judgments on it. Jung described people as sensing or intuitive types (perceptual preference) and thinking or feeling types (judgment preference).

Enneagram psychology, a spiritually-based system, has given different personality types a number designation, from one to nine, identifying particular individuals as a "Two," a "Seven" or a "Three," for instance. Some have referred to these designations as the "Sufi Numbers" in reference to their supposed origination. Whatever their origin, underlying what may appear to be infinite variation in the psychological make-up of individuals, thinkers throughout the ages have argued that there exist observable and predictable patterns of behavior, no matter how different people may appear to be on the surface. Each recognizable archetypal personality emphasizes and projects onto reality different sorts of values, goals and desires. Each has its own particular insecurities and each uses observable psychological defense mechanisms to protect and preserve the Fallen Self – the false self out of touch with its essence – the ego-protected psychological self that was initially hurt in childhood when banished from the Garden of Innocence.

In the chapters that follow, we'll examine a bit more closely the ego illusions and resulting character types associated with the perceived loss of various essential qualities in the individual. Much will be drawn from various Enneagram researchers for purposes of this analysis, without getting bogged down in the details and intricacies of the theory itself. Enneagram psychology takes spiritual matters seriously and integrates them within the psychodynamics of the ego in such a way that the distortions of the ego are best illustrated and explained. Other models explaining psychological ego function, like Freudian psycho-analysis, would be less useful to us, given its atheistic assumptions. Notwithstanding this, Freudian notions of defensiveness, guilt, denial and projection will be included in the following analysis as they are in treatments of the ego as found in *A Course in Miracles*, another important inspiration for this work.

Before we move on to our analysis of character types, however, let us remember that in the beginning, the child was in psychological paradise. At first, there was complete oneness with the world. In time, the rudimentary beginnings of self-consciousness began to appear, but to a very large extent, there was still a "merged identity" with the mother. During this period, the child's needs were almost always met. Eventually, however, discomforts arose, satisfaction of needs had to be delayed, feelings were hurt, frustrations grew, physical boundaries between self and other became more apparent, and the ego was born.

According to Enneagram theory, individuals who lose touch with their essence, are particularly affected by the disappearance of one specific *essential quality* which takes on greater importance for them. Which essential quality becomes most salient may be a matter of temperament, early parent-child interactions, or the general nature of the initial experiences causing the spiritual wound.

In truth, that quality never really leaves the child (or the adult which the child evolves into), but the individual's early-life spiritual wound convinces them that this essential quality has somehow disappeared. Subsequently, the ego gradually persuades the naive innocent child that it's through things like achievement, people-pleasing, pleasure-seeking or material acquisition that heavenly bliss can be regained.

For most individuals, mid-life informs us that the ego was a liar all along and that it's time to take another path. Life then becomes a journey for the lost treasure – one's essential being, one's true self. This is the holy grail, our gift to the world.

You and I are like the stranger lost in a strange land, yearning to return to the kingdom for the long-awaited home coming, to finally be at home and at rest. The kingdom is actually heaven where all is one. As the Bible says (Luke 17:21): "*The kingdom of heaven is within you.*"

In the context of a non-dualistic higher reality, you might even say that the kingdom of heaven *is* you. That's why the longest journey is "from here to here." It is a journey without distance, to a place without time. In fact, this place outside of space and time is your essential nature; it is your higher self; it is the real you which you experienced before your hallucinatory ego-assisted departure from the Garden of Innocence.

Your life until now has actually been like a bad dream. The

fact is you never left paradise. What has seemed so real to you for most of your life has been little more than a painful nightmare, an illusion. What's particularly distressing is that you know you're still dreaming, but you choose to remain asleep anyway, regardless of how painful the nightmare is. When are you going to wake up?

Before we fell asleep and began to dream the ego's nightmare, we were all blessed and totally absorbed with numerous essential qualities. We were created perfect, infinitely good, unconditionally lovable, pure and transparent, beautiful, open, spontaneous, joyful, trusting, and sublimely peaceful.

With the birth of the ego, however, came our separation from the garden kingdom. We all sensed that something "essential" had been lost. Everyone's experience tends to be a little different in this regard. The rest of life constitutes the journey that we all undertake to recapture the *lost innocence* of childhood. We all feel somehow deficient or lacking. In forgetting, or not recognizing, our true selves, we may have foolishly identified with the criticisms made against us by others. Their negative voices became the internalized voices of our psyches, our ego-identities. For example, if we were told that we would never amount to anything, we might have begun to see ourselves as 'losers.' If so, this became our self-concept, our self-identification, our Self.

On the other hand, wounded by having our self-worth diminished, we may have spent an entire lifetime instead trying to become successful in order to prove the world wrong. In this case, we have lived life defiant and angry against the world. *Success has become the best revenge.*

And on top of childhood messages, coming from every direction, the onslaught against us never ends as we develop and grow. Madison Avenue messages, for instance, remind us daily how we need to improve ourselves to become more desirable or more successful. If we choose to listen, we may unconsciously learn to become even more insecure, even more fearful and even more self-loathing. We hate the way we look. We're disappointed by our own performance. We can't believe how stupid or useless we are. Such insecurities constitute the materials for our new self-definition, the false-self which has usurped our true identity. In desperation, we devise ingenious strategies to protect our artificial self-image. We work out. We buy useless products to enhance our appearance. We pay consultants. We begin to accept the world's propaganda believing that "clothes make the person" or that people's worth as human beings hinges on their net income. Always fearful and anxious, we try to improve our self-concept. We make every effort to pump up our self-esteem. But deep down we know our efforts are futile because anything which needs defense and propping up is an artificial creation, not our true reality in the first place.

Our dissatisfaction with life stems from our unwillingness or seeming inability to shed the identity of the false ego-personality. All external searches to compensate for our deficiencies end with failed results. We know this unconsciously, yet we plod on. And, of course, when all else fails to make us feel good about ourselves, we can always project blame and our perceived deficiencies onto the world.

Psychological resistance to finding our true selves can be enormous for many people. Having completely identified with our personality, this is all we consciously know about ourselves. Abandoning the ego-self is tantamount to committing psychological suicide. We have to die to our previous identity to form a new one. Existential rebirth comes with a price. But add to the obliteration of the false self the anxiety surrounding the need to explore our original loss of essence in the emotional wounds of childhood, and things are made even more difficult.

What's entailed here is confronting our deepest hurts and healing our spiritually wounded "inner child".

Comparing the discomfort of doing this transformational inner work with the already familiar discomfort stemming from identifying with a false self, many people choose the latter. It just seems easier that way. Doing so, however, is like selling your soul to the 'existential devil'. This assistant to the ego may help you to keep running away from your 'shadow', the one described earlier by Chuang Tzu, but in the transaction with your devious demon, you will have to bargain away truth and the reality of your Higher Self. Unfortunately, the ego's evil agent is extremely tricky; for you see, it's actually impossible to successfully escape the shadow by running. As Chuang Tzu suggests, you'll probably drop dead first.

To strike a bargain with the ego necessarily means that you've been duped and sadly at the price of your spiritual identity. Quite a hefty price to pay for your current dissatisfaction, don't you think? For those of you who are finally tired of trying to run from your shadow, and for those who seek lasting stillness and peace, let us now explore the dynamics of the ego and corresponding psychological worldviews which until now have guaranteed your unhappiness. Release is nigh.

Draw insight and inspiration from *A Course in Miracles*:

Everything you perceive as the outside world is merely your attempt to maintain your ego identification, for everyone believes that identification is salvation. Yet consider what has happened, for thoughts do have consequences to the thinker. You have become at odds with the world as you perceive it, because you think it is antagonistic to you. This is a necessary consequence of what you have done. You have projected outward what is antagonistic to what is inward, and therefore you would have to perceive it this way. That is why you must realize that your hatred is in your mind and not outside it before you can get rid of it; and why you must get rid of it before you can perceive the world as it really is.

Part Two

LOST ESSENCE AND THE DYNAMICS OF CHARACTER

No one can escape from illusions unless he looks at them, for not looking is the way they are protected. There is no need to shrink from illusions, for they cannot be dangerous. We are ready to look more closely at the ego's thought system because together we have the lamp that will dispel it, and since you realize you do not want it, you must be ready. Let us be very calm in doing this, for we are merely looking honestly for truth. The 'dynamics' of the ego will be our lesson for a while, for we must look first at this to see beyond it, since you have made it real. We will undo this error quietly together, and then look beyond it to truth.

A Course in Miracles

Character is Destiny.

Heraclitus

Note: Before reading further about character type ego-dynamics, you might wish to complete the Character-Type Self-Diagnostic found in the Appendix of the book. Doing so will enable you to form a tentative conclusion about your own type. You can confirm your preliminary type identification with the more detailed character analyses which follow.

CHAPTER FOUR

EGO DYNAMICS IN CHARACTER TYPE ONE: *THE PERFECTIONIST*

Good, better best, never let it rest,till your good is better
and your better is best!
Perfectionist Jingle

Lost Essence:

We can begin to understand the psychodynamics of the *Perfectionist* by going back again for a moment to the Creation story in Genesis. Recall that after creating the universe, God rested on the seventh day and judged that "All was good". He was well-pleased with his work. Indeed, there was no need to touch-up any imperfections since clearly God doesn't make any mistakes. An implication of this is that when human beings, like Adam and Eve, were created, they were *essentially perfect* too. They were stained with "original sin" – and hence became "flawed" – *only after* their disobedience, banishment from the Garden, and separation from the Divine. In the beginning, however, the first human beings were morally and psychologically unblemished by design and united with God their Source in Heaven.

In a similar fashion, when children are born, they are spiritually perfect. They are at one with the universe, knowing no degree of separation between "me" and "not-me".

Soon, however, like all of us, Perfectionists begin to develop a separate ego-identity. In this case, they often experience a sense of being disconnected from their protective figure in the home.[1] This is significant for "Having another stable adult figure [apart from the nurturing figure] that the child can identify with and move toward gives the child the ability to separate from dependency on the mother and to increasingly sense his or her own individuality and autonomy. If, however, the protective figure is not adequately fulfilling his role, young Ones [i.e., Perfectionists] sense a fundamental disconnection. They realize that their real or symbolic father does not adequately fit their temperament and needs. This does not necessarily mean that the protective-figure is bad or abusive, but that, for whatever reason, a certain effortless bonding simply does not take place."[2] This can result in the child concluding that "I must father myself and therefore, I must give myself my own moral guidelines."

The One's belief that they must produce their own moral guidelines for living makes the One judge of right and wrong, not the protective figure. This is parallel to Adam and Eve's usurping the authority of God. And just as Adam and Eve felt guilty and shameful for their disobedience, young Ones feel guilty for judging, and thus implicitly condemning, their own protective figure in the process. (I know better than my father, the God-like figure in the home.) The result is that, "Ones [must] construct an identity that allows them to see themselves as good and responsible and others as lazy, sloppy, or at least less correct and 'mature' than themselves. Such self-justification becomes the bedrock of the One's identity and the emotional pattern that will be reenacted throughout their lives."[3]

By seeing others as defective or irresponsible, say, guilt is projected and the other is to blame. Such projection allows the defensive ego to defend itself against the world. Adam blames Eve; Eve blames the serpent; and Perfectionist Ones project blame onto you and me in order to protect themselves from their own guilt-ridden minds. Ones unconsciously worry about having overridden paternal authority, something they consider deep down to be wrong. As in the Garden, punishment is in order.

In recognition of this, the resulting fear and shame become unbearable emotions. So the ego conveniently buries them in the subconscious of the Perfectionist through denial and repression. Judgment, attack and blame are then projected externally in the One's fight against the world. However, for this psychological relief from guilt and shame, which comes packaged in unconscious dishonesty, the ego imprisons the Perfectionist in the illusion of an imperfect world. Everything "out there" needs correction and improvement. But remember, God makes no mistakes. The Type One's illusory self-definition as someone who is better or more responsible than others, is now complemented by an illusory world – one where everyone else is to blame. Of course, the perceived imperfections of the world are those constructed by the Perfectionist's mind. Oh what a tangled web we weave!

Experiential workshops and panel discussions with Perfectionists also reveal that young Ones are often spiritually wounded in their childhoods by overly demanding or overly critical parents for whom nothing was ever good enough.[4] Budding Perfectionists were kept on a tight leash and sharply criticized whenever they violated the rules. Emotional outbursts were considered unacceptable and so Ones learned to control their anger and put their own messy needs aside. Parents may have instilled the belief in the child that crying, feeling hurt, dwelling on one's own needs, or even asking for things are all "wrong". Feelings of joy and celebration may also have been dampened as well. For example, earning 98% on a test might have been met with parental comments like: "*What happened? How did you fail to get perfect? What's wrong with you?*" Perfectionists were never allowed to rest on their laurels. To do so would be wrong. In time,

Perfectionist Ones come to accept the idea that they are just never good enough. They begin to internalize and identify with the belief that they are always slightly deficient, no matter how excellent or proficient their performance in life.

Important to remember again is that this sense of "deficiency" was not present at birth. It was acquired through time. This deficiency does not represent our true nature as it was in the beginning. It is a fabrication of a false ego-identity. Cleverly, the ego works to ensure its own existence by diverting any awareness away from our inherent *perfection*, one of our essential qualities reflecting the reality of the Higher Self. The ego is like a double-agent. Presumably it's there to help, but if it succeeds, the need for its services will disappear. So, the One's ego deviously schemes by *appearing* to help the person find or regain their lost perfection by searching, or changing, the external world. It knows full well, however, that no lasting satisfaction can be found outside. What the ego won't do is tell the One that essential spiritual perfection is something which was never lost in the first place. The perception that it was is just an illusion. The false ego-self is in no way inclined to dispel that illusion since to do so would be to terminate its own existence. So Type Ones, like all the other character types we'll study, are just kidding themselves about why they're so upset at the world. What a cruel joke our ego plays on us in its own self-defense! And so many of us think the ego is our friend, believing that it get's us what we want.

Psychological Worldview and Compensating Strategies:

In view of those standards which were strictly imposed and sanctioned by their parents or guardians early in life, Type One Perfectionists, like us all, selectively perceive the world. Like Ones, we all notice some things and miss others. We cannot be cognitively aware of everything, so the mind rapidly and in an unconscious fashion focuses on what it values or considers interesting and important. In a way, we see what we want, and what we want, we ask for. The mind, with the help of our ego-personality, is a kind of gatekeeper which determines what enters conscious awareness.

When it comes to the One's psychological worldview, things are largely perceived in terms of right and wrong, good and evil, perfect and imperfect, excellent and poor, tasteful and boorish. For instance, entering a banquet hall for a reception of some description, the One is often quick to notice what works and what doesn't or what is acceptable and what isn't as far as things like decor and seating arrangements are concerned. The fact that there's no vegetarian alternative on the planned menu is deemed *inconsiderate* and *wrong*. Where one is directed to sit, according to the name tag placements, is perhaps *inappropriate* given one's status or relationship to the parties being celebrated. When the food arrives, it's cold and therefore *unacceptable*. Besides, it was *terribly slow* in coming and presented by an *unfriendly* catering staff. They should be *reprimanded* for their lack of professionalism. Later, the speeches were too long, too boring, or just too mundane. How *awful!*

Type Ones know they could have organized things better. They might have put time-limits on the speeches and told the speakers which topics were *verboten*. The entire event could have been much more enjoyable if it were done *right*. Somebody should tell the organizers what needs to be done for next time so things can be *improved*. (Exhausted yet?)

As the example above illustrates, for Type One individuals, there's always a better or worse way to do things and they have a special knack for knowing the better way – sometimes in truth, at other times only as delusions in their own minds. Perfectionists always see room for improvement. It's how they organize their reality. When I think about things like menu selection and social etiquette, the name Martha Stewart comes to mind. This well-know television celebrity and magazine publisher has made a living out of "doing it right" when it comes to home entertaining, cooking and decor. Her uncanny ability to present things taste-fully has made her rich and famous.

Another well-known Type One Character is Al Gore. He is a man on a mission with respect to reversing global warming. Ones, like Gore, are often moral heroes or social reformers wishing to make the world a better place. They are typically rational and principled individuals. In fact, Al Gore's recent book is entitled *The Assault on Reason*. In it, he laments the direction American society has taken with respect to its priorities, its decision-making in matters of war, and the loss of those democratic ideals articulated by the founding fathers of the nation. He sees the dangers of *unreason* when it comes to political campaigning and matters of international policy.

The point here is not whether or not we support Al Gore, but to use him as an example of someone who is a reformer, a visionary, a person of wisdom and foresight. When functioning at their best, Type Ones like Al Gore can make a valuable contribution to humanity, socially, politically, or environmentally. They are ideal-driven, and attuned to matters of values and ethics.

Two other well-known Ones are Noam Chomsky and Pope John Paul II. Both can be described as principled moralists as well. All three have worked to make the world a better place. It can be said that Perfectionist Ones are reformers who see the world as something to be improved. Wrongs need to be righted. What's broken needs to be fixed. Justice needs to replace unfairness and universal social values need to be affirmed in a world falling into the abyss of moral chaos and degeneracy.

Healthy and Unhealthy Expressions of the Perfectionist:
Individuals of all character types can be described as healthy to a greater or lesser extent in their outward expressions. The more enlightened and closer to essence one's experience of life, the healthier one is. The farther the distance, the more unhealthy is the presentation of Self in everyday life.

Furthermore, the more healthy one is, the less obvious is the character type of the individual. Those in touch with their essence are not bounded by the constraints of personality. The more unhealthy a person is, the more the personality is prominent. The fact is that it's unhealthy to identify with your personality and take pride in it. To do so is to identify with your Lower Self. Personality is not essence, your true human nature before the ego-personality arrived on the scene. Actually, it's by getting beyond your personality that you are freed from the chains of the ego. Your personality is something you should use; it should not be something which uses and abuses you. By idealizing your personality and identifying with it, the more obviously tied to the personality you are and the more imprisoned you become. So, if someone is obviously and proudly their type, this is not a good thing.

Finding your character type is not a matter of labeling people and putting them into boxes; it's a way of enabling individuals to escape the limitations of their false ego-identities. By becoming embarrassed by your personality, you have begun to walk into the Chuang-Tzu's shadow, a necessary step if you wish to find peace of mind.

The healthy Type One character has to a very large extent been able to achieve liberation from the personality through self-transcendence. The enlightened One is often on a mission in life. The mission could be based on high ideals such as social justice, equality, world peace, saving the planet, or freedom. It could involve enormous personal sacrifice and investments of time and energy in service to a cause greater than oneself. Giving of oneself in this way is meaningful and makes life worth living. The task of the enlightened One is to improve the world somehow. This is only right. For the One personality, this is what any rational and responsible person should do.

In contrast to enlightened and healthy Ones, unhealthy Perfectionists turn perfection into *perfection-ism*. The desire to get it right is coupled with highly-charged negative emotional undertones. The more dysfunctional the unhealthy the One, the more urgent or desperate is the need for perfection. Without it comes neurotic preoccupation with all its attendant forms of mental agitation. *Wanting* to improve things turns into *having* to improve them for sanity's sake. Organizing one's desk is no longer a choice, but a necessity. This brings us to the shadow element of personality.

Personal Shadow:

As we just observed, each character type can be relatively healthy or unhealthy. We saw how the healthy Perfectionist displays a serene conscientiousness. There is an emotional stability buttressed by integrity, principled rationality, and a sense of purpose. Its highly likely that enlightened Ones have already addressed their childhood issues regarding discipline, authority, and their relationships with their parents and caretakers. They have learned to deal productively with early life experiences and with the internalized messages they received in their youth. They have gone into the past and beyond it. They have come to understand how they have been shaped, but not victimized, by their upbringing. They know that they are more than their personality and are not to be completely identified with it.

The shadow side of the One becomes more obvious in

unenlightened, unhealthy individuals. Each character type has a *shadow issue*, as it were, the negative issue or attribute which the person must deal with in order to achieve true personal integration. For Type One it is *anger*. Unenlightened Perfectionists can be harsh and unforgiving judges, but find it hard to accept that fact openly or consciously. After all, anger and judgment would be hurtful and therefore *wrong;* to admit to it is to make oneself guilty of an egregious violation. Ones should know how terrible anger and judgment are; the harsh judgments they received growing up proved to them how destructive such things could be.

Repressed anger leads Ones to become *resentful* of others. They may not express their resentfulness in any obvious emotional or histrionic displays, but they don't hesitate to accept the ego's advice and project that anger externally by attacking others through criticism. For instance, Ones can resent the fact that others are incompetent at work. *"They are so disorganized or they lack commitment.They fail to display courtesy and proper value orientations; hell, they can't even spell correctly or put a proper sentence together in speech or memo-writing. Don't the others see their flaws and imperfections? Don't they care? What's wrong with them?"* asks the resentful One.*"We could do so much better!"*

The reason Ones will not directly express their resentment and irritation which is felt inside is because to do so would conflict with the virtuous self-image characteristic of the type.[5] Rather, unexpressed anger is transmuted by the ego into what Claudio Naranjo calls "intellectual criticism". By combining criticism with "constructive intent", Ones are able to justify and rationalize their feelings and yet, deny them at the same time. *"I'm not angry!"* said the One in a suppressed tone and with teeth clenched trying to maintain a cool dignified exterior. *"I'm just telling you what you should do and how you should do it!"* No wonder they are internally conflicted.

When others don't do what's right or what's expected, the stage is often set for the Perfectionist to dawn the mantle of "suffering martyr", thinking that *"If you want something done right, you're going to have to do it yourself"*. If fact, if you want it done at all, sometimes, you definitely have to do it yourself. With such thinking, anger takes on the form of *righteous indignation*.[6] The One believes he or she is mad because of what others do or don't do. *They* are the cause of any mental upset.

In reality, the negative criticisms of others are largely a projected reflection of what Ones fear is true about themselves. By a process of defensive reaction formation, that is, by obsessively striving to be perfect in their own lives, Ones try to satisfy the demands of moral conscience, what Sigmund Freud would call the *super-ego*. It's important for Ones to convince themselves that they're good, that they have ethical and psychological integrity. The Perfectionist needs to feel that they're okay. In addition to reaction formation, Ones also use projection as a defense mechanism. By projecting guilt onto others and focusing attention on the imperfections in them or in their performance, Ones unconsciously try to distance themselves from what is feared so greatly, the possibility that they are inherently corrupt, and hence, not-okay.

Despite all efforts to be good exhibited by the One, we can appreciate how this exhausting effort can only produce pseudo-integrity, however. Trying to prove your perfection on a daily and constant basis by desperately and compulsively acting perfectly is implicitly to accept the belief that you once were, or still are, corrupt and deficient or that you could return to that condition in the future without non-stop effort and unrelenting vigilance. The harder one tries, the more one is tormented by the belief.

Sadly, for the dysfunctional One, life is a continuous struggle to prove false what never could have been true in the first place. In essence, the One was never imperfect, flawed, corrupt or deficient. Our Divine Source makes no mistakes. For a One to believe or fear that they are a living mistake is to assume that they know better than God and that they are a better judge of human nature than He is. Now *that* would be wrong.

There's one more ugly aspect to the shadow side of the Perfectionist personality that warrants discussion. Unhealthy Ones have an uncanny ability to use the greatest subtlety when laying guilt trips on others. In fact, their efforts can be so subtle, that Ones themselves are often unaware that they're using the technique. They have used it so often and for so many years, it becomes second nature, an apt description. Nonetheless, laying guilt on others, however subtle or obvious, or however conscious or unconscious, is an ego-strategy used to gain dominance over others. It gives individuals using it the moral high ground. By employing this technique dysfunctional Ones try to manipulate others into getting what they desire.

"I want" is transformed into "You should". By guilt-tripping others, Ones hope to get other people to behave according to their wishes.[7] Certainly, a dishonest use of moral guilt for purposes of personal advantage reflects no true integrity on the part of the One. Ones know at some level that guilt has transformed their own behavior; they think surely it will work on others too. And often it does. Commenting on the pseudo-high-minded moralism and principled, intellectual criticism of the less than enlightened One, Claudio Naranjo writes: "Such vehement interest in principles, morals and ideals is not only an expression of submission to the demands of a strong superego, but, interpersonally, an instrument of manipulation and dominance, for these enthusiastically endorsed norms are imposed on others and ... serve as a cover for personal wishes and demands."[8]

The strain of constant judgment is virtually intolerable It is curious that an ability so debilitating would be so deeply cherished.
  A Course in Miracles

No problem can be solved from the same consciousness that created it.
  Albert Einstein

Therapeutic Recommendations for Promoting Psychological Hygiene and Finding Inner Peace:

From what we've just discussed about the One, it's clear that the Perfectionist suffers from a troubled mind. We all do to a greater or lesser extent. In view of this, the strategies that need to be developed by a Higher Reality Therapy should not primarily focus on changing the external circumstances surrounding the individual, but on changing the individual's mind about those circumstances. But please don't misunderstand. Surely, there are times when it's completely proper and fitting to actively do things to solve our problems. Taking medication to cure a migraine headache or correct a chemical imbalance brought on by a physical condition, for instance, are two situations where action is appropriate. Taking steps to leave an abusive relationship is another. Or let's say we've been wrongly accused of a crime we didn't commit. In this case, clearly we should retain legal counsel and actively mount our own self-defense to fight our accusers in court.

Complete passivity and inaction are not what's being recommended here. While essentially we are not *of* this world, we still must live *in* this world temporarily. The question is, How should we live? How should we see and organize our lives? What's important to recognize is that much of our trouble and fight against the world is unnecessary and a simply a product of our own distorted projections.

A great deal of our mental disturbance is brought on by little more than self-created ego illusions. It's these illusions we wish to dispel by our existential psychoanalysis. In light of all this, we can say that when it comes to unchangeable circumstances, some unpleasantness in life requires attitude adjustment; other manageable problems require practical action, but so much of our mental disturbance is self-generated delusional thought and hence requires us to use the mind's eye of inner vision to see through our own perceptual distortions. As Lama Surya Das reminds us, awareness is curative. "The silent watcher" observes the Lower Self in its tragic-comedy performance. It is amused, not bothered, for it has not forgotten how to laugh at the insane reality created by the ego. It rests undisturbed in the higher knowledge of that which the *eye has not seen, nor ear heard.* The Silent Watcher knows what the Stoic philosopher knows, namely, that *external things touch not the soul, not in the slightest degree.*

God grant me the serenity to accept the things I cannot change, the courage to change the things I can, and the wisdom to know the difference.

    Reinhold Niebuhr

On this note, let us turn to the first bit of prescriptive advice for the Perfectionist looking for a greater degree of mental stability. Actually, this psycho-hygienic advice applies to all character types. What we must begin to practice is spiritual discernment, rather than judgment.[9]

    Judgment is what the ego is all about. Spiritual discernment is what our Higher Self engages in. When we judge, we reinforce the separation between self and other or self and the world. We regard others as beneath us or above us. There are those who are perceived as better or worse, or more or less accomplished when compared with us. When we judge others, we project our sorry intentions onto them. Like our friend, Lance, we see them for who they are not. We often impute to them thoughts that were never theirs. We frequently imbue their motivations with projections originating from our own troubled minds. We can see imagined imperfections and find perverse enjoyment in the entire process of fault-finding. We thereby do existential violence to innocent bystanders.

As Perfectionist Ones know, when we judge ourselves, we inflict violence upon ourselves. This violence creates a great deal of internal conflict and psychological disequilibrium. We go to war with ourselves. With judgment we blame ourselves. Judgment causes us to feel guilty. It is because of judgment that we experience low self-esteem and insecurity. Pronouncing judgment on ourselves is what makes us anxious about entering a room full of strangers. Self-imposed judgment on our performance is what makes us discouraged, despondent and full of despair. Even if judgment is positive, we still worry that the next time it won't be. With judgment comes perceived deficiency, embarrassment, and self-loathing. Judgment becomes the supreme cognitive, suicidal weapon of mass psychological destruction. Even when judging targeted others, the One unconsciously feels guilty inside knowing that the critical attack on the other was dishonestly motivated by negative self-appraisal. The fear is that the One might be found out for this dishonesty and attacked in retaliation.

A quotation from *A Course in Miracles* bears repeating: *"The strain of constant judgment is virtually intolerable. It is curious that an ability so debilitating would be so deeply cherished."*

As an alternative to judgment, we should try to exercise awareness and spiritual discernment. The Essential or Higher Self observes. It notes differences, sees actions and reactions, yet it does so without the negative emotional charge of judgment. Ideas and thoughts enter and exit the theater of the mind. They come in and out of consciousness. There is no censorship. Feelings are experienced at face value without repression or evaluation. Actions simply precede and follow.

Spiritual discernment allows for neutral observation of all this. With neutrality comes disengagement, a detachment and a dis-identification with the ego-personality. There is something miraculously cathartic and enlightening about this. To catch yourself in your own habits of behavior or in your own predictable response patterns of emotion or speech creates the liberating moment for you to free yourself from your false ego-identity.

Paradoxically, when you catch yourself in the act of being yourself, that's when you gain the flash of insight that you are not yourself. You are not your ego-personality, not really the person you appear to have become. You are not the person you believe other people see. You have become consciously aware not only of your Lower Psychological Self, but also of your Higher Spiritual Self.

Now you have the opportunity to identify with your true spiritual identity which observes with *The Mind's Eye*. The Mind's Eye offers spiritual vision, not lower level sensory-based empirical perception colored by psychological defensiveness. As the witnessing presence, it plays a role as the Spiritual Decision-Maker in your life. It affords you the opportunity to choose between right-mindedness and wrong-mindedness, between peace of mind and psychological torment. It is what allows you to decide again about your true identity. It is what bears witness to the truth.

It is what recognizes the essential qualities inherent in your being and present in all other persons. Seeing life through The Mind's Eye brings one closer to others. It enables us all, Ones included, to take responsibility for the world that is observed. It can decide to perceive the unblemished perfection in others, as well as the absolute perfection in oneself. You see, The Mind's Eye views life through the optical lens of Divine Perfection. This Divine Perfection is Perfect Love. Truly remarkable is the fact that *it is through the One's essential perfection that the Divine is expressed in the world.*

Now do I finally understand something I was taught so long ago as a young child in religion class: *God lives in everybody; so how you treat yourself and others is how you treat God.*

Together, and in perfect unity with our Divine Source, is our essence regardless of the separate identity our ego would offer us. To put logic in service of therapeutic philosophy, let us say that, "If God is all, that is, if nothing can exist beyond God, and further, if God encompasses everything, and we are part of that everything, then we are necessarily part of God – undeniably perfect in Spirit. This is how we were made in God's spiritual image. Therefore, all other thinking is illusory, all imperfection a passing dream."

The lesson for the One is actually a lesson for all of us. The false reality created by the One simply revolves around the mistaken belief in imperfection more than it does for those of other character types. Though our particular psychological wounds may give rise to other preferred illusory preoccupations dealing with lost essence, we all can still feel the One's pain. We are all identical to the One in spirit.

Once truth and illusion are distinguished, it becomes easier to follow the second prescription which heals not only the One, but all of us. What the One must do is forgive themselves and others for their *perceived* imperfections. In our paradigm case of Becky and Lance, Becky never really did anything to Lance. Lance needs to recognize this and forgive her. What Lance saw never occurred in reality. Further, Becky isn't flawed or simply a "stuck-up bitch" – again, this is a delusion. She is a physical manifestation of the Divine Source. To see anything or anyone else is a hallucination.

Spiritual discernment reveals this to us, not the eyes of the ego filmed with fear and unconscious insecurity. For the One, it is time to pardon and release all those innocent prisoners who were incarcerated in the darkness of a resentful and angry judgmental mind for far too long. It is also time for Ones to see that forgiveness holds the key to their own release from the prison of psychological guilt. Self-perceptions of imperfection and deficiency are contrary to what spiritual discernment uncovers. Perfection is reflection of our true reality, our essence, the spark of the Divine in all of us. There's no longer any need to prove or defend this truth. Nothing can ever change it. There is nothing to worry about.

As it is written in *A Course in Miracles*:

Nothing real can be threatened.
Nothing unreal exists.
Herein lies the peace of God.

You may ask at this point, "But what if Becky truly were stuck-up? Or, suppose there was another Becky who really did look down her nose at Lance. Wouldn't he then be justified in criticizing her?" The short answer is no. The reason for this is implicit in things that have already been said about spirit and essence so far in the discussion.

You see, if God is All and God is Perfect and God is Love, then everything in the world must be a reflection of that Perfection and Love. Nothing is beyond God and nothing created by God is imperfect or unloving. What appears unloving is just a dream in the grand scheme of eternity. Though the ego has a hard time accepting this, spiritual discernment allows us to appreciate this fact in our perceptions and interactions with other people. If we are Divine Sparks, or embodied emanations of the Divine, then Perfect Love is what we are. An implication of this is that everything anyone does is either a direct expression of love or an indirect call for love.[10]

The stuck-up version of Becky is likely to be insecure about her self-worth. That insecurity may be transformed psychologically into haughtiness or arrogance. What is insecurity if not a desperate cry for loving acceptance? Or take the angry criticism of others, for example; it comes from a deep place of hurt, as we've seen in the One. Behind the anger is what the ego-eye does not see. There is guilt and self-blame which is too painful to bear, so it is externalized and projected onto others. This is the sad psychological strategy of someone who is delusional about their own true identity. It is a desperate attempt of someone suffering from a tormented mind. Once the One sees the mistake of their own mistaken identity, and the case of mistaken identity when it comes to how they have viewed others in the past, forgiveness becomes a real possibility and with that comes peace at last.

Finally, it's important to recognize that the peace of mind which forgiveness provides requires a dramatic upheaval of metaphysical, epistemological, and ontological assumptions about existence, human nature, reality, mind, knowledge, and God. Acceptance of a new cosmology and psychological worldview does not come easily without resistance, skepticism and doubt. You came to embrace the perspective of the ego, the one who became a good and trusted friend for years, or so you thought before the ego's treachery was revealed to you. This betrayal can be emotionally devastating and something not easy to overcome.

Another thing that Ones need not to do is confuse their "inner critic" with the "inner voice" of the Higher Self. To explain what is meant by this, let us look at an historical example.

Centuries ago, the philosopher Socrates repeatedly questioned authority and encouraged the youth of Athens to do the same. Unfortunately for Socrates, his activities came to be considered subversive and a danger to the state. As a consequence, he was charged with a crime then known as impiety. Loved and admired by many, Socrates was given every opportunity to escape the state prison in Athens and thereby avoid the assessed penalty of death. Rather than flee, however, Socrates decided to listen to his "inner voice" or *daemon*, as he and other philosophers of the time would refer to it, and accept the guilty verdict. Accepting the *Daemon's* message, Socrates drank the poisonous hemlock as punishment for his crime, though he was not convinced he had done anything wrong. By accepting the consequences of his actions Socrates wanted to "walk the talk" as it were. Drinking the hemlock was necessary to maintain his integrity as a philosophical role model for those who would follow in his footsteps. To live in Athens as a good citizen meant submitting oneself to its system of justice.

Now many of us today would likely choose to compromise our principles in order to escape death. It's often the case that we act in a principled fashion only as long as doing so works in our own self-interest. The moment it doesn't, the dishonest rationalizations and moral compromises begin. As for Socrates, his efforts to make the right decision must have been successful for many in the world today still regard Socrates as the paradigm philosopher and paragon of ethical integrity. Socrates shows us how we "ought" to live – a concern especially important for Ones. Unfortunately, acting ethically sometimes comes with a price. This might explain why there are so few heroes and saints. For so many of us, morality has become little more than an inconvenient liability in the cost-benefit hedonistic calculations of life. In cases where this is true, one might be tempted to question Socrates' choice to die. Those with moral integrity are less so inclined to doubt the wisdom of Socrates' decision.

As for Socrates' *Daemon*, that seemingly strange notion may not be easy to understand in the modern world context. To clarify, think of it as something akin to one's "guardian spirit" – that which provides inner guidance. It is what Christians might describe as the voice of the "Holy Spirit." Its counsel brings light and illumination where darkness and ignorance once stood.

Be sure to appreciate the fact that this voice is *not* the critical voice of a guilt-ridden moral conscience – what Freud calls the super-ego. The super-ego belongs to personality, not essence. Our inner guide or *Daemon*, by contrast, is part of our spiritual nature.

Sadly, in a hustle-bustle world of noisy super-highways, busy schedules, impending deadlines, mass production, consumption, materialism, and manic hyper-activity, the sound of our inner voice is barely audible. Much louder is the voice of the super-ego or inner critic screaming at us at every turn to measure up to what advertisers, image consultants, celebrities, experts, parents, gurus and leaders of all sorts set up as standards of excellence, desirability or perfection. It is the inner critic which judges, condemns, and criticizes both ourselves and others. Its moralistic voice tells us to do the "right" thing, but it does so out of insecurity, defensiveness and neurotic preoccupation.

The unbearability of the inner critic's condemnations is what leads the ego to engage in defensive projections seeing the guilt in others that one cannot stand to see in oneself. The One knows full well how harsh and unforgiving the inner critic can be. It feasts on angry retribution. It expresses itself in finger pointing and blame. It is troubling and painfully loud. On the other hand, our *Daemon* is not shrill or angry in any of its directives. It gently instructs us with a loving tone to do the right thing with the right intention. If we remain still long enough, we can hear the soothing spiritual guidance it offers.

Our *Daemon* serves as a messenger from the Divine. It whispers to us the will of our Source. It is what allows for God's will to be done here on Earth as it is in Heaven. The critical super-ego, as we know, has other things in mind. In reference to what the ancients called the Daemon, it is written in *A Course in Miracles* that *"The Voice of the Holy Spirit does not command, because It is incapable of arrogance. It does not demand, because It does not seek control. It does not overcome, because it does not attack. It is compelling only because of what It reminds you of....The Voice for God is always quiet, because It speaks of peace* (Chapter 5, p.76). This peace is ultimately the goal for therapeutic philosophy.

Father Zeus, O free them all from suffering so great or show unto each the daemon, who is their guide.
    Pythagoras

Zeus has placed by every man a guardian, every man a daemon, to whom he has committed the care of the man; a guardian who never sleeps, is never deceived.
    Epictetus, Stoic Philosopher

I myself do nothing. The Holy Spirit accomplishes all through me.
    William Blake

Healing is a sign that you want to make whole. And this willingness opens your ears to the Voice of the Holy Spirit.. .Think like Him ever so slightly, and the little spark becomes a blazing light that fills your mind so that He becomes your only Guest.
    A Course in Miracles

Of course, acting morally and doing the morally right thing are good, even if they result from the prompting of the super-ego. But, for Ones to do the right thing while beating up on themselves because they feel inadequate or flawed is not healthy. Doing the right things for the wrong psychological reasons is part of the self-deception perpetuated by the ego. Fear of failing to do or say the right things, or guilt over having fallen short of perfection, are things which ultimately cause fear, anxiety, and psychological projection. The resulting inner dialogue is one of rationalized self-justification or self-blame.

The ego allows moral conscience in this case to confuse self-condemnation with virtuous humility. The *Daemon*, on the other hand, takes no pleasure in self-flagellation or sadistic attacks on the perceived imperfections of others.

Ones need to take time for meditation and prayerful silence. To access the advice of your personal *Daemon* you will need to be still. Practice quiet meditation and learn to be present to the moment.

Put aside all thoughts. The type of meditation prescribed here does not require any type of rational, intellectual or logical analysis. In fact, such analyses would be counter-productive and self-defeating in the end. What we're attempting here is to silence *the mad monkey of the mind* as Buddhists put it.

So, when thoughts and ideas enter your mind, simply let them pass in and out of consciousness. In time, they will become less frequent. When thoughts stop racing through your mind, the great expansiveness of higher consciousness will begin to reveal itself to you. Your task for now is just to be open and aware and quiet. Out of the sublime stillness of infinity will come direction. Your Divine Source wills it. Just listen. The sounds of silence have the power to calm the troubled soul.

Finally, Ones need to regain awareness of their Essential Innocence. They can improve their overall psychological hygiene by allowing for greater spontaneity of expression, especially in their instinctual appetites and responses to life.[11]

Ones tend to be tightly wound and rather rigid in terms of their dogmatic certainty. Thus, there is a need to unwind and become less opinionated. On the physical side of things, Ones need to recognize that what is biological is part of our 'human' nature. It's not dirty or sinful. This does not imply that sex, for instance, should be pursued licentiously. There are ways of expressing human sexuality in a loving, spiritual manner. The point is that with greater open-mindedness and acceptance of not only of the body, but things in general, can come curiosity, playfulness, enthusiasm and joy – characteristics often seen in the innocence of childhood. Existential rebirth requires a return to this innocence.

Verily I say unto you, Except ye be converted, and become as little children, ye shall not enter into the kingdom of heaven.
Jesus of Nazareth (Matthew 18:3)

CHAPTER FIVE

EGO DYNAMICS IN CHARACTER TYPE TWO: *THE SELFLESS GIVER*

Don't forget to love yourself.
Søren Kierkegaard

Lost Essence:

At this point in the discussion, we're becoming much more familiar with the notion of self-estrangement. We now know that who we truly are is defined by our essence. Unfortunately, many of us still suffer from a case of mistaken identity, opting for a self-definition expressed in terms of ego-personality.

With the One we observed how the harsh judgments of parental authority were internalized and how they produced the psychological script to be enacted in the Perfectionist's day to day drama of life. Ones need to see and appreciate the reality of their inner perfection if they wish to heal. They are not flawed, stained, imperfect, or corrupt. God makes no mistakes.

Like Ones, Twos are essentially perfect, but their sense of loss or lost essence revolves more around the essential quality of Love. Like the One, the Two's sense of loss begins in childhood.

As Richard Rohr and Andreas Ebert put it:

Many Twos had a childhood that seemed gray and sad to them. Real security and a feeling of having a home were sometimes lacking, or less than they needed. Other Twos report that they have experienced only conditional love. The love of important persons in their life had to be bought by good behavior. If they met the conditions, they could, under certain circumstances, get a lot of love and security. The 'beautiful' childhood that these Twos had prevents them from becoming enraged or sorrowful that they were continually being urged to exaggerated good behavior. Some Twos also recall that early on they had the feeling of having to be a support for the emotional needs of other family members. They had the feeling that they had to make themselves useful in order to be noticed and loved.[1]

According to Rohr and Ebert, the spiritual wound of the Two results as a product of *conditional* love. In truth we are all uncondicionally loveable. Created in the spiritual image of our Maker, infinite love is simply what we are. We cannot be different from God or beyond God, for then we would have to become our own source standing outside God's omnipotence and omnipresence, and this is impossible. Furthermore, this essential quality is not something that needs to be earned; nor is it something which can be lost. It can be forgotten, however, by a mind that has become misguided.

Sadly, some children are taught in life that they are loveable only conditionally, that is, only if and when they do something for someone else. When this lesson is internalized, being 'good' is not about moral correctness – which is a fundamental concern for the One. Rather, the motivation is emotional and psychological. The wounded Two thinks: *"I need to be loved so I will do what it takes to get that love."*

In the childhood circumstances of the Two, a perverse role reversal takes place between the parent or guardian and child. In order to be loved or at least have love expressed in terms of attention or notice, the young Two has to deny his or her own needs and minister to those of the adult. The child's own needs have to be deferred and put to the side. The child eventually concludes: "*I am loved, but only when I'm ready to be helpful and ignore my own needs.*"

The result of this conclusion entails an age-inappropriate role-exchange. Those adults who should be caring for the child begin to look weak and needy, while the little helper Two begins to care for those who apparently cannot care for themselves.

The developing ego is quick to latch on to this sense of power which comes from servicing others. Around this sense of power a wounded ego-identity is born.[2]

The notion of 'servicing others' brings to mind an experience I had as a senior in high school. I remember once going over to a friend's house for a visit. My friend's little sister, still in grade school, was hanging out with the boys. I'm sure much of the conversation was going over her head, given the age differences at the time. Nobody was really paying particular attention to little sister until suddenly she brought pillows for everyone and helped to adjust them on the couches and chairs for comfort. She also brought me an ottoman so I could put my feet up and relax even more. Of course, such behavior drew our collective attention to her. We started interacting with our little hostess and we began commenting to her how nice and considerate she was. Later, she brought us drinks and popcorn. As long as our hostess was catering to our needs, she belonged to our group and was part of the action. She received attention and effusive compliments. As you might expect with insensitive and egocentric adolescents, once we got the refreshments we wanted and finished with our discussion, we departed without a moment's hesitation, leaving our little servant-girl abandoned and alone. Subsequently, each time we came over, it seemed that her care and effort escalated to receive notice. The 'pillow thing' started to become stale as such catering became an expectation on our part. Thus, she figured, more and more had to be done to deserve notice. Quite probably, recognition of this fact began to sow the seeds of personal insecurity which possibly still haunt that person today, though we should all hope this is not the case.

Psychological Worldview and Compensating Strategies:

The Selfless Giver is a feeling type individual who sees the world through the *eyes of the heart,* as it were. Opportunities are present everywhere to minister to people in need. Just look. While you and I might see a *wino* or *bum* sitting in a doorway on the street and walk by in a judgmental, self-righteous huff, the Two is much more likely to perceive a desperate human being in trouble. The Two may even stop and help or toss a few coins into the individual's begging cup. Of course, there are some people who would be quite happy to admonish the 'bum' and tell him to get a job. By contrast, the Two might be curious to learn about the person's history and the events that led him to be where he is today. Twos have a wonderful way of showing care and compassion in a cold and callous world and doing so without casting blame or judging others. They can often see through, or see past, ugly and frightening exteriors to appreciate the person inside. The ability to see the humanity in others, regardless of appearances, to recognize their hurts or needs, and the willingness to respond to them, captures the saintly generosity displayed by the Two. Mother Teresa and Desmond Tutu are probably Twos. Add to the list Mary Magdalene. More recent figures include Sally Field, Luciano Pavarotti, and Dolly Parton.

"...some things you see with your eyes, others you see with your heart."
  Littlefoot's Mother in *The Land Before Time*

As feeling types, Twos are drawn toward others. Their need to be needed is what provides self-definition for them. Their attraction to others is not always unqualified or indiscriminate, however. Twos often look for people who will inspire them or somehow move them emotionally. They look for ways to connect with such people, hoping to become confidantes, helpers or assistants of some sort.

Twos are quite happy to play a secondary role in the lives of others. After all, they learned to do this in their youth. They become the people behind the scenes who make things possible for someone else to excel. Satisfaction can be drawn from their association with 'stars' and 'winners', or with successful and 'important' individuals, those who possess power, expertise, or influence. Twos often become cheerleaders for these people trumpeting their cause.[3] They function as managers who network and do deals to ensure the continued success of the individual who motivates and inspires them.

The psychological orientation for the Two is about making a connection and moving in to make that connection happen. Their attention is focused outwardly, not inwardly. The Two spent most of his or her childhood servicing the needs of others. As a consequence, the perceptual habit to focus on others' needs, not one's own, was formed.

In service to others, Twos have an intuitive ability to read body language, energy levels, other people's concerns and interests. In fact, some Twos can anticipate what you need even before you know it yourself and they respond accordingly. This is one reason why Twos are perceived as so caring and considerate. They always appear to have your interests in mind, not theirs. No wonder Twos are so likeable.

Selfishly, we tend to like people who do things for us. I'm reminded here of an athletic event out of town, where my daughters were competing. The event was outdoors and it just happened to be chilly that morning. While my wife and I were sitting and chatting with the father of another participant, the man's wife suddenly appeared with coffee and bagels for all of us – how thoughtful! She said we might need these refreshments in light of the weather and early morning hour. Indeed we did. The woman read our minds. The ability to 'read minds', so to speak, is certainly characteristic of the Two. I suspect she was exactly that type – being so nice and so considerate.

The Two possesses the ability to don and discard multiple personas as easily as you and I can change our clothes. You see, the desire to connect and please others turns the Two into something of a chameleon. This is because the two can and does connect with more than one person at the same time.

In one set of circumstances the Two can be happily all dolled up, formal and fancy and then in another situation be all folksy, casual, and down home. The Two reads the situation and presents a version of themself that is appropriate for it. What you see in the Two is what everyone wants or needs. The Two is usually quite happy to deliver and appreciates the notice that ensues.

Because appearances are so important for Twos, they can be described as 'image types'. It's important for them to present the correct image, depending on whose wishes or needs are being catered to in any given instance. Putting on a different face or façade may be necessary to continue receiving notice and appreciation. For Twos, doing this is not experienced as something dishonest, just appropriate for the particular situation. You see, the Two's self-definition is based on the formation of relationships with others and in terms of compliance to their wishes, desires, and expectations.

Healthy and Unhealthy Expressions of the Selfless Giver:
Healthy Twos are probably the most unselfish and altruistic of all the character types that have been identified. The love they give is unconditional, with no strings attached.[4] They are not giving to get or trying to garner notice by means of doing for others. Theirs is not a deficiency-motivation. Rather, it is positive and basically other-referring. There are no ulterior motives for generosity or

unconscious schemes to get what they want. The business of maintaining an image is also not a consideration. The altruistic giving is honest and pure and the intention is virtuous.

As with all healthy types, you are more likely to see a calm radiant joy in the face of a self-actualized Two. Twos in touch with their essence are able to give in humble, yet self-gratifying ways. The giving is done freely and gladly with no expectations of return and with no resentment if appreciation is not shown. Virtue is its own reward. The healthy Selfless Giver is the person-ification of self-less love. In the Selfless Giver, we catch yet another glimpse of the Spark of the Divine, the Face of God framed in Eternal Love.

They have not lost themselves in the giving, however. The Two acts freely, consciously and intentionally in a desire to do things for others, truly for their own sake, not to achieve some dark unconscious hidden agenda.

Other adjectives to describe the Two are caring, thoughtful, warm-hearted, empathic, concerned, sincere, forgiving and compassionate. We can all learn how to live from this type of individual.

In the unhealthy Two, we witness perhaps the same giving on the outside, but with different intentions on the inside. Less-than-self-secure Twos give to others in order to establish a connection or relationship. Twos are looking for their 'better half' to complete them. Without someone else, they are not fulfilled and cannot be, at least in their own minds. In fact, unhealthy Twos define themselves in terms of the interests, occupations, successes, and prestige of other people. They try to be 'connected to' and associated with someone important, rich, influential, beautiful, handsome, or otherwise desirable. All these qualities of the 'other' compensate for all the perceived deficiencies from which the unhealthy Two believes they suffer. A committed relationship with someone who presumably will make them the person they are *not*, but wish to be, is truly a 'special relationship' but this is unfortunately almost always doomed to failure from the beginning.[5]

A common technique used by Twos to establish connections with others is flattery. Who has not been a victim of this? When people flatter us, our egos become inflated by virtue of the fact that someone else has noticed and validated us in terms of our appearance, performance, or intelligence. This flattery is certainly seductive and the Two knows it, either consciously or unconsciously. We are lured into conversation by the Two's flattery or by anyone else's flattery for that matter. We are drawn closer to them, physically, emotionally, and psychologically. The flatterer massages our ego and we like the feeling. We may even come to like the psychological masseuse, whoever they are. That is the Two's hope of course. In the center of all this ego-massage, however, can be found the hidden motivation of one person to ingratiate themselves for egoistic purposes. Perhaps compliments will be returned. The flatterer may be invited back. Most probably the recipient of the ego massage will be left with a favorable impression of the flattering Two – mission accomplished!

The Two's seductive maneuvers can often carry over into the sexual realm. In their efforts to mask feelings of worthlessness, Twos characteristically seek pleasure. This seeking can become desperate; when it does, sex becomes a convenient vehicle to self-satisfaction. Erotic love or physical expressions of tenderness become the pleasurable antidote for self-perceptions of inadequacy and lack of significance. The pleasure experienced from sex has the added benefit of satisfying and gratifying their sexual partners. The problem is that pleasuring someone else dishonestly requires one to give up one's own dignity.

In truth, nobody ever really loses their dignity, for our worth is inviolate from a higher perspective. Nonetheless, in the wrong-mindedness of the Two, the feeling of self-inflicted emotional abuse is experienced. Of course, that feeling is usually repressed as attention is focused on the other who will provide the psychologically sustaining ego-boost needed to maintain sanity.

In unhealthy special relationships, the aim of the person is to get someone else to prove to them that they are worthy of love – as if this needs proving from the perspective of our Divine Source. Establishing relationships is a way to quell the fears of the ego that one might be insignificant.

In special relationships, others are responsible for the individual's happiness. If you notice me, approve of me, desire me, and appreciate me, then I am whole. If not, I suffer in mental pain, insecure about my identity and self-worth as a person. Thus "I need you to make me happy." "Without you, I am nothing." These are the thoughts of the Two deluded about their own true identity. Their sick attachments to others manifest in a kind of *clinginess* stemming from a continual insecurity over the possibility that the other may walk out, lose interest, or find someone else more worthy. Special relationships are built on a very shaky foundation indeed. Let us say that the Two is dumped by the significant other. Well, then, the sad saga simply repeats itself. The unhealthy Two seeks out another relationship for purposes of self-validation. In the psyche of the damaged Two, it's not about truly loving the other; it's really about proving that one is worthy of love in the first place.

From the perspective of the suffering Two, the relationship is really about 'me', not 'us'. The Two thinks: *"My dull and meaningless life can be inspired by you. My insignificance can be compensated for by your importance. I'm very excited about how special you will make me look in the eyes of others. My low self-esteem can be bolstered by your interest in me. With you and me working as a team, I can deal with my personal fears about life. Just think how good we'll look out on the town together! Imagine how others will admire and respect us. In my association with you, people will be impressed by me."*

However, special relationships based on deficiency-motivations set the Two up for repeated failures. As soon as the Two no longer fulfills the needs of the other, that other is likely to leave. Recall how years ago my adolescent friends and I developed rising expectations with respect to our little servant girl. She had to do more and more to receive the same notice. After the cushions, the refreshments and the popcorn, we still needed more in order to notice her. As someone who was young and didn't know any better, she couldn't appreciate how we were using her to get what we wanted. She was apparently ready, willing and able to serve us anytime we had a craving for something.

With adults, however, there are usually limits to what they are prepared to give or sacrifice. By the time those limits are reached, the *beneficiary-other* usually has become inured to 'special treatment' and is no longer impressed. The Two may be taken for granted, treated like a door mat, ignored, abandoned or left alone, just as our little servant girl was.

The other person might also catch on to the fact that something sneaky is going on. Remember, the special relationship was based on a form of emotional entrapment. The Two manipulated the other person into liking them by giving the other what they wanted or needed.

Special relationships can fail in yet another way. For instance, if for whatever reason the other person no longer fulfills the security needs of the Two, the relationship is over once more. Perhaps the winner has become a loser or the famous has become infamous. Once attractive, the other may now be unappealing. Even when a relationship is temporarily going well, there's always the unconscious fear that it could end sometime soon.

You see, for the dysfunctional Two, any relationship is probably not right in the first place, given the insignificance the Two perceives in themselves. The disturbing thought lurks in the back of the mind that "any individual who could possibly want *me* is not worth wanting." Deep-rooted insecurity could sabotage a budding relationship rather quickly, one which otherwise would have had a dishonest foundation anyway.

Destructive special relationships are based on the principle of giving to get. If I'm taking psychological comfort from you and you're busy taking favors or getting physical pleasure from me, then we're both stealing from each other. I want what you have and you want what I have. You become a taker from me and I become a taker from you.

Ayn Rand, the 20th century pro-capitalist philosopher, would probably accept this sort of relationship insofar as it is based on a 'fair trade' agreement. In principle, I suppose, there can be fair give and take on both sides. Yet, once you no longer have the existential products, goods or services I require, then the (trading) relationship is over, either mutually dissolved in an amicable way or bitterly and with resentment given the emotional trade imbalance and all of what was done by one of us for the other. Our fair trade deal may not have turned out to be so fair at all in the end.

To regard special relationships as ideal is to dissolve the notion of life-time commitment, conventional marriage, and spiritual union. To accept this notion is to agree to selfish instrumentality in endless broken agreements. What contracts based on perverse self-interest can last forever? In the end, special love relationships are not so special. How sad are dating agencies and TV dating shows which often have single males and females listing what they *want* in their next partner. "He or she must be this or that. They must have money, a sense of humor, or a particular career."

Everyone seems to know in advance what they want from the other person. Only those with an acceptable personal and psychological profile need apply for the special relationship sought after. Applicants for the relationship also know what they want from their 'special relationship providers'. Those engaging in emotional-exchange economics should be aware, however, that there's no unqualified loyalty to the provider of affection, whoever it is. If and when the applicant's needs are not met, he or she simply disappears. *What the selfish ego has joined together, fate will no doubt be put asunder.*

Not knowing who they are essentially, unhealthy Twos form an idealized self-image based on the connections and affiliations they have made.[6] They spend their time trying to realize an image of an ideal self, rather than work on their actual self. Unfortunately, the production and maintenance of an idealized self-image may require the expression of false love and false self-satisfaction. To be seen as desirable or cool, for instance, may require 'posing' and the inauthentic presentation of one's feelings. True expressions of emotion might jeopardize things. Catering to the needs of others in order to maintain a relationship, may also require suppressing or denying one's own feelings which could interfere, say, with the idealized self-image of the 'perfect hostess', for example.

The image of positivity must always be maintained, regardless of any negative feelings. All of this self-deception, denial and inauthenticity drowns the individual in a Sartrean sea of *bad faith*. In this case, pretending constitutes an act of psychological violence against oneself.

Of course, people do not usually wish to direct violence against themselves. So the ego conveniently steps in. If and when Twos reach their breaking point – that is, when they can no longer stand their psychological sell-out to others or when their tireless efforts have gone unnoticed and unappreciated – the ego engages in forceful emotional attacks upon the ingrates – those who have failed to pay back what should have been returned for such 'loving' care.

For instance, it's not uncommon to witness Twos in histrionic displays. When they are extremely desperate and frustrated, Twos can surprise others with their angry and aggressive behavior. To others who know these care-giving helpers, such behavior comes as quite a shock. Emotional histrionic displays may include things like fainting spells or feigned suicide attempts. Such actions demand immediate attention; they induce guilt, and are designed to coerce others to give Twos what they want. The Selfless Giver will engage in any and all forms of scandalous emotional expression to get their needs met, regardless of how irrational. Reasoning with unhealthy Twos is not always productive. As feeling types, Twos are frequently anti-intellectual so the force of reason has little power of persuasion over them.[7]

In summarizing the psychological worldview of the Two, it can be said that unhealthy variations of this type tend to focus on others, seeking validation through self-sacrifice and service to them. It is believed that affection must be earned and that taking time for oneself is selfish. Presumably, good people don't have needs and should rather attend to the needs of others. Thus, Twos frequently become rescuers, gravitating to needy people they come across in their lives. By devoting themselves to needy people, they become important, perhaps even indispensable.

Twos can also adopt the strategy of affiliating with impressive people in hopes of becoming impressive themselves. They become the organizers and supporters behind the scenes. Of course, the strategy is giving to get and is largely manipulative, even if Twos are unaware of the underlying motivations of their actions. This harkens back to a claim made at the outset of the book, namely, that we're not always honest about, or aware of, our true motivations in life. The self-deception involved can have devastating emotional and psychological consequences.

Personal Shadow:

What might come as a shock to psychologically insecure Twos is the notion that their desperate attempts to connect with others or to help them rests on pride. This is their primary shadow issue which needs resolution. Often, we think of pride as emanating from boastful, arrogant, or obviously self-serving individuals. Typical Twos appear to be anything but that, at least on the surface. How can someone 'behind the scenes' be boastful? How can an organizer for someone else's successful career be self-serving? Certainly, helping the needy cannot be considered selfish; how could that possibly be?

In answer, remember that Twos need to be needed. If I, or you, or anyone else for that matter cannot live without the services of a Two, they become important to us. There's a self-satisfaction experienced by Twos in the knowledge that they have become indispensable and that we cannot do without them.

To illustrate, parents may dote on their children and give them everything they want, even into adulthood. Unconsciously, some parent Twos do this to prevent the child from ever developing personal responsibility and independence. If the child, now adult, never learns to live on their own, if helicopter moms or dads protect them at every turn, then the care-giver parents are assured that their offspring will always require help. *Translation*: The Two parent will remain important and indispensable. They may even be complimented and admired by relatives and neighbors for the boundless generosity exhibited toward their children. In this case, the motivation behind the generosity is not necessarily so pretty.

Of course, prideful motivations are not the exclusive preserve of family relationships. There is also pride in the Two's 'behind the scenes' behavior at work or in the volunteer organization. If successful and important people have come to depend on the Two, then the Two must be quite an impressive individual. By giving generously of one's time, energy, and resources, the Two often receives praise and recognition from others who are not as giving and selfless as they are. The Selfless Giver can appear almost saintly by the extent of their sacrifices for others. Most of us are 'too selfish' to do what the Two is prepared to do. Hence Twos must be morally superior or better than us – an idea that permits their pride to grow even more.

Finally, the Two's pride can come from recognition that they possess the power to manipulate other people into liking them and noticing them and thereby giving them what they want. What a perverse amusement it must be, for instance, to disingenuously compliment someone or feign real concern when the effort is all about getting noticed and appreciated for purposes of building self-esteem.

Pride goeth before destruction and a haughty spirit before a fall.
    Proverbs

Paradoxically, what produces pride in the Two is exactly what causes their mental disturbance. Twos often know that other people like them; and so they should. Twos have manipulated others' affections for their own hidden purposes. Others have been fooled into liking the Two. But what if the manipulation stops? What happens if the Two no longer gives or is too tired to give any longer?

The fear is that affection and notice will be taken away. So, in order to be accepted and loved, or noticed and admired, the Two must become someone who always gives, and never stops giving.

Twos thereby create the circumstances for their own psychological demise. They become emotionally co-dependent on others who have been manipulated into liking or becoming dependent on them.

Twos' self-acceptance is predicated on acceptance by others. The problem is that their acceptance by others has been dishonestly produced. So, the affection shown by others toward the Two is recognized at some level by the Selfless Giver as undeservedly gained, based on egocentric motivations that are too embarrassing to admit to. There must be an unpleasant tinge of guilt every time someone compliments a Two given that the Two has deviously manipulated the person into offering the praise in the first place. The emotional ambivalence about accepting people's praises must be psychologically tormenting. Clearly, it takes an insane mind to be tormented by praise.

The unhealthy Two thinks: *"The compliments I receive are needed for me to survive. The problem is that those same compliments result from my secretly motivated deceptions, and so have no worth. My psychological agenda then is to constantly try to get something I want which ultimately has no value."* This is the disordered thinking of an ego-driven personality.

When it comes to relationships, Twos produce a double-bind situation through their own insecurity. At some level, they believe that by living someone else's agenda, they might lose themselves. On the other hand, if they choose to live their own lives, they think they'll lose the other person. This either-or perspective distorts the truth and oversimplifies matters in such a dichotomous fashion that it perpetuates the Twos mental disturbance.

Logically speaking, the Two here falls prey to the fallacy of the excluded middle. Surely, there are ways to serve people without completely selling out. There are other middle ground possibilities. The fear that following one's own bliss is going to necessarily cause abandonment and isolation is irrational and falls under what cognitive-behavioral therapists call *catastrophizing*.

Therapeutic Recommendations for Promoting Psychological Hygiene and Finding Inner Peace:

As with all character types, the first thing the Two needs to do is acknowledge the problems caused by the psychological ego. You can't change what you don't acknowledge. Doing this is painful for most people, but particularly difficult for Twos. They are feeling types and are less emotionally resilient compared with some other characters that are more cerebral or instinctive in their responses to life. Any pain experienced in the discovery of one's shadow is sure to be deeply heart-felt and possibly even horrifying. Remember, the journey to self-knowledge is not always happy. It requires courage and determination. In the process of healing, we discover things about ourselves that we wish were not true, but unless we come face to face with the dark side of our personality, no lasting change is possible. The Two needs to realize this along with the rest of us.

Another thing Selfless Givers need to do is come to terms with their neediness. In the long-term, living life as 'cling-ons' is not going to endear them to anybody. If you've ever been around needy or clingy people yourself, you know how difficult it is to be fully present to them. Just imagine two needy Twos trying to manipulate each other for one another's attention and approval – not a pretty sight.

In any case, with Twos, many communications seem to be meant to serve the needs of the 'cling-on', not to establish an honest and transparent two-way meaningful relationship. Of course, admitting to neediness is simply too embarrassing for most Twos. Admission of neediness is tantamount to accepting the fact that one is lonely, worthless, and deficient – fears that are hardly bearable. If this admission is too difficult, then perhaps it's best to start with the prideful side of neediness.

Pride is somehow less stigmatized and carries more positive status in the hierarchy of human moral deficiencies. If there's pride, presumably one must have a reason to be proud. There must be some achievement or accomplishment in which too much ego is invested. Well, for the Two, the pride comes from affiliation with others or identification with them. The sad reality is they choose to identify with others and live vicariously through their experiences as a kind of existential cheerleader. The resulting positive feelings thus derive from what might be described as a parasitic existence. This is the horrifying part. There's nothing wrong with helping others and celebrating their accomplishments. However, if one's self-definition is formed around another person's life, then co-dependency results and insecurity never ends. We cannot control the lives of others or force them to like us, praise us, need us, or want us. To base one's life on hopes that they do, sets the stage for a troubled mind. To do so, makes one the architect of one's own misery.

Twos need to accept themselves. When they do, others will accept them too. To become healthy and remain so, Twos need to be less concerned about what others think of them. This doesn't imply developing a 'don't give a damn' attitude, but rather moving away from obsessing about the perceptions and opinions of others.

An examination of what actress Sally Field has said in the past gives hope to the suffering Two, the person who is not only needy, but desperate for other people's approval. It's extremely significant, in my estimation, that so much has been made of Sally Field's acceptance speech at the Oscar Award Presentations in 1985. Judging by repeated references to it on comedy networks and late night television shows, her psychological worries about being accepted obviously resonated with millions of people.

At the awards ceremony Sally Field said: *"I haven't had an orthodox career, and I've wanted more than anything to have your respect. The first time I didn't feel it, but this time I feel it, and I can't deny the fact that you like me, right now, you like me."*

Unfortunately for Sally Field, those words made her the target of ridicule for years. To admit publicly that one needs to be liked and respected is, in the estimation of many, well nigh pathetic. In researching the exact wording of her speech, however, I found some interesting Sally Field quotations which give hope to other insecure Twos.

At a later time and place, she said: "*I was raised to sense what someone wanted me to be and be that kind of person. It took me a long time not to judge myself through someone else's eyes.*"

Clearly, this statement reflects growth. Also, Sally Field has apparently done some work to shed her idealized self-image as an Oscar award winning actress. She has been recorded as saying: "*I never really address myself to any image anybody has of me. That's like fighting with ghosts.*"

So, it would seem that living up to her Hollywood image is not so important in her life, though as a Two, she remains an image-type. Let me suggest that the last two of her statements are pregnant with psychological significance and serve as proof of how far one person can go with respect to their confidence and psychological health. Once highly insecure and an object of public ridicule, Sally is now a role model for dysfunctional image types trying so hard to impress the world. She appears to have accepted herself and now communicates from a place that is authentically her. She knows she is not her Hollywood image in essence.

In this dignified authenticity she earns our respect. Congratulations Sally! Thank you for becoming our teacher. Not only have you entertained us in the past, and not only do you continue to capture our attention with your current professional projects, but now you give us hope for the future. For *that*, we really like you!

Twos have to stop compulsively attending to the needy. There's nothing wrong with helping those in need. In fact, many humanitarians and people of faith believe they have a responsibility to do so. The problem arises when the need to help the needy is uncontrollable or compulsive. When this occurs, helping others is not the point, helping oneself out of desperation is.

I guess we could call this pathological giving. To overcome this compulsion, Twos need to recognize something we learned earlier, namely, that *perception is projection*. What Twos perceive, including the needs of others, is a projection of their own state of mind.

The Two's reality, like everyone's, is a construction of that mind. The question to be asked, then, is this: What is revealed to the Two about his or her present condition that is reflected by the perceptions they have of the hurt or needy Other? The intoxicated person in the doorway can be seen as a *bum* or a *victim of social circumstances*. Those who choose to see the former, have a different mind-set than those, like the Two, who are more likely to see the latter. The task for the Two here is to examine all the other thoughts and perceptions which accompany the sight of a victim to find out what is going on inside.

The Two must ask: "What do my perceptions of the distressed individual tell me about myself?" Thus, the perception of needy others creates the opportunity for Twos to learn something about themselves. Behaviorally, it appears to be the case that Twos often minister to the needy because they perceive neediness in themselves.

They do for others as they wish others would do for them – a slight variation of The Golden Rule. The Golden Rule has a moral basis; by contrast, the Two's rescuing behavior has a psychological survival function.

Twos can benefit by working on forms of self-expression. Many Twos have, in their lifetimes, focused their attention almost exclusively on others and have thereby neglected themselves.

In trying to earn respect from others, they have in effect disrespected themselves. Learning to do things for oneself is not selfish, but necessary. If one wishes to be a giver in an honest and sincere fashion, one must give from a place of abundance and security, not deficiency and neuroticism.

A cliché that's often distorted in its meaning, but nonetheless worth repeating here is the following: *You can't love others unless you love yourself first.*

I think airline safety provides a convenient life metaphor to explain what's meant here. On any airline, the safety instructions don't tell you in the case of an emergency to put the oxygen mask on your child first, but to put your oxygen mask on yourself first, before assisting others. Initially, this may seem counter-intuitive. The point is that if you don't look after yourself first, you won't be able to properly attend to the needs of your child. To put the mask on the helpless child first may appear heroic and selfless, but actually could mean that you, the adult, fail to survive and hence, are unavailable to help the child escape by jumping down the chute with it once the plane lands in flames on the ground (forgive the dramatization). For both your sakes, it's strongly advised to ensure your own survival before you start taking responsibility for others'. By doing this, everybody is more likely to survive and no one person has to be sacrificed for the benefit of the other. The choice is not *either-or*, but *both-and*.

The lesson for Twos, then, is that they need to do things like develop hobbies or pursue interests that don't cater to the needs of others, but which serve to develop their own creativity and self-expression. Just think, by producing objects of creative self-expression, and by taking delight in their own efforts and accomplishments, Twos can share themselves with the world in a healthier fashion. The giving is no longer manipulative, but reflects true generosity and self-satisfaction in being able to contribute to others and the world in genuinely self-determined and self-defined ways.

If you're a Two who needs to give, then give the world the best you've got by becoming the best individual you can possibly be. Living someone else's life is not how you go about this.

Finally, it is important for Twos to remember their true spiritual identity. The source of the love the Two seeks is an expression of Divine Love which cannot be conditioned, withheld, or diminished.[8] Such love is not like a commodity which can be won or lost, earned or forfeited, since in its truest expression, it is not a function of the psychological ego at all. Surprisingly, *Essential Love* is not even a feeling or emotion as such. Feelings of love can reflect a deeper ontological presence in ourselves, but Essential love is beyond words and explanations. It knows no boundaries or degrees of separation. It is not something belonging to the dualistic reality of the ego and so is not an object of psychological knowledge. In fact, awareness of Love's presence is blocked by the habits and false beliefs of our personality.[9] We cannot will ourselves to love ourselves or other people; what we can try to do is simply recognize the *presence* of love in ourselves and others. Miracles come later.

No one can ask another to be healed. But he can let himself *be healed, and thus offer the other what he has received.*
    A Course in Miracles

CHAPTER SIX

EGO DYNAMICS IN CHARACTER
TYPE THREE: *THE PERFORMING STAR*

*There is perhaps nothing worse than reaching the top of the ladder
and discovering that you're on the wrong wall.*
Joseph Campbell

Lost Essence:
A quick glance at any playful toddler is likely to bring a smile to
even the biggest sour-puss. Part of the reason, is because we find
in young children a wonderful and honest transparency that
warms the heart. Kids just want to be kids. They just *are*. They
live in the eternal now with little sense of yesterday or tomorrow.
Toddlers aren't making plans for the future or regretting things
about their past. They are not anxious about next year or guilty
about what they did last year. Toddlerhood is a time in life when
a day is like an eternity – "Dad is *never* coming home from
work," or so it seems.

Unlike the rest of the adult world, where everyone is
scampering every which way to earn a living and prove
themselves to others, tiny tots are not really asking themselves
what they intend to become when they grow up.

I'm reminded here of my own experience with my son. I recall
asking him when he was about three or four years of age what or
who he wanted to be when he grew up. He startled me when he
answered by saying: "Michael." Clearly, truth flows from the
mouths of babes.

Dad, of course, in a moment of unthinking ego-insanity, was

111

picturing his son in terms of his future role or occupation, antici-pating *that* as his identity. By contrast, in his youthful innocence, my son saw himself as remaining essentially the same person throughout his life.

He was experiencing life in the present as someone who simply *is*, or *was* back then, and as someone who existed in *real time*, not in terms of imagined future possibilities. In early childhood, kids are closer to their essence than many adults.

Questions like my own are often posed with a strong wish to discover what one's children's interests or inclinations might be. Many parents enjoy watching their offspring flourish in their own unique ways, gladly accepting responsibility for creating a protective and nurturing environment around them. Emotional, material and physical support may be provided whenever needed, and on those occasions when developmental hurdles are overcome, applause is quick to flow and generously given. Unfortunately, despite the best intentions of loving parents, sometimes young children misinterpret the praise and support they receive. Correctly or incorrectly, in the minds of some young ones, there arises the belief that they are largely ignored except when they do something especially well, say, or when they accomplish something beyond their years, or when they display a skill or give a performance better than everyone else. At those times of achievement, they become a "somebody" who is worthy of attention, while for a time just before that, they felt like an insignificant "nobody", ignored.

Remember, no one is a fault here. The parents could have been outstanding people doing their best. Their intentions may have been honorable, having nothing to do with living out their own frustrated dreams and aspirations through their children – though this can and does happen on occasion. The parents may simply have been trying to promote healthy self-concepts and positive self-esteem in their children.

In light of the discussion so far in this book, such child-rearing aims may have to be re-considered. In any case, mom and dad may have had Junior's bests interests in mind all along, not their own. Junior was on the receiving end of all mom and dad's good intentions.

Nevertheless, in the cognitive egocentrism, immaturity, and inexperience of youth, Junior may have come to see such idyllic circumstances differently, becoming spiritually wounded as a result. Junior may have come to think that validation comes only with performance. "My value as a human being depends on my accomplishments." "My parents love me only when I'm performing better than everyone else."

In unhealthy parenting situations, matters can degenerate even more. The parents or guardians in question here may be trying to raise "trophy children" to make themselves look good and to raise their own self-esteem through the accomplishments of their progeny. Here, children are indeed victimized. They become pawns in the neurotic games of others who have power and control over them. Sick examples of this can be seen on afternoon TV talk shows. As we see there, some parents will go to extreme lengths to get their children into Hollywood movies, or they will dress them up and apply make-up to them in age-inappropriate ways so that their child can compete in child beauty and talent contests. Parents of athletes are sometimes no less pushy. Think of the stereotypical obnoxious soccer mom whose child plays at the more competitive all-star level. *Her child* could be so much better with a different coach, or with better support from team mates on the soccer pitch. Any lackluster play on the part of her little athlete is usually put down to the fault of others, or so mom would have us believe. *"My little darling is just so advanced and so much better than the rest..."And so am I by the way,"* thinks mom in defensive reaction to her own insecurity or self-loathing. How sad for mom. How foreboding for the child.

In their efforts to please parents, Threes gradually begin to lose touch with their childhood innocence and transparency. Life is no longer to be lived, but is to be performed. Children begin to forget they are human beings and start to view themselves as *human doings*. The Three child's value begins to hinge on the last grade report or on the quality of play in the previous game.

Junior's self-esteem may come to depend on the final standings in the public speaking contest or in the notice and recognition given by others for the theatrical or musical performance at school.

When life becomes more about performance than actually living and experiencing the moment, the essential quality of *authenticity* begins to fade in the distance. Life becomes less about being true to oneself and more about playing to the crowd in efforts to earn their praise and adulation. Without that, the fear looms that one is *nothing*.

Psychological Worldview and Compensating Strategies:

Regardless of whether mom and dad were loving and psychologically healthy or dysfunctionally insecure and selfish, Threes start out life sub-consciously internalizing the expectations of the care giving adults in their lives. They often become more emotionally bonded to the one who played the primary role of "nurturer" in the family.[1] This nurturer, depending on his or her state of psychological health, may have consciously or perhaps unconsciously and unintentionally taught the Three child to play the role of the 'family hero' or 'family star.'

Because of all the praise and support received from playing such roles, the Three child goes along with the agenda. If the child has natural talent and ability in the first place, chances are pretty good that it will excel anyway. Relatively little effort may have to be expended. Thus, for the gifted Three child, here's an easy way to get "mom and/or dad to be with me, to notice me, and to give me the attention I crave."

The emotional experience between the star child and the co-dependent nurturing figure can become emotionally incestuous. Some might describe it as addictive in nature. The experienced highs of achievement are like emotional orgasm, pure ecstasy. Child and parent may learn to love the adrenalin rushes, the celebrations, the anticipations of glory, the competitive spirit, and so on.

All of this emotional excitement serves to draw attention away from the fact that the True Self has been lost in all the competition and achievement. In the end, our Divine Source doesn't care whether little Johnny or Mary hit a home run or scored a hat-trick in the final game. The quest to win personal glory for the ego is from a spiritual perspective little more than trivial pursuit.

Unfortunately, the negative psychological consequences of seeking recognition are not so trivial. Our inflated egos do not wish us to notice this. As long as we incorrectly believe that our self-worth is based on performance, the ego is in business. But remember, the ego is a double agent helping us to get what we think we want, even if what we want will ultimately hurt us or take us away from the truth of who we really are. On this note, think about how conventional Reality Therapy is designed to help persons achieve want-satisfaction. Doing so is not always so wise. More on this in the last chapter.

Happy is the man who gets what he wants, provided nothing he wants is morally amiss.
Anonymous

The truth in you remains, as radiant as a star, as pure as light, as innocent as love itself.
A Course in Miracles

As any individual grows up, the need to impress shifts from the parent or parents to the generalized other.[2] The ego's strategy is to prove one's worth by means of an active implementation of one's idealized self-image. By adolescence, the child has learned what it means to be *successful* and for others to perceive them in this way. The experience of success leads to a vigorous pursuit of achievement as defined by the society in which the person lives.

Identity becomes inextricably linked with the image that "sells." The Three strives to be *what* others want and *who* others wish they were. In their efforts Threes often manage to achieve success in many areas of life. Typically well-groomed, well-mannered and attractive, they become the rising stars, members of the Young Presidents' Association or those who are admired leaders in the community. People look up to Threes on account of their gracious demeanor and personal accomplishments.[3]

Threes represent the personification and embodiment of socially valued qualities. They rise to the highest levels in the company or organization. They are frequently the ones driving status cars and wearing clothing labels designed to impress others with their station in life. They are the ones who are socially ambitious, continually making efforts to network, give out their business or personal calling cards, and make connections for possible future projects.[4]

Threes can be seen "working-out" or "working on themselves" in endless personal development programs. They wish to become the best they can be, at least as the ego defines them. Moms become "super-moms" and dads become "super-dads" or "supermen," going to extreme lengths to provide abundantly for the family, while managing to excel in all endeavors, while being physically fit and looking good at the same time. The energy of the Three is enormous and the achievements are often monumental. Recognizable examples of Threes include U.S. Presidents Bill Clinton and Barack Obama, and the self-help guru Tony Robbins.

All threes personify what many of us wish to be. They are

living examples of the American Dream. They are rich and famous... if only we were.

For the Three, the feeling must be downright intoxicating to think that others *"dream about being me or walking in my shoes."* Self-validation doesn't get much better than that! The question is which Self is being validated: the True Self or the False Self, that which manifests the Divine or that which is a fabricated illusion of the ego?

Beware of all enterprises that require new clothes.
Henry David Thoreau

A snapshot of the Three reveals that Threes are highly active and energetic in the pursuit of their goals. Often socially accomplished, Threes are performers for whom image and status are important.

For Threes, it's important to appear successful at all times, regardless of the true reality. Image is everything. Threes are willing to aggressively compete and fight for what they want insofar as victories and acquisitions are necessary for self-definition, at least in their own minds.

Threes are industrious individuals, wishing to make the world a more efficient and productive place.[5] Threes help to make things happen and serve as shining leaders for private corporations, community organizations, as well as for public and educational institutions. They are focused and target-driven, and gravitate to sales and marketing roles.

Threes are "blessed" to the extent they embody the values of corporate America. Their character structure allows them to *buy in* totally, or if not totally, much more so than some other types we will discuss later. The current business craze around "self-branding" was made for the Three – and was probably made *by* the Three.

By means of this technique, Threes can trumpet their personal achievements to the world. They can advertise their image. Self-branding is just like a child's way of yelling: *"Look at me... look at me!"* as they ride their tricycle around.

In drawing a parallel between the individual and society, Plato once observed that any particular society produces particular kinds of individuals who are nurtured and then rewarded with respect to what is idealized, valued or considered important to that society.

In the context of capitalist "consumer society," where sizzle and glitz often appear to be valued more than substance, where a V.I.P. is not judged by the content of his character, but by the size of his financial portfolio, the status conscious Three who has "made it" in economic terms is praised and held in the highest esteem by those who would aspire to become the next success story in the Wall Street Journal. Arguably, contemporary American society has a type Three character writ large against the sky, so to speak. No wonder those reflecting Three qualities do so well in it. Anybody who shares and personifies the values of business culture is likely to be fast-tracked to the top.

We are bound to admit that the elements and traits that belong to the state must also exist in the individuals who compose it. There is nowhere else for them to come from.
  Plato

Healthy and Unhealthy Expressions of The Performing Star:
Healthy Threes perform a great service insofar as they contribute their talents and abilities to the world. The creative synergies they produce can be utterly amazing. Their motivational style and enthusiasm to make things happen and get things done, serves as an inspiration to all those around them.

Healthy Threes like to work on themselves, and will encourage others to do the same. At their best, Threes are able to commit to other people and to goals that transcend their personal self-interests. For example, Oprah Winfrey recently established a school in Africa to help children in that school grow and maximize their potential as human beings – a goal Oprah sets for herself. Oprah has said that a guiding principle in her life is that *"we should all strive to be all that we can be"*.

Seeing people held back by things they cannot personally control like poverty is abhorrent to her. Making self-actualization possible for those school kids placed in difficult economic circumstances is a miracle in which she played a large role.

What you can't help notice about healthy Threes is their outgoing and vivacious nature. They possess social sophistication and skill. They are entertaining and bubbly individuals. They sparkle and are socially pleasing. Threes can dazzle us with their charm and intelligent wit.[6] A well-developed Three is the individual at the company party who so naturally and apparently effortlessly "works the room."

Combine charm and enthusiasm with designer apparel, well-coiffed hair, cosmetics, and management strategies on how to make an impression, and you have one powerful leader who stands out from all the rest.

Less than healthy Threes can become plagued by fear and insecurity. Playing to the crowd may not always result in their approval and that's the worry. How about if everybody else "looks at me" but they don't like what they see. What then? When the bulk of one's self-definition is based on receiving approval from others, one is placed in a very insecure position of always having to impress those others. Threes are psychologically haunted by the spiritual wounding of their youth – the occasion when they internalized the false belief that if they don't make a favorable impression by outperforming others or standing out in some fashion, they are *nothing*, at least in the estimation of their ego. Since that initial wounding, the Three's entire life has been built on proving to others that they matter, that they are *something*, as if this fact needs proof.

Insecurity can be a great motivator.
  Kermit Washington

The desperation of the Three to stand out from the crowd often shows up in the Type A personality, the one which is predisposed to heart attacks and stress-related illnesses. The excessive striving for achievement is, after all, based on anxiety stemming from the fear that one will slide into the abyss of nothingness without acknowledged achievement and praised performance. Living on the edge of the abyss, constantly worrying about the value of one's existence, can only lead to tension and a foreboding sense of disaster. Momentary successes become just brief respites from mental torment. You're only as good as your last success, and the next endeavor may not turn out as good as the last. "How will I look then?" "I may be unveiled as the imposter that deep down I believe I am anyway."

There's some justification for this fear. The "false self" created by the ego is indeed an imposter. The "true self" has nothing to worry about. The unhealthy Three has unfortunately forgotten who they are, choosing to identify with the former.

The danger is that in their preoccupation to pursue the values others reward, Threes slowly lose touch with themselves. As Riso and Hudson put it: "...their heart's desire is left behind until they no longer recognize it."[7] In the end they become distant from their own real feelings and genuine interests – which is not so terribly bad, according to the Three. Their fear is that they may not be in fashion or accepted by those who count.

By selling their souls to the Faustian devil in return for the qualities that everyone else wishes they had, an existential bargain is struck by the psychological ego. The problem is that in making this deal, Threes get to a point where they no longer know what they really want or what their true feelings really are. Such things might appear unseemly to others and so actually present a potential danger to their stardom.

"What does the Inner Self matter anyway," thinks the Three, *"I have success and recognition from others! You don't, but you wish you did! Ha! Ha! I win. See I'm better."*

In response to the Three, we should ask: *"If success and fame have made you so happy, then why are you so insecure?"*

Be extremely careful, however, about how and when you ask the question.

Unhealthy Threes can become very vindictive individuals. Woe to him who embarrasses a Three in public or uncovers their cleverly disguised inadequacies. Once in a position to do so, the dysfunctional Three will take great pleasure in revenge.

I'm reminded here of a case where a college president learned of someone who did not support her candidacy for that position at the time of her application. I presume some weaknesses in her dossier were noted and highlighted to other members of the presidential search committee. Well, the person in question was eventually hired anyway, despite the objections. Somehow, the new president got word of who had and who hadn't voted for her in her bid for the executive position. It wasn't too long after accepting the post that this new president made it a point to fire at least one search committee dissenter for what appeared to be questionable reasons. The firing could have been done in a professional and discreet manner, but in the mind of the president, this person had forfeited that right by not giving their support to their candidacy, and the embarrassment she suffered warranted telling the individual, without prior notice, in front of his entire staff, that his job would be eliminated.

The sweet revenge for the Three president illustrates how sick we can be with respect to what gives us pleasure in life. The ego may want revenge; but that's not to guarantee that what the ego wants is good or healthy for the mind. In time, that president was fired by the Board of Governors at the college. Some might describe this firing as instant karma.

All the emphasis on image and performance leaves the unhealthy Three emotionally shallow. Many Threes are perceived as superficial and insincere in their outward expressions. For Threes, feelings, especially negative ones, just get in the way of action. Hence, feelings can often remain undeveloped in the Performing Star.

The focus has always been on external factors, such as production, efficiency, goal achievement, anything but all that touchy-feely stuff inside. Threes are probably better at showing their affection in their practical gestures than by expressing it in words. Stating feelings directly is "too mushy" and besides, feelings can be inconvenient and unproductive. Feelings come to be regarded as something to be immediately harnessed, controlled or repressed. And in the case of negative emotions (apart from the quest for revenge), nothing good results, so why dwell on them?

The latest jargon and organizational double-speak used by Threes to avoid acknowledging difficulties and set-backs is often frustrating to those searching for truth or at least for candid answers. Threes turn emotionally upsetting problems at work into 'challenges;' failures into 'opportunities' for growth or reorganization, and disappointments into 'occasions to explore other possibilities.' Those who would point to problems, conflicts, and failures are quickly censured by Threes who have the power to do so. Drawing attention to such things can reflect poorly on the Three manager, for example, trying to climb the corporate ladder. Honestly calling things what they are turns out to be abrasive and counter-productive in the business towers of power, where many Threes reside.

The use of modulated, organizational doublespeak becomes the preferred mode of professional communication and is regarded as a polished human relations skill. Honest *blunt-speak* simply proves you don't belong among the successful, self-congratulatory movers and shakers constituting the executive elite.

This brings us to the Three's personal shadow.

Personal Shadow:

If Mephistopheles were acting as existential legal counsel for the Three, and presenting his case to humanity, he might argue in the World Court of Public Opinion that there's absolutely nothing wrong with his client seeking success, material rewards, and recognition. The point might be made to the ladies and gentlemen of the psychological jury that it's only the "losers" in life who have any objections. The "winners" don't seem to mind so much, and don't we all wish to be winners, just like the Three who is accused here of some bogus crime against humanity? Who wouldn't want more than less? Who wouldn't want greater recognition rather than lesser recognition? What's wrong with being admired?

In response to our devilish advocate, I suppose we could conduct some sort of empirical investigation of people's views on status and materialism, that is, if we wished to find out if what he said was so – but this is not the point. What is salient is *how* and *why* such things are sought by the Three.

In answer to the "how" question, let's say the person's methods are not entirely honorable. The dark shadow issue for the Three is that much revolves around *deceit*. In their efforts to get what they want Threes become the "mask" they wear in public, sadly identifying with all their false and phony affectations.[8] By promoting and advertising themselves, they've made themselves into a commodity to be bought and sold in the marketplace.

There's an eager readiness and willingness to change one's attitude, appearance or fashion as the situation requires or as changing social market conditions redefine what "sells" in the world today.

In this respect Threes, like Twos, are chameleons. In selling themselves, through things like self-promotion and self-branding, Threes begin to believe what is often only their own embellished publicity. They come to identify with the idealized image of themselves that they have presented to the world. In the process, they begin to deceive people with the "glowing picture" of themselves that they present to others.

To the extent Performing Stars start believing their own self-generated press reports, they also deceive themselves. The self-deceit is motivated by emotional wounding.

Cognitively, it is based on the confusion between conditional extrinsic validation with unconditional intrinsic worth, the sort which characterizes every human being, in essence.

Our Divine Source doesn't place conditions on our value. Sadly, the Three tries to earn significance in the eyes of man, a significance initially and irrevocably bestowed by the hand of God. When the estimation of man supersedes the value given to us by our Maker, then we do suffer from spiritual insanity and we do need help.

Speaking of insanity, in answer to the "why-question" above, Threes seek recognition through the creation of a "false-image" because the early life need to receive attention was frustrated. As we have learned, this need to be noticed translated later in life in the need for applause. Thus, the real reason behind all the self-promotion, competitiveness, fame-seeking, ambition, and hard work, is to heal to the narcissistic emotional wounds of childhood.[9]

In less than healthy Threes, the desire to stand out and be

noticed can lead to compulsive social comparisons and never-ending competitions, all designed to prove one's worth as a person. Others' efforts may have to be sabotaged or their successes usurped and claimed as one's own. Résumés may have to be "talked up" or falsified and accomplishments invented.

The desperation to prove that one has value might even manifest in gross exhibitionism.[10] This can take all forms. To use a sexual example, when Threes become exhibitionists, they display themselves in ways designed to seduce others, thereby reassuring themselves that they are attractive and valued. A dysfunctional, exhibitionistic Three is the one who will dress to attract attention, but who, once this attention is gained from someone else, is likely to dismiss the admirer saying something like, "Buzz off." The image-conscious Three needs our notice, not our real affections. Attention is usually what is sought, not long-term relationships, unless of course they make me look good!

I never lost, I just ran out of time.
Rationalizing Three

The need to impress can also manifest in workaholism. This is because so much importance is placed on career and occupation in today's society. Things like pay raises, promotions, and positive work evaluations serve as drug-like ego-boosting injections, dangerously addictive in their effects. The actual work done itself may become secondary in importance. What's really valuable is the notice or public recognition that work brings. In this case, work takes on an instrumental value. Doing the task no longer presents any intrinsic reward. Work that brings with it no obvious material benefits or social kudos is not worth doing.

A belief in this notion is what probably contributes to the Threes' emotional underdevelopment and superficiality as far as psychological depth is concerned.

Inner Work doesn't get much notice these days. Isn't that primarily for weirdo hermits, monks, gurus, and people in recovery or rehabilitation programs? "Why bother?" says the Three.

I do not know the thing I am, and therefore do not know what I am doing, where I am, or how to look upon the world or on myself.
A Course in Miracles

Therapeutic Recommendations for Promoting Psychological Hygiene and Finding Inner Peace:

Threes need to begin their self-healing by recognizing their psychological sell-out. When people's choices are not *inner directed*, and when individuals don't even know what those choices would be even if their choices were to be inner directed, a terrible sense of self-abandonment and self-alienation is present. Having played to the crowd for so long leaves Threes ignorant of who they really are inside. They are out of touch with their own true feelings, thoughts, and desires. They've been busy finding those that sell in the existential marketplace of life. They've achieved their goals, but they lost their soul in the process.

Threes need first to recognize the psychological violence they have perpetrated against themselves. The aim of this recognition is not then to find reasons to flagellate oneself out of guilt. Healing does not come from laying blame on oneself – or on anyone else for that matter. Rather, to recognize the psychological damage that has been done is to acknowledge that a problem exists. Remember, you can't change what you don't acknowledge. In this case, Threes need to accept the fact that what has been done has been done out of personal ignorance and early emotional wounding. Life until now has been largely nothing more than a grand convoluted scheme to prove one's worth to the world. The psychological strategy of the ego has simply been the Three's best attempt to get what they *thought* they wanted, when what they *really* wanted from the beginning was recognition and a sense that they were valued for who they were. Sadly, but truthfully, the ego's efforts have all amounted to a bad dream, with all of its frenzied efforts and empty pursuits. In the end, the dream fantasy has turned out to be little more than a nightmare. So much anxiety and so much mental disturbance, all for nothing.

You see, the Three's value was never in question from a Divine perspective. What happens in the space-time continuum does not impact on one's essential nature. Sadly for the Three, eternal peace of mind, what some would describe as the Peace of God, was exchanged for a brief ovation or a short moment's notice from others. This was the Faustian bargain that has required psychological re-payment for a long time until now. Fortunately, a Spiritual Lender is nearby to forgive the Three's debt with no interest payments, and with no conditions in the fine print, I might add!

Like all of us, Threes need to stop searching outside of themselves to get what it is they think they want. What's true for all individuals out of touch with their essence is that they believe they are *deficient* in some way. Based on early childhood experiences, each character type develops its own strategies to make up for these *perceived* deficiencies.

Of course, in our essential reality, no deficiencies exist. Nonetheless, in our insanity, many of us still believe we are flawed from birth and must remain "guilty" of that deficiency for a lifetime. This guilt is what produces "shame" – which is a state of living Hell for the Three.

The problem for Threes, as for all types, is that they become compulsive and obsessive about rectifying a non-existent deficiency. There's an addictive quality to their actions as they desperately attempt to escape their mental pain and get themselves out of the hole they have dug for themselves. However, the more they dig to get themselves out of their predicament, the deeper the hole becomes. To continue doing what got you into emotional and psychological trouble in the first place makes no sense. To want to do it with greater proficiency and then to take pride that you can accomplish the task of digging the hole deeper and faster, and thus better than anyone else, is insane.

The blunt truth is that nothing *outside* will heal. *The answer lies within, so why not take a look now.*

In light of this, Threes need to abandon the ego's self-inflation projects and turn their attention to what's true inside. Nothing outside can provide the lasting peace we all seek. Our past efforts to find happiness somewhere *out there* have all turned out to be futile. If we continue doing what clearly does not work, as verified by our own experience, then perhaps we are slow learners needing spiritual special education classes! I know a few good teachers.

The suggestion here is not that Threes should remove themselves from the world or stop being productive. As we know, it's possible to live *in* this world, but not be *of* this world. Threes can do more or less the same kinds of things they've been doing until now, only they need to recognize that their worth as human beings does not hinge on the results of their efforts. Once this fact is accepted, the desperate, addictive part of productivity disappears. There's nothing more to prove to oneself or others. Insecurity no longer becomes the chief motivator in life.

Threes can begin to enjoy their successes and more importantly, the work that produces them. Also, when Threes are no longer desperately searching to find the cure to their existential ailments in the outside world, they can spend more time sharing themselves with others. For example, they can share their true feelings – ones they now recognize, own, and communicate with integrity. Ah, what a relief that is in itself. With self-honesty and integrity, more's to miraculously follow.

Threes need to abandon the image created by the ego. To function in a healthy fashion, Performing stars must rip off their "masks." It's all right to have a Hollywood image, but it's quite another thing to believe you *are* that image. In one interview, David Bowie, the singer-songwriter, admitted to overly identifying with his stage-presence alter-ego "Ziggy Stardust" in the 1970s for a period of time in his life while he was on tour. The "image" was so powerful that he psychologically merged with it, dissociating from his original identity as he perceived it at the time – which was likely still his ego. He admits this caused him psychological difficulty and problems in his relations with others. For a significant duration, Bowie forgot who he *really* was.

Well, one could argue by analogy that Ziggy is to the ego-personality, as the ego-personality is to one's true identity – one's essential Self. The former is confused with the latter in both cases. Identifying with Ziggy put Bowie's personality in crisis mode. Likewise, identifying with personality causes serious problems when it comes to expressing our essence in the world.

It's time for Threes, and all of us quite frankly, to quit dreaming about who we'd like to be and accept the reality of who we really are. It's easier that way. Nobody can be better than us or outshine us when it comes to being ourselves. In that, victory, success, and accomplishment are guaranteed and peace comes at last.

You got some big dreams baby, but in order to dream you gotta still be asleep.
Bob Dylan

Another recommendation for Threes is that they need to practice being still and alone. In the competitive market-place of western society we are all encouraged to be motivated, aggressive, self-starting individuals who are willing to pay the price for success. Initiative and hard work and a little bit of luck can combine to make the "American Dream" come to fruition, so we're told. This is the dream the Three has bought into hook, line and sinker. To use the vernacular, they've been *fished in* more than most on this dream.

However, as we know, the Three needs to stop all of their frantic activity. In response to the Three who is likely to say to subordinates at work: "Don't just stand there, *do something*", we have just the opposite advice for this type, namely: "Don't just do something, *stand there*."[11]

Threes need to learn to simply *be,* to exist without the constant desire for social approval. As Claudio Naranjo puts it: "...these people who usually have difficulty in being alone and in extricating themselves from over-acting achievement can particularly benefit from the task of facing themselves and from bearing the 'loss of face' entailed by not looking into the social mirror."[12]

An emphasis on this "non-doing" can help Threes work on their interior landscape. Lack of development in this area is what leads others to perceive Threes as superficial. Paradoxically, this should be enough to get Threes motivated to "do" something about this problem.

The proper motivation should not come from the fear of looking flighty to others, but from the realization that one lacks self-knowledge. This should be motivation enough. Appearing deep, but remaining shallow, is no solution to the Three's psychological disturbance. That would be like faking sincerity – which might be good for business perhaps, but not good for life.

Deep understanding of one's Self must be genuine, not feigned, or else we go back to where we started – in an emotionally wounded state with nothing but snake-oil remedies for our troubled minds.

As proverbial wisdom reminds us: Money – *and success* – I add, can't buy happiness. Just think of all the rich and famous people whose personal lives are tragic wrecks. It's curious how so many still wish to be like them.

Wanting what will hurt you most is a symptom of spiritual immaturity. As suggested before, we are truly like young infants wishing to play with sharp scissors and we have no hesitation about screaming and yelling to get what we want, even if what we want is a threat to our well-being. To fantasize about becoming a self-destructive star is sheer lunacy.

"What a piece of work is man!" [13]

A good way for Threes to get in touch with themselves is through engaging in creative activities. The products of these activities should not be meant for display, however. The purpose should not be to impress others or we're right back into the troubling psychological pattern the Three is trying to escape. No. The painting, pottery making, writing, drawing, journaling, musical composition or playing a musical instrument is intended to get Threes in touch with their feelings and innermost intuitions. By *getting in touch* Threes can bring themselves into better psychological alignment. [14] They can enjoy themselves and their own experiences, for a change, not the reactions of others.

Rather than play to the impersonal crowd, Threes need to join with others they trust and with whom they can share their anxieties and vulnerabilities. [15]

Threes may be surprised by how endearing they become when they're not always putting on a show. We're all human and we all have our insecurities. For Threes to admit theirs is a refreshing change – honesty usually is. Once the psychological guard is put down, and honest expression leads the way, less energy needs to be expended defending oneself in public. There is less need to be guarded, lest one's image be tarnished. Room is made for greater spontaneity and humor centered around one's own foibles and limitations. Learning to laugh at oneself is incredibly liberating. Once able to do this, the Three is free, free at last, free from the chains of the ego that began all this insanity in the first place.

Into eternity, where all is one, there crept a tiny mad idea, [i.e., of real separation from our Source] at which the Son of God remembered not to laugh [at the ego that was born].

A Course in Miracles (my insertions)

CHAPTER SEVEN

EGO DYNAMICS IN CHARACTER TYPE FOUR: *THE DEEP-FEELING INDIVIDUALIST*

People understand me so little that they fail to understand when I complain about being misunderstood.
Søren Kierkegaard

Lost Essence:

As with other character types, the Four experienced a childhood that could make us all cry. This claim should be qualified perhaps: The Four had a *perception* or *experience* of childhood which could elicit tears from any sensitive, empathetic person. Whether or not that childhood was, objectively speaking, actually as tragic as the Four would have us believe is another matter.

Some might say that, like beauty, *tragedy is in the eye of the beholder*, so what seemed so terrible from the Four's perspective may not have looked so bad from an impartial point of view.

The Four's reply: *"You just don't understand!" "You don't know what it's like to be me!"*

Fours typically did not bond with their parents or caretakers early in life. This was not necessarily because they were absent, negligent, or emotionally unavailable. Those who looked after the Four could have been quite loving and nurturing. The problem arises because the Four may not have seen things this way or simply did not identify with those responsible for raising them. In psychotherapeutic jargon, they were not "mirrored in the eyes of the parental other".

There thus arose in the child's mind a perception of difference. Feeling a psychological separation, they came to conclude that they were much *unlike* those who brought them into the world; Fours consequently became psychologically disconnected from them.[1]

It's not unusual to hear Fours relate their impression that they were not *seen* by their parents for who they were. Sometimes Fours wonder about the possibility that they were mistakenly 'switched' in the hospital at birth and given to the wrong mother. Others query whether they may have been orphaned and then adopted.[2]

On the subject of perceived separation and difference, imagine, for instance, that someone was born gay or was genetically determined to be homosexual from birth. That person, from the earliest experiences of childhood, may not have felt comfortable "playing daddy", identifying with daddy, or trying to be just like daddy. Mommy, on the other hand, may not have physically appeared to be the same either, making identification with her even more difficult.

The example of the homosexual illustrates how bonding between parent and child can fail to occur with no one at fault. The failure to bond does not necessarily make someone guilty of a psychological crime.

To use another example: In a large family, where other siblings were present during early childhood development, the parents' attention may have had to be split or shared with other children. It's possible that these other siblings became the Four's rivals for parental notice.

If the parents were unable, under busy or difficult circumstances, to give the Four everything they needed or wanted *on demand*, including attention, this should not be seen as some sort of indictable offence.

However, from the cognitively egocentric perspective of the Four-child, split-attention meant that he or she became an *innocent victim* of others' callous indifference. *"But I did nothing wrong"* thinks the child. *"Why do they ignore me as if I don't exist?"* *"Don't I matter?"* *"Who are these people anyway?"* *"I'm not anything like them."* *"When I grow up, I'll be sure to act differently."* *"I will give my children the attention I didn't receive." "I never want to be like my parents!"*

Here we see the youthful face of innocence screaming at *perceived* slight and violence against the self. It is precisely at this moment that the ego rushes in to save the emotionally wounded 'victim' and with the ego's effort comes the seal of psychological separation from others and the world. *"I am myself, myself alone"* says the ego on the Four's behalf.

Because Four children did not experience the initial psychological mirroring that is so important in developing their self-concepts, Fours begin life with an identity crisis. Little do they know that even if they form a fairly stable self-concept later in life, they still won't know who they *really* are!

"If I'm nothing like my parents and do not see myself in their eyes, then who am I?"

Out of this identity crisis arises the thought that "there must be something *wrong with me.*" *"I wouldn't be ignored if I were the star of the family. Others would notice me if I were more charming like my older brother."* *"The talk at the dinner table would revolve around me more if I showed greater confidence or if I were more assertive like my sibling sister."* *"Am I just an anti-social loser, a worthless no-count who can't even gain the attention of my parents? I must be defective as a human being."*

With thoughts like these firmly planted in the back of the Four's mind, so life begins.

Given the early childhood experiences of the Four, we can see how even in youth, the Four already suffers from a troubled mind. The essential quality of *equanimity* is lost in the little person's experience of the world.[3] Equanimity can be understood as the full embodiment of Being. It manifests in a sense of completeness. Nothing is absent or missing; nor is anything wrong.

The experienced fullness of equanimity results in a deep and abiding contentment. One just *is* and one is just happy to be as one is, wherever one is. There is nowhere else that is better. There is nothing one is deficient without, and there is no one else one would rather be. All is in perfect balance.

Oh, that we could all return to our Essential Being without the misguided hope that we could be different – different from who we are at our core – a strange hope, really, and no doubt futile in the end.

Trying *not* to be yourself is about as silly as trying to be someone you're *not*. Also, always wishing to be somewhere you're not guarantees you'll always be unhappy where you are.

We're reminded here of Buddha's wisdom concerning the insight that our cravings or desires are what cause our dissatisfactions with life. Also, defining happiness in terms of what you don't possess and locating it where you are currently not situated is also insane thinking.

Don Riso and Russ Hudson sum up the experience of Essential Equanimity from the psychological perspective of the Four. They say:

> From point Four, we experience *Equanimity*. Once we open to the riches of the heart and to the inexhaustible wonder of living in truth, we are filled from moment to moment with a kaleidoscope of powerful impressions, sensations and feelings. Equanimity gives us the capacity to contain all these ever-changing qualities without being swept into emotional reactions to them... Equanimity allows the identity of the

Essential Self to participate in the cornucopia of experiences and inner qualities without clinging to or fearing any of them and without regretting their passing. In this way, the sense of oneself continually deepens so that powerful experiences are fully felt but do not overwhelm the Essential Identity. We are able to feel both the heights of ecstasy and the full intensity of suffering without becoming lost in either.[4]

Psychological Worldview and Compensating Strategies:

The first thing to notice about Fours is that they are rarely satisfied to live in the present, the here and now. Their focus of attention tends to wander away, either to the past, to the future, to the absent, or to the hard-to-get.[5] For example, this could involve thinking about an absent friend at a party or focusing their attention on how things were better in the good-ol'-days.

Fours amplify present negatives or deficiencies so that what is, or what is currently being experienced, looks far less appealing than it might be. On the flip-side, Fours tend to unconsciously amplify the positives of that which is missing, lost, unavailable or somewhere else.

If truth be told, were the missing object or person actually present, things quickly wouldn't look so positive. Something or someone else in the distance would again begin to look more attractive.

This perceptual tendency is what leads Fours at a very deep level to appreciate the saying that: *the grass is always greener on the other side of the fence.*

Fours are feeling-type individuals. Thus, to fully understand their psychological worldview, it's important to carefully examine the role which feelings play in their personal existential psychodynamics. To do this, it's useful to point out that not just Fours, but all of us, give off 'vibes', to use a 60's hippy expression. Whenever we enter a room, an emotional tone is set by our presence. We may send 'good vibrations' or give off 'negative vibes', so to speak. This no doubt contributes to the first impressions we all make on other people.

The tonal vibrations we set by our personalities might alternatively be described as the *emotional climate* which surrounds us, envelops others in contact with us, and influences our perceptions of reality. Things often look different on a grey and overcast day compared to how things appear on a clear and sunny day. Likewise, one's emotional moods color one's perceptions of reality. You get the point.

Furthermore, the emotional climate established by our personalities cannot help but affect others who come into contact with us. If talking to you is like walking into a storm, then it is not experientially the same as speaking with a mellow fellow with whom conversation is like taking a walk through the park on a bright summer's day. What's your emotional forecast, or should we say 'broadcast,' today? Will being with you make it a day for a walk in the proverbial park or will you force everybody to start running against the wind?

Now, as far as the Four's general emotional climate is concerned, almost everything about the Four's life is influenced by it. It is the 'inner affective atmosphere' or emotional weather system in which life is lived and experienced.[6] Let's see how it is distinct by doing a comparison with the character types we have already studied.

With respect to the Perfectionist One, you'll recall, the emotional climate surrounding this character type often entailed an overly serious attitude and unease which manifested from the One's pent-up anger or tightly controlled resentment toward the world. The emotional restraint and harnessed affect of the dysfunctional One could leave others in their presence feeling strangely guilty about whatever they had done 'wrong' – even if nothing untoward had occurred.

It's difficult for the moderately unhealthy One to be easy-going and happy, especially when everything from his or her perspective appears flawed, needing correction, or less perfect than it should be. The energy around the struggling One can be uncomfortable with a sense that something is about to burst – perhaps the storm clouds of anger. Psychologically turbulent weather, lightning bolts of criticism, and thunderous judgment seem certain to come with time.

As for the healthy and high functioning Two, by contrast, being in their presence is like basking in the summer's day sun. There's no cool wind of judgment, no need to pack up and run before the torrential rains of criticism begin. Healthy Threes, of course, bring excitement. Sunshine and comfortable tempera-tures are what they're all about. We feel like getting out and being active in their presence.

As for Fours, their inner affective atmosphere creates a psychological mood or external emotional climate around them which is typically subdued, often melancholic. For less than optimally healthy Fours, life is like a cloudy, rainy day in late November. Raindrops of melancholia are gently falling on the bare branches of a solitary tree in an empty field. The barrenness of the tree reminds the Four of something lost or something that will never be quite the same again. Less than healthy Fours live much of their lives under the rain clouds of perpetual sadness. How dark these clouds are in fact, how much of the sky is overcast, how much rain falls, and what rays of emotional sunshine are allowed to pop through the clouds of despair all depend on the Four's level of health. It's difficult sometimes not to feel both sympathetic, but unwelcome in their presence, sensing some sort of sad hurt deep inside, a private hurt that *we* are simply incapable of understanding.

The Four's emotional depth is great – too much for most of us to bear, at least for those of us who are superficial happy-hoppers. It's likely the case that Bob Dylan is a Four, as is The Artist (formerly known as Prince), Janis Joplin (now deceased), the Canadian singer/songwriter Sarah McLachlan, and actor Marlon Brando. The philosopher, Søren Kierkegaard, is also a Four.

It's amusingly synchronistic to find that, like The Artist, Kierkegaard also used alternative identities in creating his works. He wrote under various pseudonyms. For example, *The Concept of Anxiety* was authored by Vigilius Haufniensis. *Stages on Life's Way* was edited and compiled by Hilarius Bookbinder. Of course, both books were actually written by Kierkegaard himself.

So, in the person of Søren Kierkegaard, (formerly known as Vigilius, and Hilarius), we find The Artist's kindred spirit exhibiting those psychological traits and characteristics typical of the Four. As for Kierkegaard's alter-ego Vigilius, some would say that when attempting to communicate indirectly through some kind of puppet-identity, he is indeed Hilarius!

However insightful Kierkegaard's philosophy, or however creative his methods, there's nothing really funny about identifying with, or communicating through, an artificial image created by a false-self, masking one's true Identity. Psychological excavation in the search for one's Essential Self simply becomes much more onerous. There's a lot more 'fool's gold' to throw away!

Since my earliest childhood a barb of sorrow has lodged in my heart. As long as it stays I am ironic- if it is pulled out I shall die.
   Søren Kierkegaard

Like Twos and Threes, Fours are also *image-types,* people for whom appearances are extremely important. Twos like to look attractive to others so that they can feel needed or desired. Threes like to look successful in ways defined by society in order to bolster their perceptions of self-worth.

As for the Four, the self-image involves the perception of difference. Fours see themselves as fundamentally different from everyone else.[7]

We can now appreciate how this stems from their early childhood orientations. The idealized self-image of the Four is used as a compensating strategy for the Four's fears and insecurities. Their fear of difference, of being an outcast or outsider, now becomes a virtue. The self-idealization comes in at least a couple of forms. Some Fours view themselves as *aristocrats,* loving refinement, culture and sophistication. Such Fours may regard themselves as belonging to the elite or upper classes – set apart from the common riff-raff. In this case, they can look elegant and classy and carry themselves in complementary fashion.

Other Fours see themselves as special in another more *bohemian* way, highly unique or idiosyncratic in their expression and self-presentation to the world.[8] Following popular trends dictated by others or being a slave to cheap mass-produced fashion is anathema to this sort of creative Deep-Feeling Individualist. With the bohemian, the Four's image is not fashioned to please the audience. Unlike the Three, they are not playing to the crowd. Hence, their outward appearance can be rather shocking, even outrageous. Whatever image is presented, healthy Fours, at least, create it primarily for themselves.

Most Fours live a rich and profound existence in their imaginations where the terrain is for them much more interesting than the world of social interaction where conformity and identification are often asked, if not required.

Their credo is captured in the words of Keats: *Beauty is truth, truth beauty, That is all you know on earth, and all you need to know.*[9]

With respect to the Four's rich and complex inner life, Helen Palmer sums up the Four's worldview beautifully:

Fours say that the highs and lows of their emotional life open up an intensified level of existence that is beyond ordinary happiness, a level far richer than that for which other people seem to be willing to settle. There is the sense of being an alien outsider to ordinary reality, of being unique and strangely different, of being an actor who is moving through the scenes of one's own life. To give up the suffering of a heightened emotional life would mean sacrificing the sense of being special that drama tends to generate. For a Four the prospect of becoming happy can also threaten to close access to an intense emotional world. Worst of all, there is the risk of settling for a pedestrian vision and an ordinary life.[10]

... Fours say that they prefer the richness of melancholia to what other people describe as happiness. It is a feeling of sadness that calls up imagery and metaphor, and the sense of being connected to distant things. Melancholy is a mood that elevates the life of an abandoned outsider to a posture of unique temperamental sensitivity.[11]

I'm a rose in a field of daisies.
Bubble Wand

In fashioning their idealized self-images, Fours have a strong tendency to become introverts, withdrawing from the world and moving into a more or less solitary space.

This tendency to withdraw is shared by Fives and Nines, a couple of other character types we'll get to later. By withdrawing from the crowd, the Four is able to remain in the bitter-sweet state of melancholy more easily. This emotional experience appears to be the feeling of choice for the Four. Through the optical lens of melancholy, ordinary events in life can be faced as aesthetic experiences. Depression can be transformed into a *poetic appreciation for the human condition.* Waiting for someone at a train stop can be transformed into *yearning for the beloved other*. The odd thing, seemingly perverse from the vantage point of others, is the Four's choice to remain melancholic, regardless of circumstances. This melancholy is something special, not to be lost. On the subject of the Four's melancholy Helen Palmer says the following:

Melancholy is a mood that elevates the life of the abandoned outsider to a posture of unique temperamental sensitivity. It's like being a character in a story, a character whose been put under adverse circumstances. I'm in this world as an outsider, and no one understands who I am, which makes me feel different and misunderstood. It also brings on a kind of contained desperation. Nobody gets me, I'm an outsider and therefore tormented by not belonging, but I'm also intense inside because I am tormented. I live at the outer edges of whatever human beings can stand in the way of feelings. I remain mysterious to myself, and I am absolutely different from anybody else.[12]

With their perceived separation and isolation, Fours often report that they feel something is missing in their lives. What's missing is seemingly so easily possessed by others, be it willpower, social ease, self-confidence or emotional tranquility. This insecure sense of deficiency leads Fours to play a game of 'hide and seek' with others. By hiding-out, Fours hope that people will notice their absence.[13] They usually put the onus on others to seek them out; far less frequently do they take the friendly extroverted initiative to make contact. In the privacy of their minds, Fours can 'test' others to confirm how much or how little interest others take in them.

In the end, the *longing* or *yearning* for connection may be experienced as more pleasurable than the contact itself. Once contact is finally made, the Four will likely soon pine for how things were before.

"I wish to be alone now".

Wherever they are, there's something that's missing. What's not where they are is exactly what they want. And what they have in the place where they are is precisely what leaves them dissatisfied; it is what they don't want And so the sad story of perpetual dissatisfaction continues....

It is better to drink of deep griefs than to taste shallow pleasures.
William Hazlitt

Healthy and Unhealthy Expressions of the Deep-Feeling Individualist:

Healthy Fours are individuals who are honest with themselves. To use existentialist terminology, they display *authenticity*. Their unique dress, for instance, is no longer a means to reinforce distance and separation from others, but rather becomes a genuine form of self-expression, often trend-setting in nature.[14]

Gone are the pretensions of elitist nonconformity – displaying them constitutes a rather sad way to feel good about oneself anyway. But an impressive capacity for aesthetic presentation is present and presented. They may indeed be artistic. Certainly, the ability to create beauty is one of the Four's greatest gifts. We are all enriched by the Four's exquisite taste. When healthy Fours combine their creativity and originality with deep feeling, and introspective insight, the results can be stunning. (Go back to the list of well-known Fours for proof of that).

Given the depth of their feelings, healthy Fours are especially well-suited to work with people going through some sort of personal crisis or grief. No stranger to depression and other forms of mental anguish, Fours display remarkable stamina for helping others to live through intense emotional episodes in their life. For example, they may be quite willing to stick with a good friend through long periods of recovery, from addiction, disease or emotional trauma.[15] Fours 'get it' when it comes to pain. They are not likely to minimize the significance of other people's feelings or discount them in some sort of insensitive fashion. Emotionality and sensitivity are what the Four is all about. When such things are put in service of others, self-transcendence occurs as Fours open their hearts to others, for the sake of others. The bitter-sweet taste of isolated self-pity diminishes as one experiences the joy of caring for others in selfless love. Joining produces joyful jubilation, not the sick satisfaction of feeling dishonestly superior in lonely isolation. Such uniqueness comes with a hefty psychology price. Commenting on positive dimensions of the Four, Riso and Hudson remark:

Fours are the deep-sea divers of the psyche: they delve into the inner world of the human soul and return to the surface, reporting on what they have found. They are able to communicate subtle truths about the human condition in ways that are profound, beautiful, and affecting. In a fundamental way, Fours remind us of our deepest humanity – that which is most personal, hidden, and precious about us but which is, paradoxically, also the most universal .[16]

Unhealthy Fours have placed themselves in a bind. Because their idealized self-image is based on how *unlike* they are compared to everyone else, their self-definition is a negative one. *"I am nothing like you."*

Second, recall that this negative self-image is largely a defensive reaction to feeling deficient. The elitist nonconformity or bohemian persona are nothing more than a Freudian-like defensive reaction formation, fashioned to cover up a deeply feared lack, namely that one does not possess a stable identity worthy of notice by others. Thus, the unhealthy Four's self-definition rests on a bed of affectation and existential inauthenticity.

Remember that this false ego-identity was initially sparked by early feelings of abandonment and victimization. The Four saw themselves as excluded and as outsiders. Hence, a feeling of melancholy took over their psyches, so much so that melancholy came to be perversely cherished and incorporated psychologically. The Four identified with melancholy. It became part of the Four's self-definition, seemingly preferable over the 'superficial' happiness of the mindless crowd that was guilty of rejecting the Four in the first place.

Now, for a Four to acknowledge their intrinsic worth, good qualities, or Essential Goodness would be tantamount to losing their sense of ego-identity as a *melancholic outcast* or *suffering victim*. To accept themselves and let go of their *perceived* flaws (the true Higher Self has no flaws) requires that Fours give up their cherished personality. But, who likes to give up their personality, their cherished sense of self – certainly not the ego? To do so is like losing oneself completely. However, refusal to let go of their ego-identities for fear of losing themselves in the process requires that Fours remain in depressive misery. So here again we see that the ego is not really our friend, though it claims to be.

From the vantage point of the lower psychological self, the options *appear* to be fear or misery, at least in the misguided mind of the Four individual: *"I'm trapped in my mental pain and there's no way out!"* To get out is to lose myself and fall into the abyss of nothingness. *"Don't worry,"* says the ego. *"We can enjoy your pain together! I'll be with you for every melancholy moment. How sweet it is!"*

As Fours become progressively more unhealthy, they go beyond normal introversion, and withdraw almost entirely from social involvement. Feelings of shame and expectations of humiliation become so overwhelming that Fours don't even want to risk being seen. Such feelings certainly cause problems outside of the home. Insecurities can become so debilitating that many Fours become unable to work productively in any consistent fashion or long-term basis. They may neglect responsibilities or the responsibility level may be reduced, and they may be fabricating rationalizations for why everyone else is guilty for *forcing* the Four to quit the job, to take the educational detour, or to minimize the demands of life which have been *put upon* them against their will.

At extremely unhealthy levels of development Fours become hateful and to the extent this is still possible, even more alienated. They come to reject everyone and everything that does not support their self-concepts or their emotional demands.[17] Isolated and withdrawn, it is difficult for dysfunctional Fours to directly and openly express their rage, though make no mistake, emotional histrionics are not beyond possibility for the Deep-Feeling Individualist.

Nevertheless, rage generally tends to be internalized as depression, apathy, and constant fatigue. This introjected rage could also translate into Fours hating everything about themselves that does not conform to their idealized self-image. This self-loathing could be complemented by also hating others for failing to come to their emotional rescue, to be there when they were most needed.

The clinically-depressed, self-loathing Four may very well sabotage whatever good remains in their life. When this happens, all that is left is despair. Fours may come to believe that there is no point in living and that they have wasted their entire lives chasing after meaningless dreams. They may come to believe that their life has been a total waste. In desperation, they may engage in overtly self-destructive behaviors in vain hopes that someone will finally *notice* them, thereby validating their existence. Suicidal attempts can become the ultimate insane call for notice. Such actions say: *"I am. I exist. I have worth. And I deserve to be seen! Just wait until you discover I'm dead. You won't be able not to notice me then!"* Through actual or attempted suicide, the insane Four tries to affirm the value of his or her life to the world by destroying it or at least attempting to do so. This is psycho-logic indeed.

It's always darkest before the dawn.
   Proverb

Personal Shadow:
You will recall Chuang-Tzu's advice that we must all step into our personal shadow if we wish to stop being chased and harassed by it. It's not by running away from our shadow that we escape its torment. For the Four, this means confronting the issue of *envy*. It is envy which mostly influences the inner emotional atmosphere of this character type.[18]

In the Webster's Encyclopedic Dictionary of the English language envy is defined as: *Pain, uneasiness, mortification, or discontent excited by the sight of another's superiority or success; a feeling that makes a person begrudge another his good fortune.*

Enneagram researcher Claudio Naranjo puts it this way: The emotional state of envy involves a painful sense of lack and a craving toward that which is felt lacking; the situation involves a sense of goodness as something outside oneself which needs to be incorporated.[19]

From these definitions of envy, we learn that it is largely based on comparative judgment. Someone else has something that we don't. That something is outside of ourselves. What someone else has is judged as better, while what we possess, or are left with, is inferior or somehow less desirable. Comparative judgment shows us the discrepancy between what we have and what we don't have, but want. It has us comparing ourselves with others who appear to have already become what we would like to be.

In others, we see a life we wish we enjoyed, but don't. Being less than we wish to be and not possessing what others have presents a bleak horizon. Our envy, then, is driven by a perceived deficiency, what can be called *a voracious dearth, a yawning emptiness.*[20] This is bleak indeed.

As if wishing to be more like someone else or wanting what someone else has isn't cause enough for mental disturbance, with envy also come other negatives such as anger and hatred.

As Sandra Maitri states:

> What adds maliciousness to envy is both the sense of unfairness about not possessing it [i.e., the desired object or quality] and the despair that we cannot learn, develop, or acquire that superior thing. We feel a sense of hopelessness about having it as our own. It will perpetually reside outside of ourselves. This is terribly frustrating, to long for something and feel at the same time complete despair about ever getting it. This leads us to feel hostility toward what we consider goodness. We start to hate the source of our envy, because it makes us feel so devastatingly lacking and helpless to do anything about it.[21]

Thou shalt not covet thy neighbor's goods.
Old Testament Commandment

Envy is most likely to occur for the Four, as indeed it is for anybody, when comparisons with another are both negative for the self and pertaining to a domain or area of life that is particularly important and relevant to self-definition.[22] In other words, if someone is deficient compared to someone else in something they care little or nothing about, envy is not likely to occur. It's when the comparison 'matters' to them, when it somehow impacts on the Four's self-image, that envy will rear its ugly face. Envy is not a random occurrence. It is targeted and very specific to the individual.

Another thing to note about envy is that it is *not* the same as jealousy. Jealousy, more often than not, involves relationships. Usually there is a rival-other threatening us in one of those life domains we consider important to our self-definition. This could involve an intimate relationship, for example, where someone more attractive or alluring presents a sense of danger that our partner might be taken away from us because of someone else's superior qualities. We jealously guard our partner believing that the rival-other has no right to our partner's affections. Jealousy has a 'mine or thine' quality about it. Only one of us can get what we both want.

Distinguishing between jealously and envy, Maitri expresses the differences in the following fashion: "Jealousy is an intolerance or suspicion of rivalry or unfaithfulness, hostility toward a rival one believes holds the advantage, and a vigilant guarding of one's possessions. On the other hand, envy is a painful or resentful awareness of an advantage enjoyed by another joined with the desire to possess the same advantage."[23]

An example might be useful here: I may envy someone for having had a wonderful vacation and wish I could have one too, without suggesting that the other person didn't deserve it, but I did. It's not that the other's vacation robs me of what I want or what is rightfully mine. In principle, we can both have vacations to the same or different destinations at the same time. For the Four, however, the thinking is that what is possible in principle will likely never occur, hence the resentment. *"I can never seem to get what I want, yet they can!"*

The role which envy plays in the existential psychodynamics of the Four is tied up with psychological projection. Recall that perception is projection. Our inner affective atmosphere is what determines the psychological weather outside. More simply, what we see in our experience of life is a projection of our current state of mind.

We learned this at the outset of this book in our discussion of

Lance and the new girl in class. Recall that in Lance's case, we observed how he projected his own insecurities onto Becky, thereby externalizing what he didn't like about himself.

This is how projection works much of the time. With the Four, however, the psychodynamics are somewhat different. Rather than project their insecurities onto others, Fours tend to project their ideals onto them and then envy others for better approximating what they themselves want to be or achieve. Others' lives are so much better than the Four's. Others' lives are so full, so complete. They are so happy and so satisfied. From the Four's vantage point, others seem to have everything the Four does not –close relationships and meaningful friendships, material possessions, children or the ability to have children, skills, abilities, opportunities, invitations, and so on and so forth. No wonder the Four feels chronically sad. Compared to others, they feel so deficient, even in the face of their own holidays, career, social life, singing talent, relationships, home or children.

Whereas jealousy can lead to bouts of open warfare, the very dark side of envy is a little more subtle or indirect. Unhealthy Fours can take secret delight in the losses and suffering of those who are envied. *"Ah... so sad your face has been scarred for life!"* says the Four! *"Oh, wasn't he was fired from his executive position..."* *"Oh, failed the test... don't worry you'll do better next time..."* (thinking in the privacy of one's mind: *"I hope not!"*)

Surely it takes a sick puppy to derive pleasure from the misfortunes of others.

Another dark aspect of envy is that it serves as the breeding ground for gossip, slander and backbiting.[24] It's extremely difficult for the unhealthy Four to constantly see what is idealized in others, but is apparently so lacking in oneself and one's own life. In others, the Four sees the positive and the good. This perception eventually becomes unbearable, however, given the yawning emptiness felt deep inside. So, in sneaky fashion, supported by the ego, the Four goes after the one who is recipient of this positive projection. Fours often try to bring individuals down a notch, that is, those who seemingly display qualities perceived as absent or less developed in themselves. This can be done by talking behind the person's back, diminishing the other person's accomplishments, or otherwise trying to harm those who are envied. For example, a Four with failed ambitions may unfairly criticize a successful person for being ruthless in pursuit of their own goals. In this case, by cutting down someone else's ambition and devaluing it, the Four tries to convince themselves, largely unconsciously, that they needn't feel so bad about being less accomplished. Smooth move Four!

Do you *really* feel better about yourself when you do this? Or, is suppressed unconscious guilt more likely to contribute further to your feelings of self-loathing? Aren't you really contributing to your own misery when you do this? Aren't you really the chief architect of your troubled mind?

Therapeutic Recommendations for Promoting Psychological Hygiene and Finding Inner Peace:

The first thing Fours need to recognize is that yesterday is gone and tomorrow will never come. All of life must necessarily be experienced in the *present* – the precious *now* is all there is. Yesterday's *tomorrow* and tomorrow's *yesterday* are both *today* – nothing more than *today*. In the present are captured what your past will become and what your future will turn out to be.

This is important for Fours to realize, of course, since their yearnings and longings depend on focusing on other times and other places. For Fours, living is like driving forward in an automobile with their eyes firmly planted in the rear-view mirror to see what they have just missed or what might have passed them by on the road of life. And when they are not looking backwards, wishing they had gotten a better look, Fours are impatiently looking too far ahead of themselves, wondering why their trip is taking so long. They pine for arrival at their destination, and in the process, they miss all the beautiful scenery of life along the way. Surely, there must be a better way to travel on life's journey. Focusing almost entirely on what's behind is certainly dangerous as far as making progress and moving forward is concerned. Furthermore, always focused on some distant horizon means that you miss how much ground you've already covered and how sweet the ride so far has been.

Thus, Fours should try to catch themselves at frequent intervals throughout the day determining their space-time coordinates. They should ask: *"Am I experiencing reality right here and now, or am I absent in thought dreaming about some other place and time?"* Whenever their attention is focused elsewhere, one should simply chose to return to the present moment, to what's happening now.

As we've learned in this chapter, even when Fours are living in the present, there are still problems. Fours tend to selectively focus their attention, amplifying the present negatives and exaggerating the positives of the future, or some other place, or some other person.

The truth is that the present is not *all that bad* and the future, the past, or some other place is *not entirely good*. No doubt the envied idealized-other has his or her flaws as well, just as we all do – at least at the level of the psychological ego.

Truth be told, no time, no person, nor any empirical situation is absolutely perfect. Nothing will be exactly how the Four wants. Fours need to recognize their cognitive tendency to see their life predicaments as *just so terrible* and everyone else's as *just so much better*, regardless of the reasons.

As pointed out, this delusion is based on selective perceptual distortions. Fours need to make the conscious choice to perceive things differently, in a more balanced fashion. There will be pros and cons no matter who is concerned, no matter what the situation is, or where life is taking place. Recognition and acceptance of this fact should help Fours find greater contentment in their present circumstances.

The green grass on the other side of the fence has its yellow and brown patches too, if you look closely enough.

Appreciating this fact lends to the Four's maturity and confidence. There needn't be all of this crazed yearning and searching and melancholic self-pitying any longer when the Four comes to terms with the complexities and vicissitudes of life. Everyone has good times and bad. At a psychological level we all have our foibles and deficiencies.

Appearances can be deceiving. Think again of the image-conscious Three, for example, who has fooled us into thinking they are a complete success, masking the deeper reality that they are someone whose life depends on our favorable opinion of them. They are actually a slave to the crowd.

Now that doesn't look so good, does it? *The grass isn't so green, is it?*

To idealize any person or character type as better than oneself or one's own type is foolish. We're all entrapped to some extent by our self-serving, destructive, egos. We all have our shadows, our defenses, and our compensating strategies for dealing with life's difficulties and disappointments.

It's all so amusing to watch from the perspective of Perfect Being where Goodness is eternal and infinite. From that vantage point, *Life is a carnival! Here for only a limited time engagement.*

If you're a Four, you need to forgive others and accept yourself. We saw before how Fours project their values and ideals onto others whom they quickly come to envy. Fours see in others what they believe they lack in themselves. Since the ego can't stand conscious envy for too long, that envy becomes transformed into hatred targeted at the envied other. From the ego's perspective, hate is easier to live with than envy – which is such an admission of failure and inadequacy. In the so-called *real world*, hate has some kind of perverse status associated with it. We're tough when we hate.

We're confidently right in our criticism and moral condemnation. We're okay, they're not okay. The defective other deserves our attack and judgment. When we judge someone, we assume we're better than the person being judged. That individual displays a flawed character, one that needs psychological repair.

Of course, the *Idealized Other* did not ask for the Four's projections. More often than not the Idealized Other is not aware that someone has made an idol out of them, an idol soon to be knocked off the pedestal that the Four has awarded them. From afar, they have been idolized and destroyed in quick succession, without their knowledge. They have been unknowingly glorified for their attributes and then, without notice, they've been attacked, criticized, judged, labeled, stereotyped, and resented in the fantasy land of someone else's troubled defensive mind.

Insofar as this is true, Fours need to review in their minds all those people they have held in envious contempt. They need to forgive those others for what they never did, namely intentionally go out to hurt the Four. Fours, and all of us for that matter, often *do unto others as we would never want done unto us*. In this case, an assault is launched against an unsuspecting innocent. If anyone can understand, surely the Four should be able to understand the emotional pain of someone who suffers at the hands of others, even when they've done nothing wrong to deserve the maltreatment. The targeted victim of the Four's venom could say: *"You don't understand... You don't know what it's like to be me! Who are these Fours who have chosen to make me their hero, without my permission, and now make a villain out of me? I didn't ask for this!"* What can the Four honestly say in reply?

The Four's own insecurities have unconsciously created the

object-other that now appears to deserve judgment and attack. With a deeper appreciation of the complexities of life, the complexities of people's personalities, and the workings of one's existential psychodynamics, Four's can now come to see more easily how a disturbing world, a world of ambivalence oscillating between admiration and attack, is really a psychological projection for which they need to accept personal responsibility. Appreciating how the undeserved assault on the envied other is based on self-ignorance, the Four need not judge and condemn themselves either. Rather, they need to *go and judge no more.*

Fours should not waste their energy in feeling guilty for their projections and hateful attacks. They need to understand better what gave rise to them. Just as figuring out the trick robs magic of its wonder, uncovering the deceptions of the ego robs it of its power to wow us with its apparent effectiveness, which was all based on illusion anyway, just like magic.

There's another wrinkle to all this attack and judgment. Ironically, attacks on envied others were indirectly attacks on oneself for the Four. Feeling deficient from childhood, Fours never did identify with their positive qualities; rather they projected them externally. By attacking others onto whom those positive qualities were projected, Fours attacked themselves in effect.

Now, by accepting in others what was projected onto them unconsciously, the Four is better able to accept themselves. Releasing others from guilt has the effect of releasing oneself from the tormenting thought that one is deficient at the core.

You see, previous attacks were ultimately based on self-hatred. This kind of hatred or self-loathing, however sad its beginnings in the formation of the ego, was never justified for it was based on ignorance of one's Higher Being. With respect to this, there are no deficiencies; there is nothing to feel guilty about.

In the space-time continuum we cannot impact on the

Essential Being of another and the other cannot really affect us in our Essential State.

To understand all is to forgive all.
  French Proverb

"External things touch not the soul," the Stoic philosopher tells us. All the perceived hurt, attack and judgment occurs in the ego's playground, a virtual reality illuminated by fires of hatred, fires fueled by psychological insecurity. This virtual reality of the ego is the mind's living Hell.

The mind is its own place and in itself, can make a Heaven of Hell, a Hell of Heaven.
  John Milton

As with all types, the major existential task for the Four is to stay in touch with one's essence.

For Deep-Feeling Individualists, the biggest challenge in this regard is to regain the virtue of equanimity. Fours lose balance in their lives when they identify with that part of the self that coincides with their idealized self-image. Fours are indeed special in this regard.

To explain by way of comparison: with Ones, the idealized self-image is the Perfectionist. Twos are the Selfless Givers. Threes identify with success and do everything to realize themselves in terms of it. Fours, however, identify with that part of the psyche that *fails* to fit the idealized image. That idealized image is projected onto others and then those others are envied from afar. Because Fours are then left to identify with what's missing or what's lacking , happiness seems only a very distant possibility.

"I am a misunderstood melancholic outsider," says the Four with some perverse satisfaction stemming from a sense of elitist

nonconformity. Identifying with pain is never good.

In view of all this, what Fours need to recognize is the fact that what they see in others is a *projection* of themselves. It's not all that infrequent that Fours are complimented by others for having qualities or abilities that they envy in others, but fail to see in themselves. For instance, a Four could be depressed over the fact that a rival is much more eloquent or articulate in speech than he or she is. Yet, the eloquence of the other is only recognized because the Four possesses the ability to appreciate it. That person's 'genius' requires a genius to see it. As the saying goes: *"It takes one to know one."*

The importance of projection in perception cannot be overstated. Each time we see another, we are in some ways looking at ourselves. Perceived reality is a construction of our minds. Sometimes we see our insecurities, as Lance did in Becky (see Chapter One). At other times we see our values and ideals.

When Fours develop the habit of seeing the Good in others and understand that their perceptions are a product of their own minds, then they will see similarities between themselves and those others. The Goodness they witness in others, then, will become the Goodness they perceive in themselves. This Goodness will bring light to the mind darkened by melancholy, depression, and despair. And with illumination comes joyful bliss.

The holiness in you belongs to him [your brother]. And by your seeing it in him, returns to you.
    A Course in Miracles

CHAPTER EIGHT

EGO DYNAMICS IN CHARACTER TYPE FIVE: *THE OBSERVANT THINKER*

I think, therefore I am.
René Descartes

Lost Essence:
Nobody emerges from childhood totally unaffected by the events experienced during that developmental period. While our early childhood upbringing does not necessarily determine in any one-to-one causal relation what our characters will turn out to be, or how we will behave as adults, it certainly does act as one very significant formative influence on the creation of our personalities.

People who have self-identified as Fives often report that they had an unhappy or troubled childhood. Compare this fact with the Three, for instance, who was continually praised and rewarded for their achievements. The Two will also have received endless psychological strokes for being so nice and helpful. Of course, the young Two and Three didn't know what devastating emotional consequences all that praise and recognition would have for their later emotional well-being. At the time, receiving strokes felt good.*"Mommy and daddy always take me out for ice-cream when I get an A on my report card,"* said the Three. *"Or when I clean my room,"* replied the Two.

Little did the recipients of those rewards know what was in store later on. How unintended were the results of all that loving parental attention. Who could have known?

As for the Five, the childhood story is usually not so sweet. Fives more often than not had parents or guardians functioning at one of two extremes. At one extreme, parents of the Five were terribly intrusive. They frequently invaded the child's space, either physically and/or emotionally. Rather than allow the Five to live at his or her own pace, mom and dad imposed themselves, making their endless demands and suggestions. Their parental involvement was *inflicted*, not welcomed.

This is particularly upsetting for, temperamentally speaking, Fives tend to be introverted individuals even in their youth. This predisposition toward introversion makes unannounced and unexpected visitations unwanted, almost constituting an act of violence against the self. Because Fives felt a danger of being overwhelmed by their parents or caretakers in their early developmental histories, they did not feel safe in their family setting – undoubtedly the one place of refuge where safety and security should be guaranteed, at least for healthy psychological growth.

The result is that they retreated to the safety of their minds. It is in this inner tabernacle where many Fives choose to live most of the rest of their lives.

At the other extreme, it's sometimes the case that Fives were physically and/or emotionally abandoned. Nurturing may have been erratic; perhaps the parents were emotionally disturbed or alcoholic or caught up in a loveless marriage, for instance.[1] In all these cases, the parents did not offer consistent and dependable sources of love and reassurance for the Five.

This abandonment could also have involved parental separation and divorce. In this situation, one parent is completely absent, perhaps estranged. The remaining parent could have been more concerned about their own needs than their child's. Trying to make it through the week or until payday was perhaps the primary consideration in the single parent's new situation. In circumstances such as these, the Five child is left to fend for themselves. They are desperate to survive under very adverse conditions. 'Conveniently', the ego arrives on the scene for purposes of emotional rescue and gradually begins to take a more prominent role in the life of the Five as he or she matures.

After repeated and long-term disappointments when it comes to getting their basic psychological needs met, the ego helps to articulate a kind of social contract, one which lays out the terms in the following fashion: *"I won't ask too much of you if you don't ask too much of me."*

The psychologically damaged, neglectful, or overburdened parent is glad to agree to the deal. *"Look at how nicely Billy plays all by himself for hours at a time... He's such a good boy... so independent... so low maintenance."*

The parent's ego is relieved of responsibility and the guilt associated with not fulfilling it. Unfortunately, the contract, which is signed and sealed with egoistic stamp, will often have an enduring effect. In the immediate future, it will certainly make life temporarily easier for the suffering parent, even if it does cause lasting psychological problems for the child.

Adding to the grief, however, that parent may come, in time, to experience even more suffering in the form of intensified guilt, if and when their neglectful ways are consciously acknowledged or brought to their attention later in life by their grown children. The 'deal' which was agreed to by the child-Five, which was one made out of perceived necessity, can become a source of resentment as maturity and understanding increase. The Five was treated unfairly and so the agreement was really a raw deal. *"Nobody ever gave me what I was entitled to growing up as a child,"* thinks the Five. *"Life is unfair. Nobody cares. All they ever want is something from me!"*

A Five child growing up in a dysfunctional marriage situation often witnesses angry or at least unpleasant exchanges between his parents. Screaming and yelling may have taken place; dishes may have been thrown across the room; the apartment landlord or police may have even shown up at the front door to quell the domestic violence.

For the young Five, occurrences like these are terrifying and psychologically confusing. So are times when parents irrationally exert their authority or just barge into the room, take what is needed or stop the activity currently under way, for apparently no good or obvious reasons.

For young Fives, then, life typically begins with fear and insecurity stemming from worries about personal violation or abandonment. The demands of reality force them to defend and protect themselves against harsh forces in the external world.

Early in life, Fives begin to realize they are on their own. Their basic needs will not necessarily be met or satisfied by their caretakers and so they become fearful and insecure. Thus, the perception of *deficiency* arises – as it does for all the character types. This sensed deficiency can be generalized and diffuse. Not only do they risk losing or never getting what they need, child Fives sense they are quite different from everyone else. They feel there is something wrong with them, though they can't always put their finger on what. They're like outsiders looking in.

Furthermore, a look around reveals there may not be enough to go around. The Five may be overlooked, or their preferences may simply be ignored as others trample over them. In response to all of this, the Five can experience a kind of *stunned affective state or emotional paralysis* – emotions may be denied or repressed in the unconscious. They are too painful to experience in the moment.

The experience of separation between self and other is heightened as the Five no longer spontaneously engages with others, but warily observes to see what new unpleasantness will be forthcoming. *"What will they want from me next?"* the Five asks.

Playfulness diminishes, joy evaporates, and others become perceived sources of threat or intrusion. So goes the sad story of the Five.

In their efforts to cope, direct experience of life is often replaced by an effort to understand. Rather than being immersed in the immediacy of experience – just hanging out or being with people, the emotionally wounded Five begins to distance themselves from the potentially painful experience, trying to figure out or analyze the intentions, motivations, feelings, and thoughts of others who have proven to be unreliable or invasive in the past. They could prove to be so in the future.

Psychologically, Fives remove themselves to observe from above or from a distance, as it were. Life starts to be lived from the sidelines. In the process, Fives become disengaged from others, and alienated from something essential in themselves.

There's an expression that goes: *"One cannot see the forest for the trees."* This usually means that one is so involved or so immersed in something, that one lacks objectivity. The Five's problem is that they *can* see the forest from a distance but they don't know what it's like to experience the beauty of the individual trees from inside. Their objective perspective, though not necessarily bad in itself, is limited because it becomes the only distanced perspective from which the troubled Five operates.

In the process of separating from others and from one's experiences in order to safely analyze them, Fives lose sight of an essential quality which they, and all of us possess; namely, a *Higher Mind.* This Higher Mind or *Divine Mind,* as some refer to it, allows for a type of *direct knowing.* By means of this Higher Mind, one accesses a knowledge which transcends the space-time continuum of ordinary experience by way of interior, intuitive means.

This sort of knowing harkens back to our discussion of Plato and St.Thomas Aquinas. Remember that after Aquinas experienced Divine Revelation while serving Mass, he never wrote again, believing that human language could not express the truths that were revealed to him.

In his conception of knowledge, Plato also spoke of 'direct intellectual acquaintance' with the higher forms of knowledge – Goodness in particular.

Both thinkers pointed to some higher way of knowing that is unmediated. This form of knowing is not dualistic, nor is it based on linguistic or scientific or logical categories. It involves no degrees of separation and hence is beyond all ego and matters of personality.

This knowledge is knowledge of a Higher Reality. Unfortunately, the experience of oneness in direct knowing is replaced in the Five by the ego's lower mind which accepts dualism and separation – things on which rational objectivity is predicated. The lower mind takes history personally and allows that history to have an effect on the personality psychologically.

In other words, 'the lower mind *does allow* for external things to touch the soul, and it does so in the highest degree.'

This thinking is opposite to the Stoics. Of course, in truth, the soul remains unaffected, but the Five who identifies with the lower mind of separate ego identity is psychologically impacted by its illusory hurts. Like phantom-limb pain, the experience seems real, but just as the external body part which ostensibly causes the physical pain does not actually exist, neither does the psychological ego, at a higher level . And furthermore, just as the amputee balks at the notion that his or her pain is unreal, so too does the *dispirited* Five rebuff any notion that the hurts stemming from a separate and false ego-self are actually illusory. What's meant by 'really existing' is called into question here.

The notion of the Higher or Divine Mind is difficult to capture in language, since what it refers to transcends common experience. Describing what 'direct knowing' is all about is plagued by the same problem. In their efforts to explain what's at issue here, Riso and Hudson put it this way:

> "Direct knowing... is quite distinct from the ego's form of thinking, which is generally characterized by inner talk or inner visualization, often accompanied by a process of sorting information and 'data retrieval.' In direct knowing, however, the mind is silent and open, and we are supported by the awareness that we will know whatever we need to know as we need to know it. Even the acquisition of new information, skills, or experiences will be guided by an inner knowing that does not arise from the ego's feelings of insufficiency. Direct knowing arises out of a direct experience of the pristine empty space of mind: it allows us to be free of attachment to any particular perspective. We know that in different moments and situations different perspectives may be more useful, and that our Essence will guide us to the perspective that is most suitable. This inner clarity allows us to be unattached to the phenomenal world: when we are functioning in this capacity, we see all objects and events as arising and disappearing within a vast and unfathomable mystery. We see the world as an dance of exquisite gestures and movements within the shining void."[2]

In short, having forgotten what direct knowing is all about, Fives lose the *Omniscient Quality of Higher Mind*.[3] They attach themselves to worldly knowledge whether it is found in common sense, pet theories, empirical science, or the rarified abstractions of academic philosophy, for instance. All such knowledge is based on dualistic reality, something beyond which a Higher Transcendental Reality exists.

The way to God must pass through silence, going beyond words and thoughts.

Anthony DeMello

Psychological Worldview and Compensating Strategies:

As we've seen, in response to their painful early childhood experiences, Fives begin withdrawing from the world. They try to minimize contact with others, while at the same time simplifying their needs. It becomes very important to Fives that they find a protective private space and if they cannot find one, they need to create one.[4]

Fives are probably the most introverted of all the character types we'll examine in this book. They most closely resemble what Carl Jung labels the *Introverted-Thinking Type*. Though Fours are commonly a withdrawn introverted type as well, and quite private too, they yearn for connection in a way that Fives do not. At a conscious level at least, Fives are often quite happy to lead the reclusive life of a hermit.

This is preferable for them as getting involved with others would likely involve forming relationships and with relational attachments come obligations – something Fives experience as coercive, given their early childhood interactions with intrusive parents.

On the other hand, if they had parents who were not intrusive, but neglectful at the other extreme, then those needy, uncaring, or otherwise dysfunctional caretakers probably demanded things they themselves should have offered to their Five offspring instead, things like time, help, money or affection.

Worried, then, about being enveloped, or sucked dry, Fives compensate by hiding out. Emotional attachments are felt to be a drain.[5] Fives come to believe that connecting with other people may force them to sacrifice their depleted energy reserves or what little resources they've managed to accumulate on their own, without the help or support of others. Remember, little has come easy for the Five. Addressing the Five's joy of privacy, Helen Palmer writes the following:

> Fives come alive when they are alone. They often need to get away from people in order to recharge their batteries and to let out feelings that were suspended while they were in the presence of others. A Five's private time is filled with reverie and interesting things to think about. They love the company of their own minds, and unless privacy deepens into feelings of isolation, they are rarely depressed or bored because they have nothing to do.... Although Observers [Fives] can appear to be lonely and socially isolated from the point of view of the more extroverted types, Fives themselves prefer to be alone. They are, in fact, remarkably independent. They do not look to others for approval, they prefer to be economically self-sufficient, they insist upon being able to come and go as they please, and they want to remain free of the emotional drains of dependency relationships.[6]

Alone, but not lonely.
   A Five's Adage

As we have just learned, the Fives' preference for non-involvement means that they are highly independent and self-sufficient individuals. Autonomy becomes an idealized need. This need often translates into living the life of the mind, where independence from the exigencies of everyday reality is maximized. In the mind, one can develop expert knowledge or master some sort of special skill. Such expertise and mastery provide the Five with a sense of psychological place, a niche where one is safe and where one belongs and is nourished, if only intellectually or in an impersonal professional way.

Quite frequently, Fives are attracted to the unusual, the overlooked, the secret, the occult, the bizarre, the fantastic or the unthinkable.[7]

By intensely focusing on such things, they become 'the expert' and produce an idealized self-image around their expertise. Fives project an image of someone who has something unusual and insightful to say – and often they do.

It's probably the case that a disproportionate number of philosophers are Fives, including the European philosophers René Descartes, Jean-Paul Sartre, Immanuel Kant, as well as The Buddha. Other Fives who have made a great impression on how we think, include the computer software magnate Bill Gates, the scientist Albert Einstein whose impact was the Theory of Relativity, the best selling horror author Stephen King, the poet Emily Dickinson, and the British anthropologist Jane Goodall who theorized on what separates humans from apes.

In their efforts to achieve expertise or mastery, Fives often seem to be in a perpetual *preparation mode*.[8] They appear to be always preparing for life, but never really feeling ready to live it. Degree may be stacked on top of degree; or one course on top of another as the Five prepares to enter the workforce. *"With just one more course, one more certificate, or one more degree, I'll finally be ready to embark on my career,"* says the Five. However, whenever that course is completed and the certificate or degree is obtained, there magically appears just one more preparatory step that needs to be taken before starting out. Until then, it's back to the ivory tower or hermitage, either literally or figuratively.

By living a life of the mind, Fives adopt a *cognitive orientation*.[9] Emphasizing the cognitive, intellectual side of human existence, Fives become keen analytical observers. Wishing to remain rationally objective and not biased by personal attachments, they seem to replace the actual living or experiencing of life with an understanding of it. This could involve dwelling on abstractions, while at the same time avoiding concreteness.[10]

For instance, a Five might be more interested in historical definitions of 'love' than in experiencing love itself. If a Five is able to write the definitive book on the subject of love, so much the better in their mind. *"Most people who say they are in love can't even define what they're experiencing,"* says the observant thinker. *"What do they know?"*

And if the Five in this case is not writing about love, then they are probably reading about it. Reading about life can become a replacement for actually living it

Books are like maps, but there's also the necessity of traveling.
George Gurdjieff

Still on the subject of the Five's cognitive orientation, it's interesting to note that while any one of us might have a particular experience, it's not unusual for Fives to have the same experience – three times. Fives like to rehearse or prepare ahead of time for the experience they anticipate having. For example, the Five could imagine what a party will be like while traveling to get there. "Who will be there? What will the topics of conversation be?" Questions such as these preoccupy the mind as they rehearse whole conversations and responses in their head.

Then there's the experience of the party itself, where the Five is likely to be somewhat of a wallflower or aloof observer of the proceedings. Finally, there's the debriefing phase after the party when everything is mentally repeated. Comments that should have been made, but never were, can now be made in the Five's mind. In that safe place, emotions can be silently expressed, arguments can be won, people and things can be analyzed and evaluated.

It's as if life requires a period of processing and debriefing after every episode. From the outside, Fives often seem detached and may even seem to be lacking emotion.

Such a perception fails to grasp the fact that Fives' feelings have a 'retroactive' dimension to them.[11] They are felt and experienced after the fact, in the third part of the lived experience.

Healthy and Unhealthy Expressions of the Observant Thinker:
Healthy Fives are extremely curious individuals. As children, they probably asked the 'Why?' question more than anyone else in their families. They like to probe and uncover the reasons why things are the way they are. Fives display a deep need to understand how the world works, how the mind works, or how the machine works, in fact, how just about anything works. From a distance, Fives can look very intense in their probing intellectual investigations. Their focused concentration for long periods of time can yield awesome discoveries.

Not only are Fives likely to be the most private of all the types, they are also usually the most perceptive. They see things in the surrounding physical or social environment that most of us overlook. They notice the minute details; they read between the lines, they understand the implications, and are able to uncover the underlying assumptions or presuppositions of anyone's argument or point of view.

More often than not, they are able to express their ideas at a level of detail that's so precise that their high definition intellectual clarity is truly amazing. It's almost always fascinating to talk to a Five about their latest project, whatever that might be.

Fives invest a lot of energy and enthusiasm in those things that interest them most. They have found their niche when they have mastered some body of knowledge or become expert at some skill which allows them to confidently move forward in their lives.

When talking about their interests, Fives are at their social best – unreserved, animated, and excited about life. There's much to learn from Fives. You may have noticed this by their dissertation style of communication! Personally speaking, as an academic, I've always found it intriguing to watch the nervous and avoidant Five professor emerge from the uncomfortable pre-lecture gathering to then command attention on stage behind the podium with great confidence and flair. It's just as intriguing then to watch the same professor go back into their shell after-wards, unless of course somebody wishes to discuss the content of the lecture that was just given.

It's not unusual for high functioning Fives to become pioneering visionaries.[12] As astute observers of nature and people, or as rational analytical thinkers of the highest order, they can produce important, original and creative works. The list of Fives provided earlier, which included people like Albert Einstein, who have made breakthrough discoveries or theories, illustrates the point here. Through detailed observations, critical analysis, new discoveries, innovative ideas, or by synthesizing already accepted ideas in hitherto unthought-of ways, they can come up with novel and profound forms of understanding, or make lasting contributions to humankind. By standing back from reality, they gain an objective appreciation of the truth better than those blinded by convention, past teachings, or by their own prejudiced and largely subjective views having limited or questionable validity.

Fives are usually careful to remain impartial and disinter-ested, trying to make sure their perceptions are not skewed by their own theoretical or personal bias. They are able to de-center from their own subjectivity and see things objectively from an external point of view. A Five is likely to find it more compli-mentary to be described as rational, objective, and fair, as compared with emotionally warm, personal, and preferential in treatment towards family, friends and acquaintances.

While healthy Fives often observe things that most of us miss or can't see, unhealthy Fives begin to witness things that aren't there. Perceptions of reality become little more than defensive distortions, or even worse, hallucinations and projected delusions of their over-heated minds.

Life can start to be filtered through the Five's theoretical lens so much so that his or her interpretation of reality does not fit most other people's – and this is not necessarily because the majority is blind or wrong in this case. The habitual desire by Fives to stand back and experience life from a distance can have the effect of removing them from the real world almost entirely. In extreme instances, they may suffer from schizoid withdrawal.[13]

In view of what was discussed at the outset of this book, it should be clear how everyone's reality is in fact constructed from their own psychological perspective, so that we all do what the Five does. The point is that extremely unhealthy Fives start making cognitive connections that don't make any sense, connections that impede their ability to function in the world. When their idiosyncratic perspective begins to seriously conflict with publically accepted norms and socially accepted definitions of reality, trouble arises. 'Pseudo-objectivity' may remove the Five so far from reality that they lose touch entirely. In the Five, we're reminded that there's sometimes a thin line between genius and insanity.

Unhealthy Fives confuse their detachment from life with the virtue of *non-attachment*. Buddha taught us that craving things or clinging on to them was the original source of suffering and that if we wished to experience Nirvana, or at least a greater degree of peace of mind here on earth, we would have to minimize our worldly attachments. Remember, nothing lasts forever.

On the surface, it may look like minimalist Fives have been successful in reducing their cravings. By settling for little and by withdrawing from the world to observe it with emotional detachment, it appears that Fives are sticking with The Buddha's program.

Yet, unhealthy Fives are more accurately described as *Unenlightened Buddhas.*[14] What the detachment is that Buddha had in mind is not the same as the dysfunctional Five's. Fives originally detached from their parents early in life in fearful, defensive reaction to either emotional abandonment or intrusiveness.

They feared being helpless and incapable. They were also worried that their personal resources and capacities were limited, so they responded to their anxieties by downscaling their activities and needs.[15]

Fives also came to avoid situations where others might expect from them more than they could give. Thus, in fear, they retreated to the inner sanctum of the mind in order to find refuge from what they perceived was a hostile and uncaring world.

In the process, unhealthy Fives became masters of one skill they may not wish to acknowledge publically, namely *avoidance.* They became masters of *noninvolvement* in their psychological efforts to protect themselves from ever having to feel and experience the fears and desires of ordinary life.[16]

By contrast, Buddha did not advocate becoming immune to feelings. He didn't depart from the world, but chose to remain within it. Why else would he have been called The *Compassionate Buddha*? Buddha saw the suffering of others and empathically felt their pain. This is why he chose to become the *Bodhisattva*, the Enlightened One devoted to helping others and relieving their pain.

On the other hand, to see the sick Five's non-involvement and avoidance of others as good is to adopt a perverse understanding and application of the universal wisdom captured in Buddha's teachings on non-attachment. Buddha appreciated the transitoriness of life. To want to cling onto things that can never last is the source of suffering according to Buddhist tradition. However, letting things come and go, understanding their fleeting and transitory nature, is not the same thing as the Five's habit of running away from life or refusing to enter into the lives of others out of insecure fearful detachment.

In no way is this defensive retreat a virtue. To think of it in this way or to define it as so would be intellectually dishonest. Unenlightened Fives are guilty of existential bad-faith when they try to make defensive psychological withdrawal into something praiseworthy. *"It's like trying to make a silk purse out of a sow's ear,"* as the saying goes.

On the subject of the sick Fives' unhealthy detachment, Riso and Hudson remark:

> Fives are the type of persons who cut themselves off from most human contact. Once isolated, they develop their eccentric ideas to such absurd extremes that they become obsessed with completely distorted notions about themselves and reality. Ultimately, unhealthy Fives become utterly terrified and trapped by the threatening visions which they have created in their own minds.[17]

The most unhealthy of Fives become dangerously reclusive and entirely isolated from the world. Feeling anxious and divorced from any meaningful human contact, they can also be drawn into a nihilistic worldview.

Their lack of stability and fearfulness surrounding the need to meet others' expectations leads the dysfunctional Five to reject and repulse others, as well as all social attachments. Their obsessive ideas can become terrifying to them as they lead to gross distortions of reality and phobic reactions. At worst, Fives experience psychotic breaks with reality.[18]

Personal Shadow:
We have seen so far how Fives display a tendency to detach from people and life in general. They avoid action and prefer to live a

life of the mind. They sequester themselves in their little area of expertise or skill mastery and thereby suppress any negative feelings they might have, many of them having to do with fear and anxiety. All of this emotional suppression and avoidance leads to an impoverishment of experience, an experience of emptiness.[19]

We have also learned in this discussion how the Five compensates for this impoverished existence through developing an idealized self-image of *thinker* or *curious and critical outsider*. That image might also take the form of *master* or *objective and detached observer*.

In light of their childhood deprivations and later compensating minimalist lifestyles, it might come as a shock to Fives that their psychological shadow falls on the problem of personal *avarice*.

To understand what's meant by this, it's important first to distinguish between avarice and greed.

Greedy people want more and more; they are never satisfied with what they have. No amount is ever enough, whether it be money, property, or other material possessions. Greedy people are constantly grasping to get more, to increase their wealth, to have more.

Avarice, on the other hand, deals more with retention and holding on to what little one has. The Five is not going out into the marketplace of life to aggressively compete with others for resources. Rather, the Five is more likely to take what little they have and find contentment with that, usually in some private place where they are safe emotionally, psychologically, and physically. Fives minimize their needs to avoid dissatisfaction. Greedy people, on the other hand, go out to get more if they're unhappy, thinking that increasing what they have will be the solution to their grief.

As part of their minimalist retreat from life, Fives' avarice comes in the form of *stinginess*. They frequently show a lack of generosity toward others. Understand that this stinginess is not necessarily all about money. Fives can be stingy with their time and energy as well. Hence, they may be slow to make themselves available or to volunteer themselves for greater responsibilities at work or in the community. Fives have rarely been on the receiving end of other people's benevolence, especially in terms of their childhood relationships with parents, and so sometimes they come to feel like they don't owe the world anything. In fact, they may believe that they're barely surviving or holding on as it is. What they have, they need; there's nothing left over to give.

Furthermore, whatever little they've managed to achieve in their lives, they've accomplished themselves, more often than not with no help from others. There's often an embittered reluctance to give to others when the occasion arises. Charity workers who show up at the Five's front door or who call for donations over the phone should know they do so at their own peril. They have invaded the private space of the Five and have the audacity to ask for something on top of that. It would be far better to approach the Five indirectly through mail when asking for a donation in order to give the Five a little time to think about the merits of giving in advance. A sudden and unexpected request at the door or over the telephone is usually experienced as a rude intrusion. *"How dare people invade my space or take up my private time at home. And then they ask for something! There should be a law against this!"*

While stinginess may appear awfully mean-spirited to others, it's worth remembering its source in the Five. The Five is not some unfriendly miserly person by nature. In fact, in essence, the Five is nothing like this at all – nobody is. The psychological traits and compensating strategies that Fives exhibit turn out to be the result of their best efforts to cope with a life of abandonment or intrusion as they perceived it and experienced it early in childhood. The next time you witness the stinginess of a Five, it's helpful to remember the source of that behavioral trait.

Therapeutic Recommendations for Promoting Psychological Hygiene and Finding Inner peace:

Fives are astute observers of human nature. They frequently observe in others what those others don't notice. For their own benefit, Fives need to take their perceptiveness and direct it at themselves for a change. In this instance, it's important for Fives that they notice when they are leaving the body and retreating into their minds.[20]

Through such self-observations, Fives can engage in something we all need to do, namely, *catch ourselves in the act of being ourselves.* Fives have a tendency to disengage from feelings in order to observe. Their *inner observer*, or *Mind's Eye*, what some call *The Third Eye of Spiritual Inner Vision*, needs to catch the lower ego-self in its tricky maneuvers.

In the end, the ego is not really helping, but hindering Fives in their efforts to find psychological security. Premature withdrawal from emotional pain is not the same as spiritual detachment. Fives can't get things like help, validation, love, respect or nurturance from others if they're always hiding out from them. The ego is not about to remind the Five about the truth of this. It's very existence is predicated on the Five's psychological identification with the ego and the idealized identity the ego has fashioned. That means the ego's job is convincing the Five to stay in one's head and isolate from others, while at the same time leading the foolishly self-satisfied, but *Unenlightened Buddha Five*, into believing he or she is on the right path to enlightenment.

However, to perceive detachment from others as real is to perceive dualism and separation, things not part of Higher Reality, nor the Essential Being of the Five, which is beyond space and time. The ego's promise of safety and comfort is therefore dishonest in principle. In empirical reality, this dishonesty has been verified by the Five's persistent dissatisfactions with life as they've been experienced until now.

Fives need to experiment with risk-taking. As fear-based character types, Fives are notoriously anxious or apprehensive *vis-à-vis* the external world. Their insecurities are what causes them to retreat to the inner castles of their mind for protection. One writer has described this place of refuge as a "womb with a view."

Unfortunately, when hiding out in the castle, it's like being under siege by reality. What's out there is experienced as alien and dangerous. The forces of reality must be prevented from jumping the moat of psychological defensiveness or scaling the walls of ego-isolation. It's the job of the Five's personality to be ever vigilant and to make sure that these dangerous, alien forces don't invade or somehow make their way into the secret kingdom. The Five must decide when the drawbridge will be lowered and if, or when, efforts will ever be made to make peace with others or peace with the world.

Hell is other people.
Jean-Paul Sartre

The results can be surprisingly wonderful when Fives give up analyzing and judging experiences even before they have them. Fives sometimes believe that they know what things will be like, even before they occur. This is 'part one' of their threefold experience of the world mentioned earlier. In their minds, they may think: *"The party will be so boring, the conversation so mundane – why even go?"* This kind of quick and dismissive *pre-judgment* is evidence of the way Fives attack in order to protect themselves from having to engage socially.

By charging others of being guilty for being so stupid or

uninsightful, say, the Five's ego uses arrogance as a intellectual weapon. It's time for Fives to put down the weapons, to open the doors, and let others in. This unilateral disarmament is likely to reap huge benefits.

First of all, the world will miraculously become a safer place – trust me. As a Five, you will come to see that a lot of worry in the past was for naught. Furthermore, rather than fire-bomb the castle, those *intruders* outside may arrive actually bearing gifts. Who knows? Fives won't until they take the risk and invite others into their heavily guarded private worlds.

Furthermore, they need to venture outside so that they can get fresh psychological supplies. As Fives well know, resources keep dwindling inside the castle walls. Like the saying goes: *"Nothing ventured, nothing gained."* Just imagine, by risking social engagement, there'll be so much more to know and think about. There will be so much more to analyze and understand. Now, if that's not some motivation for the Five to change, then nothing is!

Fives also need to get into their bodies. In their lifelong retreat into their minds, Fives not only lose touch with their emotions and with other people, but also with their own bodies. It's important that they fully appreciate the fact that their earthly existence is not one merely of a disembodied mind.

To be a human living in this world is not just to be Descartes' *Cogito* or *Thinking Thing*.

Though in ultimate spiritual reality, the body as a separate entity, does not exist, for the time we walk the face of the earth, we all have to deal with this temporary, albeit illusory, inconvenience.

The physical state of the body can impact on our psychological moods, energy levels, ability to function effectively or even concentrate mentally, as Fives so much like to do. Paradoxically, while we are not a body, we can't seem to get rid of it. The body serves as our physical transport in our journey of life.

Now, growing up on the sidelines or secluded behind closed doors in the bedroom reading books, means that most Fives failed to develop their physical coordination and athletic skills in childhood. Fives were likely the most *nerdy* of all the children in school. Especially if they were emotionally or personally abandoned early in life by their parents, they probably didn't receive any encouragement to develop their physical skills in organized sports, dance, or other after-school athletic activities which would require practice, transportation, and cost. All this would require too much attention be paid to the child.

Even if Fives did somehow find a way to participate, uncaring or dysfunctional parents were likely absent in their capacity as cheerleaders, coaches, and loving onlookers. Without help and encouragement at home or on the playing field, many Fives just drop out and go back to their room – something they're good at. The net result is they often look physically awkward and undeveloped in their youth. This underdevelopment is carried into later adulthood.

All is not lost for adult Fives on this account. What Fives need to do is reacquaint themselves with their bodies. The simplest thing to do is to start a program of regular exercise. One could join the gym to engage in a regimen of weight training, for example. Doing yoga is another possibility. Or, the exercise could be something as simple as going for walks. Over time, the actions taken to get back into the body could be combined with joining a walker's club or running club. Perhaps a beginner's hockey or soccer league is a possibility once physical stamina, strength, and coordination have improved sufficiently.

For Fives who have always felt insecure about their bodies and physical skills, no time in life is too late to relive their childhoods, and to now do with confidence what was once done only with paralyzing insecurity.

Fives might discover that they are not as useless as they believed themselves to be when they were growing up. If all this physical activity occurs in the context of a team or club, the Five also has the opportunity to make friends and informal social contacts in the outside world. With a social life, better physical health, and a newly found feeling of confidence, stemming from the mastery of physical athletic skills, Fives are able to reach out and form contacts with others and maintain better psychological balance.

They don't have to abandon their attachment to knowledge, of course, but they don't have to use it as a defensive retreat from reality either. Living more in the body means life is fuller and there's less need to fill the emptiness of one's life with the pursuit of knowledge – something which is noble it itself, but not so when used in defensive retreat or as a psychological weapon of judgment and attack.

The unexamined life is not worth living.
    Socrates

The over-examined life is not living at all.
    Enlightened Five

CHAPTER NINE

EGO DYNAMICS IN CHARACTER TYPE SIX: *THE COMMITTED LOYALIST*

Fear and I were born twins.
Thomas Hobbes

Lost Essence:

To explain how Sixes lose touch with their essence, let me start off by relating a personal story. Years ago, when my children were young, I remember playing a little game with them on the living room sofa. Sometimes while I was relaxing on it, they would climb up and stand tall on the armrest or back, then suddenly fall forward without making any effort at all to support themselves. They just expected me to catch them in the air before we smacked heads or before they crashed to the floor. I remember this game as being lots of fun. I found it endearing insofar as it made it obvious to me what incredible trust my kids had in their father. They knew I wouldn't let them get hurt. Their protective daddy would make sure nothing bad would happen.

It's probably true to say that most parents, most of the time, make conscious and deliberate efforts to protect their children from danger and to keep their offspring out of harm's way. Little doubt there's something instinctive or biological about this tendency. This inclination to protect is what gives young children an early sense of safety and security. Whenever there's an occasion for fear, there's always mommy or daddy to run to for assurance, protection, and comfort.

In such a loving and supportive situation, it's possible to have faith in people and, out of this faith, to develop a basic trust in the goodness of humanity and the world. With a deep sense of trust and security, the universe is experienced as beneficent and loving.[1] A.H. Almaas calls this dimension of the soul's experience 'cosmic' or 'divine love.'[2]

When we are aware of it, we are in touch with our essential Being. We feel loved, solidly supported and optimistic, confident that in the end, things will work out for the best. Think of this as a kind of "faith in the future".

Contrast this with worrying about tomorrow, "having butterflies in the pit of your stomach" or feeling anxious and uncertain about what's going on around you right now.

If your life is currently filled with worry and anxiety, you've somehow lost touch with your Essence. Pure Being is not about panicky disorientation. It is about feeling grounded in eternal peace.

In faith, we find confidence. The faith here is not so much belief "in" something; rather, it is a real immediate knowing that comes from experience.[3] This is what brings reliable guidance.

As Riso and Hudson put it: "When Essence emerges... Sixes... have a certainty that they are grounded in Being in a way that is immutable and absolute. Being supports them because they are part of it: their own existence has Being because it cannot *not* have Being."[4]

Look at the birds in the sky; they do not sow or reap, they gather nothing into barns, yet your heavenly Father feeds them. Are not you more important than they? Can any of you by worrying add a single moment to your life-span?
Matthew 6: 26-27

Sadly, not all children are raised in psychologically safe and secure environments. Sometimes they are brought up in chaotic situations, by cold and overbearing parents, by parents who were frequently absent, or by unstable parents who were somehow out of control.

Sixes often come from households where there were many "family secrets" or where authority figures, who were initially idolized, went on to become sources of betrayal later on.[5] The son or daughter of alcoholic parents, for example, may not always have received the kind of loving support and comfort that young children need to feel safe. Mom and/or dad may have been too worried about replenishing their dwindling liquor supplies. In moments of sloppy drunkenness, the parents may have lost control, engaging in violent or destructive acts. At other times, they may have become embarrassingly generous or inappropriate with their expressed affections toward one another or the children.

What could have become still more confusing is when these same parents turned cold and uncaring when hungover, emotionally unavailable and seemingly lost in some mysterious distant psychological world of their own. So, in the home of alcoholic or otherwise disturbed parents, it could be the case that the child finds the situation entirely unpredictable – which is not a good thing. If a child is suddenly punished or beaten, without apparent reason, and then loved and adored before inexplicably being ignored or coldly dismissed in the next instant, a sense of insecurity quickly begins to grow in the child's mind. The child never knows what to expect; people's reactions don't seem to make sense. The child can never tell how others are going to act or what they're going to feel or say or do or what their real intentions actually are. Sometimes their reactions are pleasant and reassuring, whereas at other times they are unpleasant and threatening. There appears to be no rhyme or reason to explain how they'll behave in any given situation. They don't make sense, and by extension, neither does the world.

Unpredictability is the first experience of the child's reality and eventually it is this same unpredictability which determines the child's view of the world. In the mind of the young Six child, raised in such an erratic situation, life is scary. People simply can't be trusted.

In the words of the political philosopher Thomas Hobbes, an archetypal Six, "... *the life of man [becomes] solitary, poor, nasty, brutish, and short."*

It's not surprising that Hobbes should have written these words given that his own father was unruly and quarrelsome, given to much drink. In fact, after one embarrassing drunken-fight episode on the steps of the church where he was the vicar, Hobbes' father abandoned the family, leaving Thomas not completely alone, but with a highly anxious mother in some financial difficulty. Life for the young Hobbes was clearly not ideal. He yearned for structure and stability.

Years later, when formulating his political philosophy, he wrote the following (in old English) about the state of nature without a ruling monarch or absolute authority (Leviathan) to control people:

Hereby it is manifest that during the time men live without a common Power to keep them all in awe, they are in that condition which is called Warre; and such Warre, as is of every man, against every man.[6]

Where there is no common Power, there is no Law, where no Law, no Injustice. Force and Fraud are in warre the two Cardinal vertues.
Thomas Hobbes

To those who would argue that Hobbes has a very fearful and overly pessimistic view of human nature, he replies by saying the following (in old English again):

...what opinion he has of his fellow subjects, when he rides armed, of his fellow Citizens when he locks his dores; and of his children and servants, when he locks his chests. Does he not there as much accuse mankind by his actions, as I do by my words?[7]

In the context of Enneagram psychology, it's quite interesting how Hobbes' political philosophy reflects to a very large extent the worldview of the Six. This is not to suggest that we must therefore reject his thinking; this would be to commit a logical error of reasoning known as the genetic fallacy.[8]

Identifying the source of a claim or explaining how a philosophical position came to be does not necessarily nullify it. Nevertheless, it's interesting to acknowledge how even philosophers see reality through a lens of limited vision and with the selective perceptions of their own character structures – structures that had their formation in early childhood experiences. Intellectual perspectives on life are conditioned by the influence of one's cognitive unconscious whose interior psychodynamics have a developmental history.

Early in life, Six-children seek security from the protective parental figures in their lives. They feel anxious when they do not receive it. If protective support is not forthcoming, they typically shift their attention to substitutes such as charismatic leaders and civil or political authorities. In the case of political authorities – like Hobbes' Leviathan for instance, we witness how they become the newly found substitute sources from which security is drawn.[9]

However, original frustrations *vis-à-vis* security needs leave the Six ambivalent toward the protective authority figure – most commonly the father. That person may not have delivered security consistently or delivered it at all. In the end, outward obedience may be shown toward that protective figure, but only as a thin veil masking the inward rebellion inside.[10]

Sixes psychologically need authority figures, but resent it when protection is not always provided. They may learn to ingratiate themselves to get the protection they need or in classic defensive reaction-formation, they may rebel and become defiant toward authority.[11] Of course, the defiance toward authority is clear evidence that authority still matters very much.

On the subject of famous or well-known Sixes, here are a few others: Sigmund Freud, Adolf Hitler, Woody Allen, "George Costanza" (Seinfeld TV series), George W. Bush, "Archie Bunker" (*All in the Family* TV series), Princess Diana, and Don Cherry (Former Boston Bruins Coach and current *Hockey Night in Canada* commentator).

Central to Freud's theory of psychoanalysis were conflict and anxiety. For him, biology was interminably in conflict with civilized society. Inner instinctual urges could unexpectedly explode at any time into inappropriate sexual or aggressive behaviors.

Hitler projected his psychological fear in maniacal paranoid scapegoating of Slavs and Jews.[12] George W. Bush declared to the world after 9/11 that you are either an ally of the United States or an enemy who supports terrorists. *Archie Bunker* stood tall in unwavering support of his country and the authority of the president.

Princess Diana, with that lowered glance, felt constantly under attack, fled the paparazzi, and feared for the privacy of her children. The television character George Costanza was constantly insecure in every episode of *Seinfeld* and suspicious of just about everything. For him, everyone was a 'suspect.'

As for Don Cherry, he is loyal to Canada, the military, the police, firefighters, and competitive pugilists on the ice, as long as they obey the unwritten "honor code" of those who play the game. Players who break the unwritten rules are considered cowards and enemies deserving our disrespect.

In typical Six scapegoating fashion, Cherry often singles out Europeans and Russians as deserving our special contempt, claiming they are dirty players and "gutless." He frequently laments the fact that these "foreigners" are taking the jobs of more-deserving Canadian hockey players.

Sixes, like all of us, are always looking for someone to blame to make themselves feel better. In the case of Sixes, it's important to identify the "enemy" if one is going to protect oneself. Once our adversaries are identified, our ego loves to hate them; its' how the ego stays in business. Special hate relationships are established helping us to form our identities as "people-opposed-to-so-and-so" or "defenders of the faith against the infidels."

Every man takes the limits of his own field of vision for the limits of the world.

Arthur Schopenhauer

Perspectivism need not be presented as an absolute truth; it can be presented as an account of how reality looks from where one is situated. It does not thereby cease to be of value. The account of the game given by the winning coach cannot claim to be THE truth about the game: other accounts must be taken into account, including those from the losing coach, the players, the referees.... But that does not mean that we do not listen with attention to what the winning coach has to say about the game.

Merold Westphal

Psychological Worldview and Compensating Strategies:
In response to all of the fear and uncertainty in their lives, Sixes begin to construct a worldview designed for self-defense. There's nothing wrong with defending yourself when the occasion arises, but for Sixes the time for self-defense is virtually constant. This posture could be described as psychological defensiveness.

Though we are all defensive to some extent, the Six is almost defined in terms of defensiveness.

From the vantage point of the Six's ego, the world is perceived as dangerous. In a perverse way, the "politics of fear" are custom made for the Six. Sixes are probably the most inclined to check out the US. Homeland Security Advisory System before heading off to work in the morning. "What are the chances I'll be killed in a terrorist attack today?" asks the paranoid Six. "Is the risk green, yellow or red – low, elevated or severe?"

In childhood, the Six typically experiences many violations of trust. They are held out of the loop by family secrets. Or perhaps broken promises too often lead to disappointed expectations. Nothing ever seemed the way others said it was in the household of the Six.

To ensure its own survival, the Six's ego had to remain ever on the lookout for external threats, whatever their nature. This hyper-vigilance becomes the driving force of the Six psyche. Sixes are, if not the most alert, surely the most anxious of all character types. Sixes make an effort to be superhumanly clear-headed, paying intense attention to their surroundings, but at the same time doubting their own perceptions.[13]

Like Fives and Sevens (see Chapter 10), Sixes are fear-based personalities. Fives are afraid of the external world – hence the retreat into the mind. Sevens, as we'll discuss later, are afraid of the inner world, with the result that they are preoccupied with frenzied activity in the outer world.

Sixes, by contrast, don't trust what's going on inside themselves; nor do they have much confidence in what's happening around them. It all looks bad. The worst could happen at any moment. For Sixes, *the sky is falling... or it will likely be falling* any time soon! Why worry about that later, when you can begin your worrying right now? For Sixes, *only the paranoid survive!*

To cope with what might or could happen, Sixes analyze a lot.

They become devotees to the intellect. This devotion may translate into fanatical allegiance to reason or unswerving adherence to philosophies like scientific rationalism, for example. The Six's rational, intellectual orientation makes them questioners of the highest order.[14] Their questioning orientation gives them the appearance of terminal sceptics.

In their efforts to avoid what could go wrong, Sixes not only query, but resort to problem-solving and problem-seeking. This helps them to feel safe.[15] Through pre-emptive efforts to deal with what *could* go wrong, the hope is that nothing *will* go wrong.

In addition to reason, authority plays a big role in the life of Sixes. Like Thomas Hobbes, who sought peace and good order in society through submitting to the authority of the great Leviathan – that is, a supreme authority or governing assembly of men – Sixes look for security from some sort of external source since they did not find it forthcoming from their parents in their formative years, and they cannot find it within themselves.

They are not very inner directed at all. Sixes are not only fear-based, but compliant individuals as well. The authority they seek could come from a rigid faith in the Christian Bible, the Jewish Torah, or the Islamic Qur'an, following the creed to the letter rather than the spirit of their spiritual law.

A stronger sense of security could come from obeying the commander-and-chief of the armed forces, the Pope, the corporation's chief executive officer, or the neighborhood gang leader.

This constant searching for authority and security outside themselves comes essentially from an overriding sense of self-doubt. Sixes question their own motivations, impulses and abilities.[16] Feeling deficient and lacking confidence, they look to others for direction.

A Six-professor once complained to me about his departmental chairman saying: "He's not a very effective leader; he never makes it clear what we're supposed to do." Apparently, this Six wanted clear instructions about his duties and responsibilities. The chairman, who might have been perceived positively by another more independent faculty member as laid-back and flexible or open to suggestion from members of the department – all adults and experts in their field - was perceived instead as ineffective, which may simply have been a projection of the Six's insecurity and his ego's desire to be told what to do.

As we see again, reality-as-perceived is always a projection of the ego. Our perceptions of reality are more reflective of our wants than of things-in-themselves or things as they "really" are. If we don't like what we see, we should turn inwards and examine ourselves.

We're reminded here again of the Delphic Oracle's injunction repeated by Socrates to "Know Thyself."

The kingdom is perfectly united and perfectly protected, and the ego will not prevail against it. Amen.
A Course in Miracles

On the subject of projection, Sixes are very likely to attribute aggressive motivations to others. The result is that others are perceived as much more malevolent and threatening than they really are, hence, their constant fear. What the Six doesn't recognize is that others have often been invested with the Six's own disavowed belligerence.[17] Even when some danger is present, the associated fear is often too intense and out of proportion with the actual threat.

The explanation for why comes from the past or personal history of the Six. Current circumstances act as trigger to stir up feelings of helplessness which originated in childhood. The Six unconsciously relates to the present as if he or she were still a frightened young child.[18] This underscores an important insight from *A Course in Miracles*, namely, that what we see before our eyes is actually our past projected outwardly by our mind. The threat is really a projection of our own fear.

As Pogo says: *"We have met the enemy and he is us."*

Another cognitive aspect of Six-psychology involves dichotomous thinking. Sixes do not tolerate ambiguity very well for obvious reasons. Where there is ambiguity, there is likely no agreement, no clearly stated true or false, no absolute right or wrong. For the troubled Six, the grey fog of ambiguity offers only uncertainty and grief. So, in the real world, there are only "white hats and black hats," "good guys and bad guys," "those who are with us and those who are against us," "those who are saved and those who are going to hell."

The Six professor I referred to earlier used a binary system of marking. Students received either one hundred per cent or zero for their homework assignments. Their computer programs either worked or they didn't. In the professor's mind, the students could do the programming assignment or they couldn't. It can really be that simple in the mind-set of the Six.

To speak of levels of knowledge in this case, or to take a nuanced or conditional position on any issue, is likely to be perceived as weakness or hypocrisy. "Real men" are able to take a strong stand and stay the course. Those who don't are indecisive, backsliders, or cowards. They are the "chickens" who "cut and run" to use an expression used by some Republicans to criticize Democrats who initially supported the war in Iraq, but then objected to it once new intelligence information surfaced regarding the *non-existence* of weapons of mass destruction. One could question the wisdom of "staying the course" when the original destination was misguided in the first place. For counter-phobic Sixes, however, *it's better to be confidently wrong, then hesitantly right.*

Of course, the bravado is just a veil of insecurity. Acting or speaking tough puts others on the defensive and thereby reduces the threats to oneself. But the imminent threats allegedly coming from others, are nothing more than a projection of one's own intentions. In this regard, and in light of events in the Middle

East, one could ask George W. Bush, as a Six, whether the USA was a bigger threat to Iraq than Iraq was to America prior to the outset of the war. The same now can be asked *vis-à-vis* Iran, as the sabre rattling in Washington continues into the winter of 2009, as these words are being written. Does a "wimp" deliberately pick a fight with a Herculean opponent, knowing that defeat is inevitable? Does one nation provoke another nation, knowing its own destruction will be the likely result? What does Iran gain by provoking the United States? Is it, in fact, provoking at all? Who is actually threatening attack? Who, really, is a threat to whom?

Could George W. Bush just be a counter-phobic Six projecting his disavowed belligerence? Historical psychoanalysis will determine that, I suppose. (See discussion below for an explanation of what 'counter-phobic' means.)

Iran was dangerous, Iran is dangerous, and Iran will be dangerous if they have the knowledge necessary to make a nuclear weapon.
George W. Bush (The Guardian Dec. 5, 2007)

Our projection forms a kind of blanket that darkens what we perceive, both around us but also within ourselves, blocking out the luminosity that is present and more fundamental to the nature of everything.
Sandra Maitri

"...dictatorships and all systems that operate on fear are afraid of nothing so much as being unmasked through laughter, mockery, and satire."
Richard Rohr

We see then, that in the dangerous world of the Six, the truth is hidden, while appearances and motivations are suspect.[19] There's a preoccupation with authority and a hyper-alertness.[20] The Six exhibits a state of chronic arousal in carrying out the task of interpreting any potentially dangerous reality.[21] The Six's hyper-vigilance is always on the lookout for buried meanings, hidden clues, and anything untoward. As you might guess, Sixes do not like sudden change; they would prefer to move about within the security of well-known boundaries and established procedures. They seek out situations with well-defined guidelines and rules.[22]

The Six is interesting with respect to its two diametrically opposite compensating behavioral strategies used by the ego to cope with a perceived threatening reality.

Sixes divide themselves into two basic types: *phobic* and *counter-phobic* personalities. On the surface, these two variations of the Six character appear quite distinct. Their intent, however, is the same: to fend off fear. Phobic Sixes appear timid on the outside. They are uncertain and hesitant, lacking self-confidence. As a result, phobic Sixes actively seek out authorities and belief systems as a way of assuaging their uncertainty.[23]

Counter-phobic Sixes, on the other hand, can sometimes look like aggressive Eights (see Chapter 11). They can appear tough and confident, not afraid to speak their mind. They might also choose vocations or engage in activities that others might describe as dangerous – policing or sky-diving, for example.

For counter-phobic Sixes, it's better to confront their fears directly; at least that way the danger is not lurking somewhere in the bushes. It's right out front where it can be seen, experienced, and dealt with. War, for example, is dangerous but at least you know who the enemy is. A fighting soldier can obey orders, do his or her duty, serve, and remain loyal to the country.

This is how the aggression of the counter-phobic Six distinguishes itself from that of the Eight. Eights are more likely to stand up for themselves. Sixes fight for a cause, a mission, some group objective, or in service to a higher authority. They don't try to prove their superiority or take control over others as (unhealthy) aggressive Eights wish to do.

Healthy and Unhealthy Expressions of the Committed Loyalist:
If finding a dependable friend is a goal of yours, then a Six is someone you wish to seek out. In Enneagram circles, Sixes are said to travel in "Six-packs." The Six is no lone wolf or free and independent spirit off on solitary adventures. The Six likes to participate in groups (not necessarily in six-packs, but you get the point).

The Committed Loyalist is a trusted friend, a "joiner", someone actively involved in church-group activities, social causes or institutional organizations. Sixes are likely to build friendship networks and have people around for supportive companionship. Healthy Sixes are people you can count on to help whenever the need arises. Of all the types, they are probably the most loyal to friends and the most loyal to belief-systems. They are some of the most religiously devout, patriotic, and service oriented people you can find.

In addition to loyal dependability, healthy Sixes exhibit a superior ability to anticipate problems before they arise. Using clarity of vision and thought, they foresee problems better than most and thus are able to provide valuable input into projects in the planning stages. It's like they have radar for trouble.

Allowing them to serve as questioner, loyal sceptic, or devil's advocate can head off disasters. By taking their advice the need for unforeseen detours can be avoided. The perennial optimist who charges ahead with large-scale grand planning, for example, is well-advised to consult with a Six before proceeding too far. This step could forestall disappointments and unanticipated delays. The Six is always on top of what could go wrong. The Six offers prudent caution to potentially reckless *gung ho* decision-making.

Unlike some isolated and forlorn existentialist Fours, who feel lost and alienated from the rest of humanity, healthy Sixes are grounded by tradition and conventional norms. They enjoy doing things 'right' in established ways. No doubt doing things in a traditional fashion helps them to build a sense of identity. A Six might say: "I'm a Scotsman who loves the 'pipes' and always eats haggis during Robbie Burns' Week." Another Six might comfortably add, "We always have a fish dinner on Good Friday." Or "Any good loyal Canadian always wears a poppy on November 11 to honor the war dead."

Such comments, commemorations and remembrance rituals give Sixes a sense of place in the world. Such things are highly symbolic and psychologically meaningful for them. Thus, given their ties to history, ritual and tradition, when it comes to "donating to the cause" or volunteering help for group celebrations, the Six is usually one of the first in line.

Another feature about healthy Sixes is that they display a deep sense of responsibility. As mentioned, they are quick to volunteer, becoming role-models of cooperation, commitment and service.[24] Sixes display a strong sense of duty and do what duty demands. You can plainly see how their loyalty, a service-orientation, and sense of duty can all combine to make one an excellent guard, police officer, soldier, corporate executive, defender of the faith, politician or firefighter.

When working for something greater than themselves, they display tremendous courage and endurance. In seeking this greater good or higher purpose, Sixes find security in numbers; they do not wish to go it alone or amass power and authority for themselves personally. The Six is generally the person you want to back you up when the going gets tough. Sixes can and do take on leadership roles, as evidenced by George W. Bush, but when they do, they depend highly on coalitions and loyal supporters to function properly. More often, Sixes prefer to support leaders rather than stand out themselves as targets of criticism and attack.

On the downside, a major problem with unhealthy Sixes is that they are blind to much of the goodness and benevolence that forms the fabric of existence.[25] Spiritually wounded religious

Sixes from all three of great western monotheistic religions have apparently forgotten Genesis 1:31, where it is written:

And God saw everything that he had made, and behold, it was very good.

For the Six to think otherwise is actually evidence of *hubris*, a belief that one knows better than God. Now that would be a violation against the Highest Authority and perhaps a real justification for fear! (Not that I would agree that God is a punishing judge). For non-religious Sixes, let us say that by obsessively focusing on what could go wrong, one is not paying attention to what has gone right and what positive things might also occur in the future. Unhealthy Sixes are too busy catastrophizing to notice.

The inability of unhealthy Sixes to see goodness and light causes them to suffer from high levels of anxiety. Worried about all that could go wrong, Sixes are, as we've learned, racked with insecurity, indecision and doubt. In fact, highly troubled Sixes even doubt the reasons for their own doubts, thereby exacerbating their inability to make decisions. Immobilized and paralyzed by doubt, plagued by over-thinking, and questioning the justifiability of their own doubts, they desperately look for someone or something to save them from their predicament. For sick Sixes, the "answer" does not lie within, but without." So, the desperate search for security continues.

This "doubting of one's own doubts" and seeing only the future's "gloom and doom" contributes to the unhealthy Six's mistrust in dealings with others. If others are invested with the Six's disavowed belligerence, they are understandably perceived as potentially dangerous.

The Six's psychological projections provide good reason to be suspicious of other people; after all, Sixes can't even trust themselves, so how could they possibly trust anyone else? Of course, then there's the chronic doubt over whether one's suspicions are warranted, perhaps they're not? But then again, they might be? Who knows for sure? But suppose they're not and I treat people like they are? Or, suppose my suspicions *are* warranted and I treat others like they're not....then what misfortune is likely to befall me? This line of questioning points to where the unhealthy Six is heading – toward an unending circle of insecurity.

The troubled Six's inability to feel secure by the fabric of existence – what some might term the providence of God or the benevolence of the universe – leads the Six to confuse Being with authority.[26] Certainty and confidence are found in playing the existential game of "follow the leader." In this game, aggression is typically shown to those below and unquestioning obedience to those above in the authority hierarchy.[27] This strict adherence to authority leads the Six to form what has been dubbed the "authoritarian personality" or "Prussian character."[28]

This type of dutiful character is rigid and tense, displaying an intolerant attitude toward ambiguity. One cannot help but think of the obedient soldier following orders from superiors, not allowing themselves the opportunity for questioning or independent judgment. To do so would be to jeopardize the entire hierarchical structure of the military. Chaos would be the result, and we can't allow for that. Security is found in obedience, or so the obedient believe.

False obedience is the rotten fruit of fear.
    Richard Rohr

Jawohl mein Kommandant!
    Obedient Reply of the Nazi Soldier

Personal Shadow:
As we've learned, all character types repress unpleasant thoughts and feelings. Twos are often unaware of their pride and manipulation when they help others. Threes suppress their dishonesty as

they try to present a successful image and impress people. Of course, Twos and Threes in this instance are both insecure, trying to prove their self-worth, as if that needs proving. With Sixes, by contrast, fears are much closer to the surface of conscious awareness. What may not be so recognized by the Six are the self-deceptive strategies used to divert attention from their shadow issue, namely cowardice.

Even the counter-phobic's "reckless courage" or risk-taking is testimony to this. The counter-phobic Six looks like anything but cowardly but alas, there's the self-deception. Recall how counter-phobic Sixes cannot bear the possibility of danger lurking in the bushes. It is less fearful to deal with threats and risks directly, than to let anxieties fester over them.

Sixes were previously described as friendly and loyal. It was said that you could trust them to back you up when the going got tough. The question is why? If troubled Sixes are self-aware and honest with themselves, they will frequently admit that such loyalty and friendliness arise out of fear. Sixes worry that others will abandon them, reject them, or harm them if they don't come through. It's like the Two worried that if they don't serve others, others won't like them anymore. For the Six, being accepted requires friendliness, being responsible, and showing loyalty. A great deal of the unhealthy Six's camaraderie stems from personal insecurity and a desire to make sure everything is still okay.[29]

Claudio Naranjo describes the Six's behavior here as "ingratiating friendliness."[30] In his words, it represents "the compulsive search for protection through cowardly affection."

The Six's cowardice is also masked by exaggerated faithfulness to individuals, causes, and belief-systems. The Six defends against his or her own anxiety by identifying with leaders, parties, religions, political ideologies, group ideals, associations and so on. The phobic Six seeks ties with authorities and stronger individuals as sources of strength and power perceived to be lacking inside. The greater the identification with the authority and their mission, and the greater the bombast relating to their loyalty or principled commitment, the greater the fear.

There's certainly nothing wrong with commitment and loyalty, but for the anxious and neurotic Six, such things comprise elements of self-deception designed unconsciously to make one feel better. Were the fear absent, the principled commitment and defence of the 'faith' would not be so existentially important. In other words, to continue the existentialist allusion, there's some "bad faith" going on (pun intended). Believing out of fear is really a form of self-defence. It's a dishonest way to find security and make oneself feel better. One could say belief motivated out of fear is not 'true belief' at all.

Religion is the opium of the people.
    Karl Marx

Sixes also need to recognize their tendency to point fingers and lay guilt, both on themselves and others. Since feeling guilty is unpleasant, the Six strategy is to use "mechanisms of exculpation through projection and creation of outer enemies."[31] Others become threatening and others are at fault somehow. It is others who become the enemy. However, so-called threats are often just the Six's fears staring the Six right in the face. Of course, the threats seem real to the Six and so they should; the Six is looking at a reality that their own egos created.

There is nothing to fear but fear itself.
    Franklin D. Roosevelt

Therapeutic Recommendations for Promoting Psychological Hygiene and Finding Inner Peace:

There's a variety of things that Sixes can do to relieve their troubled mind and achieve the inner peace they so desperately want. If you're a Six and you doubt this, you're doing it again! Doubting and questioning, that is. *And how's that been workin' for ya?* Hopefully, by now, you've come to see how your sceptical mind is one of the greatest obstacles to your own inner peace. I'm not asking that you unquestioningly accept the recommendations here, hoping that this character analysis can bail you out of your troubles. That would also be a blind-faith "Six-thing." What I'm asking is that you simply suspend judgement temporarily and let personal experience be your guide. Don't decide in advance what is surely to fail, what won't work, or what's a dead-end street. Also, don't mindlessly accept directions and suggestions provided here. Experiment and try them out. Then decide for yourself.

Allow your feelings and gut-level intuitions a role to play before intellectually dismissing guidance which could help you in the end. Trust your instincts just this one time and see what happens.

If absolute certainty were always required before moving forward, then we would never move an inch in our lives. As the philosopher points out, what you know with absolute certainty (e.g., that 1+1=2) doesn't tell you much about the world and what you can know about the world, you cannot know with absolute certainty. So, I guess the first bit of advice is to quit looking for perfect solutions and certain outcomes in the so-called real world. If the philosopher is correct, to do so is futile and self-defeating. Uncertainty is part and parcel of life – everyone's life.

To the extent misery loves company, Sixes can take solace in sure knowledge of the fact that they're not alone in their worries about future outcomes. The trick is not to succumb to them in terms of psychological paranoia.

Another thing Sixes need to do is to be present to the moment. As Almaas has taught us, "presence" is the closest thing to "essence." The objective here is to still the mind through disciplined meditation.[32] Such meditation should focus on the body. By placing attention on the breadth and also, by focusing on different parts of the body and releasing tension in those different areas, the so-called "relaxation response" can be achieved.

"The *relaxation response* is a physical state of deep rest that changes the physical and emotional responses to stress....and the opposite to the *flight or fight response.*"[33] It can be consciously elicited; it can quiet the disquieting internal dialogue plaguing Sixes; and it can facilitate the experience of oneness with the universe. [34] Of course, flight is the preferred strategy of the phobic Six; fight is strategy of choice for the counter-phobic Six. Though different in form, both are responses to fear, stress, and anxiety. Focusing on the body gets the thinking Six out of the head, first of all, and allows a changed physiology to still the mind.

If you're a Six who has trouble meditating, you might try to review the many worries that have troubled you over the years. The aim here is not to stir up past upsets, Rather, the point is to illustrate that much of your previous worry has led to naught, or in most cases very little. If you, as a Six, want to worry, then you should worry about the time you're going to waste in the future worrying about things that will never happen! Our past provides conclusive proof how many times worry has been useless and unproductive. Once you intellectually understand how worry is largely a waste of time and once you become emotionally fatigued by your own chronic anxiety, you can then accept with deeply-felt conviction the insight from *A Course in Miracles* that: *There must be a better way.*

The time is now to commit yourself to personal transformation, not to another cause to be used as a defensive shield against perceived external attack. Such commitment is inauthentic, though it may not look that way to outside observers. Only you can know your true intentions. Are your commitments for the right reasons or just strategies to alleviate your anxiety? Being loyal for the right reasons is honorable. Being loyal out of psychological defensiveness is a sham. What's the real aim of your loyal participation? And what about your friendliness? Is your friendliness genuine, or as Claudio Naranjo puts it: cowardly affection?

Asking such pointed questions and answering them are necessary if you are to escape the shadow that hauntingly follows you. Recall what Chuang Tzu taught us: If you wish to rid yourself of your tormenting shadow, you must enter the darkness. Only then will the shadow disappear. Darkness can be scary, I know. It takes genuine courage to enter into it. The journey must be taken alone, however, not in a "six-pack." Walking into the darkness is a hero's mission that we all must accept for purposes of personal liberation. If you wish to be liberated from your fears, enter the darkness now. Out of that darkness, you will emerge into the light.

Sixes can also greatly benefit by learning to savor their personal successes.[35] If you're a Six, rather than worry about how you might fail in the future, it's useful to remember how you have succeeded in the past. What was accomplished? How did it feel? What was learned by the success? Take these lessons with you into the future. Support yourself with fond memories of achievement. Bring those moments of confidence to mind and dwell on them. Appreciate them. Be emotionally nourished by them. Learn to remember what went right and imagine how things can go right in the future... how you can be successful in the future as you've been in the past. Stop being surprised when you succeed or when others look to you for support and direction. Clearly, when they do, they see something in you that you fail to see in yourself.

If success troubles you, be happy, don't worry reflecting on the words of Jules Renard: *"There are moments when everything goes well; don't be frightened, they won't last."*[36] (This quotation was meant as a joke, in case you were wondering!)

Speaking of jokes, humor and the ability to laugh at one's exaggerated fears can also help the Six to drive fear away.[37] "When we laugh from the heart, fear can't remain very long."[38] This brings to mind one of the rules of life taught by Nick Nolte's character, nick-named Socrates, in the movie *Peaceful Warrior*. The rule is: *Keep a sense of humor, especially about yourself. It is a strength beyond all measure.*

Sixes would be well advised to abide by this rule. When one disconnects from the ego, and learns to laugh at it, and observe from above, as it were, fears and insecurities miraculously disappear. Those who take themselves too seriously are the ones who should proceed with caution. They are the ones who become architects of their own troubled minds.

One of the biggest challenges for Sixes is to find their own inner authority.[39] They must find faith in themselves and in so doing, they will learn to have faith in others and the universe. It's ironic how some insecure Sixes do not wish to become leaders or role-models for others, appreciating their own fallibility; yet these same (unhealthy) Sixes sometimes give blind allegiance to other authorities who are no less fallible than themselves.

If, in the mind of the insecure Six, others would be foolish to follow the Six's leadership, given what the Six "knows" about themselves, then it would seem to follow that it's equally foolish sometimes to follow others, given they are essentially no different than the Six – at least when it comes to the ability to provide absolute truth and certainty. Sixes need to recognize this and practice making decisions without always asking authorities for permission and advice.[40]

Accepting that no decision is perfect and that mistakes are a normal part of living makes it easier to establish inner authority and achieve the confidence it brings. The Six can learn from errors and resolve to do better next time. This is a mature and intelligent stance to take. It permits mistakes without devastating losses to self-esteem.

Finally, quit being so suspicious. By now you've learned how we're all a little 'sick' when it comes to our ego-obsessions, projections, and distortions of reality. People do what they do in their best efforts to get what they want, even if what they want is misguided or their behavior is somehow crazy.

Making one's own ego laughable and recognizing the craziness of one's own psychodynamics, we can become more forgiving of others' behaviors and dispositions. Dis-identifying with our egos also makes it less likely that we will be emotionally threatened or hurt.

Remember: *External things touch not the soul.*

As always, healing must in the end be spiritual, not merely physical or psychological. To identify yourself exclusively with the psychological ego is to choose trouble and pain.

CHAPTER TEN

EGO DYNAMICS IN CHARACTER TYPE SEVEN: *THE ETERNAL YOUTH*

Truly, I say to you, unless you change and become like children, you will never enter the kingdom of heaven.
Matthew 18:1-4

May your heart always be joyful, May your song always be sung, May you stay forever young.
Bob Dylan

Lost Essence:

Childhood is a time filled with joyful spontaneity. Indeed, *joy* is one of the essential qualities which emanates from our higher nature. It is perhaps most obvious in us when we are young. Witness the way that children are open-eyed sponges, soaking up all of the experiences life has to offer. Every flavor is a new taste sensation. The sight of a "moo-cow" next to the country road is a cause for jubilation! The arrival of somebody at the front door is like a celebrity guest appearance. The sound of a beloved one's voice on the telephone is pure ecstasy. Joy somehow magnifies the ordinary. One could say, where there is joy, there are no ordinary moments.

When we are in touch with our essence, joy is experienced not as a momentary response to a single event or situation. Rather, it's more like an enduring state of mind. It's like an emotional aura accompanying us on our travels. People who have joy in their lives display a soft sunny presence. They may not be screaming with excitement like today's lottery winner, but there's a quiet gratitude about just being alive. This gratitude can be displayed by a seemingly ever present smile or the twinkle in a person's eye.

True joy seems to be impervious to the many slings and arrows of outrageous fortune. Just like the rest of us, joyful people experience misfortunes, but somehow remain resilient, able to see the silver lining in the storm clouds of life.

Sevens, in particular, understand the saying, "It's always darkest before the dawn." Tomorrow is new day with a whole new array of possibilities.

In contrast to the kind of happiness which might come from achievement, recognition or luck, Rollo May says: *"Joy... is the emotion which accompanies our fulfilling our natures as human beings. It is based on the experience of one's identity as a being of worth and dignity."*

One doesn't earn joy or win it; neither is it bestowed on us by others. Joy is in us. Joy is us.

When Essential Joy manifests, we are filled with a kind of humble confidence knowing that we're heading in the right direction. When we experience joy, we feel grateful for the wonderful and mysterious gift of our lives, and experience a profound wonder and curiosity about our journey.

We deeply feel the presence of our true spiritual home, and feel it calling us back. As Essential joy arises in us, we know where true value lies, and are fortified to do whatever is necessary to return to what our heart truly desires. We know what we love, and joyfully open to deeper aspects of our True nature."[1]

'Pan, who and what art thou?' [Hook] cried huskily. 'I'm youth, I'm joy,' Peter answered at a venture, 'I'm a little bird that

has broken out of the egg.'

....So come with me, where dreams are born, and time is never planned. Just think of happy things, and your heart will fly on wings, forever, in Never Never Land!
     From *Peter Pan*

If we read the experts on enneagram psychology and listen to anecdotal childhood reports of the Seven, we find some inconsistency. Some Sevens recall a childhood that was happy; almost picture-book in quality,[2] while others reveal a childhood that was happy at first glance, but painfully troubled when the surface was scratched. The pain could have arisen from divorce, abandonment, shuffling among relatives or just being ignored.[3]

Some Enneagram researchers have also concluded that Sevens experienced largely unconscious feelings of disconnection from the nurturing figures early in their lives.[4] The claim is that such disconnection led to very deep frustrations requiring compensating strategies to alleviate their psychological upset and emotional pain. These deep frustrations are typically not visible however. You'll find little residue of bitterness on the Seven resulting from past hurts. Sevens are not people who hold grudges or keep scores.[5] Consciously or unconsciously, Sevens have decided not to be like them, that is, like the hurtful people in their lives. They simply move on. There's no point in dwelling on what's unpleasant.

Psychological Worldview and Compensating Strategies:
The Eternal Child exhibits a worldview which is characterized by "cosmic okayness".[6] For Sevens, life is for enjoyment; the world is one big amusement park. Constraints and boundaries are counter-productive, they interfere with the Seven's *laissez-faire* attitude.

Also, such things are often inconsistent with the Seven's

egalitarian stance toward life. Being forced to stay within boundaries oneself or preventing other people from doing things they would otherwise do would mean either undermining The Eternal Youth's pursuit of pleasure or using some sort of coercive sanction against others. Violating boundaries contributes to feelings of guilt when authorities are not obeyed. Serious effort – not fun – is also required to enforce authority; leading to unpleasant feelings all round. Boundaries, limits, authorities and penalties are all contrary to the Seven's existential Law of Enjoyment: *Seek Pleasure and Avoid Pain.*

I like persons better than principles, and I like persons with no principles better than anything else in the world.
   Oscar Wilde

Nature has placed mankind under the governance of two sovereign masters, pain and pleasure. It is for them alone to point out what we ought to do, as well as to determine what we shall do.
   Jeremy Bentham

Sevens are also characterized by their future orientation. They are not gloomy people who like to dwell in the past. They regard life as an adventure and are buoyed by the belief that life is unlimited.[7] In contrast to Sixes who habitually imagine the worst that could happen, Sevens are predisposed toward the positive, imagining best case scenarios and minimizing worries about problems and potential obstacles.

   This best-case scenario thinking reflects the Seven's selective attention. Their imagination is skewed in favor of optimistic outcomes and expectations. Sevens tend to overestimate the positive and underestimate the negative. Related to their positive, idealistic, future orientation is the fact that a Seven's habit of attention drives in several directions at once.[8]

   They are habitually pre-occupied. They have many irons in

the fire at any given time, not satisfied with concentrating their focus on any one thing. That would be limiting and potentially boring.

As Helen Palmer puts it: *"Attention moves through experience and on to more experience, in a headlong rush to the next fascinating enterprise... attention can move fluidly between sweet memories, fascinating thoughts, and interesting future plans."*[9]

In what some might describe as their exhausting and frenzied lifestyle, Sevens somehow believe all of their disparate interests will lead somewhere and come together with unified coherence – a grand synthesis, as it were.

On this note, it's worth pointing out that the grand plan is not to achieve some socially admired goal like success. Seven's are not so much goal-oriented as experience oriented.[10] What's the point of achieving something if there was no fun or excitement to be had in the process. One could safely say that unlike workaholic, ambitious Threes, Sevens work to live; they don't live to work.

It's probably the case that Sevens more than others look forward to weekends, fantasize about vacations, and plan escapes in their minds. *How much fun we'll have! It'll be great C'mon along!*

Sevens respond well to society's new normality of changing jobs every few years rather than working at the same place for an entire lifetime. There are so many exciting possibilities waiting for all of us out there. How wonderful!

Another feature about Sevens is their attraction toward the exotic, the inaccessible and the eccentric.[11] If the choice is between re-visiting a previous vacation destination or going somewhere new and different, they will choose a new adventure rather than a tried and tested old haunt. For Sevens, variety is the spice of life. With respect to hobbies, doesn't Inuit throat singing sound more exciting than hiking? Been there; done that.

This also helps to explain why so many Sevens are epicures. If they're going to dinner, why go out for a steak dinner at the local chain restaurant, when sushi, curry, and pad Thai await in one of the interesting ethnic neighborhoods around town? Those restaurants are unique and the ambiance is refreshingly different compared with the formulaic and contrived alternatives produced by large-scale restaurant conglomerates. The Epicure Seven is *oh so above this*! Given a choice between a well-known domestic blend of coffee, and some exotic brand, you can guess which one the Seven will select. Put water in a bottle, give it a foreign name, and put it in chic bistro, sell it with an accent and the Seven is almost orgasmic with delight, regarding those who fail to see the value of this bottled water as philistines.

I have simple tastes. I am always satisfied by the best.
Oscar Wilde

This "aesthetic sophistication" which Sevens perceive in themselves translates oftentimes into a kind of condescending narcissism. Some Sevens possess an idealized self-image leading them to believe that they are superior relative to others. The expression of this superiority is usually indirect, however. It would be "tasteless" to be in someone else's face about how inferior they were. It's better to just cavalierly dismiss those considered vulgar and turn to more interesting people and things. Less trouble that way and less waste of time having to deal with the plebeians. Besides, who cares?

As Oscar Wilde, an archetypal epicure once wrote: *"I'm the only person in the world I should like to know thoroughly."*

Because of their self-perception that they possess a natural superiority of endowment, Sevens assume that they can master multiple things with little effort, and indeed, more often than not, they can. They delight in future challenging events, intoxicated with their own imaginations. *"I'm so good....so adept!"* the

Seven thinks. Hence the frequent invitation to *"C'mon and do what I suggest (namely, something I can do so much better than you with so much more ease! ...It'll be fun...Don't worry, I'll show you how to do it."*

You will probably detect the indirect expression of superiority in the invitation.

In matters of intellect, Seven's tend to over-focus on their own brilliance, while undervaluing that of others.[12] They are prone to think things like: *"Most people are simple-minded, unsophisticated boors, unable to appreciate the esoteric and finer things in life."* And say to their friends: *"Let's go to the foreign film festival – what it's screening is so much more interesting than the latest blockbuster release."* Thinking to themselves: "That *Bimbo over there is going to rent the latest Hollywood flick at the big-box movie rental outlet. There's nothing worth watching in that place."*

Unlike the Four, who can be very much the aesthete as well, but is too preoccupied with deep feelings of envy and self-loathing, the Seven's preferences are meant to serve as visible proof to others of their tasteful superiority.

In addition to the acid wit of Oscar Wilde, some other well-known Sevens include the comedians Robin Williams, Joan Rivers and Jim Carey. The composer Wolfgang Amadeus Mozart, and the eternal fictional character "Peter Pan" were Sevens, along with actors Bette Midler, Goldie Hawn, and Jack Nicholson, as well as radio talk-show host Howard Stern.

Anyone familiar with these fantasy and real-life characters can appreciate their playfulness and youthful exuberance. Notwithstanding the thinly covered underbelly of the Seven's cleverly disguised superiority complex, their enthusiasm for life is infectious, making them so endearing to others.

In the light of the preceding discussion, it is perhaps surprising to learn that Sevens are "fear-based" individuals, like Fives and

Sixes. As children, Sevens may have been extraordinarily afraid of loud noises, bumps in the night, or the darkness in the closet. They may even sleep with the lights on as adults. They may also have had traumatic experiences which they did not feel equal to.[13]

In this case: "In order to avoid the repetition of this pain in the future, they ... evolved a double strategy: First they repressed or whitewashed their negative and painful experiences... Secondly, they...[went] into their heads and [began] to plan their lives so that every day [would] promise as much 'fun' and as little pain as possible."[14]

Though the outside world became a playground for excitement and exploration, the inner world for Sevens promised only scariness, depression, pain, and discomfort, so they stayed away. Inner life is often too dark and foreboding to invite examination. It is a place the undeveloped Eternal Youth avoids like the plague. Besides, as adults, why would anybody want to "screw themselves up" analyzing themselves to death when the joyride of life is about to embark for another thrill?

The point is that Sevens use their varied interests and activities as a diversion from mental and emotional pain. As long as the frenetic pace never stops and one stays "busy...busy...busy", there's never any time to feel unhappy or become upset. Manic diversion is a major strategy used by Sevens for the purposes of pain-avoidance.

Too many of us seek to fill our emptiness with food, or drink, or drugs, or obsessive and frantic activity. The much-lamented pace of modern life is not inevitable − it is a cover for its emptiness. If we keep in motion, we create the illusion of meaning.
Carol Pearson

If you're going to stay busy, it's necessary of course to be constantly planning the next activity. In this regard, Sevens are always thinking – indeed they fall under the classification of "thinking type" personalities, incessantly trying to organize and scheme and figure out different ways of getting what they want. On Mondays, Sevens are already planning what they're going to do on the weekend.

Young-hearted Sevens always seem to have a Plan B to follow up Plan A and if both of those don't work out or don't feel right at the moment, then there's always Plan C. Contingency plans must always be at the ready for possible frustration and disappointment – things which are not handled well by our Eternal Youth, as is also the case with children. The Seven's *raison d'être* is to have places to go, people to see, and things to do. That amounts to a full life, a life worth living.

In view of Chuang Tzu's wisdom, it is a person running away from their shadow. Nothing wrong with activity and human interaction; only in Chuang Tzu's view, they shouldn't be used as a psychological escape from oneself. You can't outrun your own shadow, at least as long you continue to run under sunny skies. Furthermore, the beautiful rainbows which make life such a joy must result from storm clouds and rain. No clouds, no rain, no rainbows. That's just the way the world works.

A Seven would be well-advised to learn the lesson. Much to their own disadvantage, Sevens who fear being engulfed by unpleasant aspects of their emotional life retreat from it and move into their minds where fantasy, imagination, planning, and dreaming can take over.

Speaking of lessons, Sevens learned early on that being cheery and light had its advantages. A pleasant disposition earned approval from others and helped them get what they wanted.[15] Sevens learned, in other words, that keeping things pleasant, not complaining or criticizing, and cheering up family members had its rewards. In time, they learn to laugh about adversity, stay upbeat and remain optimistic. All of this endears the Seven to others at home and more generally to others in the outside world. *"Oh how charming and polite...Isn't 'so-and-so' so nice! And so well-spoken."*

Of course, making such a favorable impression opens many doors of opportunity, contributing still further to the Seven's optimism. It's a mystery to Sevens why people choose to be "downers" and pessimists. There is no bleak or harsh reality on the horizon in the mind of the Seven. All looks good. As well it should. Sevens seek out environments and people that either reinforce the Seven's positive self-image or who are mesmerized by the Seven's magic.

However, the not-so-nice reality is that the unconscious goal is to gain narcissistic validation of their personal self worth. One can imagine a Seven thinking: *"It's well-nigh intoxicating to ponder how much others like and respect me, how much they want me around, how often I'm invited. I'm so special."*

The trick is to be full of yourself without appearing so. A little self-deprecating humor usually works. The attention remains on me and the humor suggests humility. *Et Voilà*, magically, narcissism becomes a form of charming and disarming modesty. What alchemy!

Healthy and Unhealthy Expressions of The Eternal Youth:

The healthy Seven is the quintessential Renaissance person.[16] You'll usually observe in the healthy Seven a gifted mind, as well as good hand-eye coordination.[17] Intelligent, graceful and physically coordinated, the Seven is able to partake in all manner of activities and be rather good at all or at least most of them. They can absorb large amounts of information, learn facts, and master procedures. They are likely to display quite the knack for sports and activities requiring manual dexterity. It's truly amazing how good Sevens are at so many things. I once observed a Seven go out waterskiing for the first time and master the slalom technique, using only one ski in a matter of minutes. By contrast, it can be amusing to watch other less-coordinated beginners do multiple "face-plants" in the water before finally getting up on the double ski-boards. Sevens are generally spared such embarrassment.

Of course, learning a new and different skill is always fun and what's fun is worthwhile for this character type. There's pure joy when the Seven masters a new skill. Think of the bright-eyed child who takes its first few steps and begins to spontaneously laugh with excitement with mouth wide-open; that's what it's like for our Eternal Youth. You can see the expression of joy on their face when mastering new things.

It's hard not to like a Seven. They are admirable in their personal qualities and disarming with their charm. The egalitarian, anti-authoritarian stance of the Eternal Youth contributes to the person's cooperative spirit. Sevens don't like to dominate or hold sway over others, even if they do like to hold forth. This cooperative spirit is inviting to others and entices them to get involved in whatever the activity is. Sevens are able to be quite persuasive by using their charm, without using any threats or tactics of intimidation. Subordinates of healthy Sevens are treated respectfully and inspired to participate on the job, with friends, or at the local club.

Given their varied interests, their energy, and their quick minds, Sevens are very good multi-taskers at work. They can juggle different responsibilities simultaneously. This movement from one thing to another can be very exhilarating. Life is filled, things are brewing, situations call for attention, and *"It's my job to plan and organize it all,"* says the Seven, *"Does life get any better than this?"*

Pre-occupied with everything that has to get done, the healthy Seven can feel the adrenalin pumping inside. *"It's so busy, it's crazy....Don'tcha love it!"*

Others simply watch in amazement or leave exhausted by the energy displayed.

Because of their boundless energy, their enthusiasm, quick minds, and cooperative spirit, healthy Sevens are typically accomplished individuals in life. They enjoy a high measure of material success and often rise to positions of prominence and power.[18] Who wouldn't want a charming, inspirational, intelligent, able, and friendly boss? For this reason, their people skills as much as their other abilities, it's the Seven who often gets "fast-tracked" to the position of corporate executive or CEO.

The values of modern North American society are tailor made for the Seven's enjoyment and personal benefit... fun-loving, intelligent, optimistic, youthful in spirit, bright, athletic and energetic... the Seven has it all. In fact the Seven embodies the whole package. On this note, I've mused to myself that if the good-looking Seven has one endearing dimple, then vice-president is that person's destiny. Give me two dimples and we have president and CEO for sure!

While youthful enthusiasm is a wonderful thing, it can become unhealthy if taken too far or if used as a shield against unpleasantness. Those who have "issues" with Sevens often comment on their immaturity and superficiality. Immaturity shows itself when Sevens often use the strategy of generating alternatives to avoid responsibility and commitment – two indicators of mature development.[19]

When one option appears to be turning out badly, there's no need to worry; other options have already been identified. All that's required is a quick about-face and movement in another direction. Pain is not felt, as the focus is quickly shifted. Thus, there's no failure or need to deal with unpleasant consequences. However, an inability to face up to the consequences of one's actions or decision-making is not psychologically healthy. Rather than responsibly deal with the inevitable unpleasantries of life in an adult fashion, Sevens tend to avoid them and run when the going gets tough.

This avoidance and escape strategy prevents genuine engagement with that psychological underbelly of life mentioned earlier, with things like longing, loss, and tragedy. It contributes to a lack of interiority, the sense of soulful self exhibited by the Four or Deep Feeling Individualist.[20]

So, as charming and up-beat as Sevens are, they can be extremely superficial, lacking depth of emotion, sensitivity and empathy toward others. How can you feel someone else's pain when you refuse to feel your own? So, when it comes to close personal relationships, emotionally needy, dependent, or otherwise troubled people should beware. To buffer themselves from their mate's problems, if things get intense Sevens will conveniently schedule things to be away from home. If things get too tense, they will be just as likely to leave permanently, bailing out of the relationship.[21]

We can appreciate how insensitive and ineffective Sevens are by looking at another strategy they use to shield themselves against unpleasant sticky emotions. When confronted with other people's pain, unhealthy Sevens often make fun of the problem. They might trivialize it or regard it as ridiculous. Behind the fun-poking, however, lies an unconscious anger. If you look carefully, just beneath the joking smile hides a hostile, condescending sneer. *"Better to be angry than to be afraid, even if I don't know what the anger is all about."*

Another major problem with unhealthy Sevens involves their inability to make commitments. To decide and focus on one goal and to invest that goal with one's complete disciplined commitment is a dangerous proposition for the Eternal Youth. Making commitments reduces choices, increases psychological risks of disappointment or failure and seriously reduces options in life, all unwelcome bad news.[22]

Suppose escape alternatives have not been envisioned in anticipation of the possible future failure; then the failure will have to be dealt with head-on. Who likes failure? Who wants to deal with that? Why set yourself up for failure? Better to deal with that possible eventuality by having Plan B lined up. Maybe the decision to commit was wrong in the first place? I'll just keep things open-ended. Besides, committed people are boring. Their lives are so one-sided, the anxious Seven thinks. Discipline and single-minded focus are things the unhealthy Seven must disparage to rationalize their own fearful and scattered lives.

The defensive rationalizations of the unhealthy Seven point to their dishonesty. Helen Palmer describes them as "charlatans."[23]

The charming talk and pleasant style you get from Sevens is a way for them to hide from being seen. Usually attractive, Sevens have a desire for people to adore them. Others are wowed with thoughtful gifts, flowers, and "sharing the very best of times."[24] Sevens may even come to feel entitled to recognition and support, given their specialness. The fact is that all of this charm and pleasantry is an outward focused strategy which leaves large regions of true intention and unconscious fear unexplored.

In this same vein, Sevens are masters at "bluffing."[25] Their scattered attention and inability to "specialize" and focus on one thing leads them to cleverly combine a little bit of this and a little bit of that to create a comprehensive image of competence or expertise. They sometimes seem to know just about all about everything, when the truth is they are more likely all-around dilettantes[26] pretending to be *"all that and more,"* to use a collo-quial expression. Being able to bluff with enough enthusiasm and charm can get one quite far in life. So, it's not only the healthy Sevens that are professionally and materially successful.

Problems arise, however, when others finally figure out there's not a lot of substance behind the sizzle. Just before that happens, however, the perceptive future-oriented Seven is likely to move on to the next adventure, never getting caught up by one's own psychological ruse and hence, not being required to face up to one's own unconscious escapist tendencies.

A man who finds no satisfaction in himself seeks for it in vain elsewhere.
La Rochefoucauld

Personal Shadow:

We learned earlier in the context of *A Course in Miracles* that the ego survives by first creating fear and then promising to alleviate it for us. Generally speaking, most of us forget about the ego's first tactic and then turn to the ego to help us out. We lose sight of the fact that our "savior" ego is in fact the cause of our suffering. Also remember, the ego doesn't want to put itself out of commission, so it employs deceptive techniques and strategies which it assures us will bring us happiness, so that we will identify with it.

Pride is taken in being ego-identified as the Eternal Youth, the Enthusiast, or the Epicure. In the case of Sevens, we observed the ego in action, trying to lighten things up by promoting a *laissez-faire* attitude, attention to positive experiences, fun and excitement, attraction to pleasure, optimism, an idealistic future orientation, a sense of adventure, egalitarianism, charm, and pleasantness.

The bag is filled to the top with delicious possibilities. What will it be today? Will it be pleasurable pursuits, an optimistic attitude, fantasizing about future adventures, or getting together with friends to have some fun and excitement? Maybe all of them at the same time. There's so much that's so good!

What the ego doesn't reveal to Sevens is that it's like the corner drug dealer giving potential users freebies until they get hooked and start having to pay for the highs that the dealer offers. Who doesn't like emotional highs, the adrenalin pump of excitement, the wonders of nature, the varieties of taste and sound, or all the endless possibilities and opportunities of life. The challenge for the ego is to get people hooked on such things, and in the case of Sevens, the ego succeeds in its mission.

First, the ego works through the unconscious to convince Sevens that they are deficient. This requires a separation from Essential Being. Any perceived deficiency is what *The Course* calls *sin*. Remember, sin does not actually exist in the spiritual non-dualistic universe. Regardless, like everyone duped by the ego, Sevens experience some sort of incompleteness inside, accepting the dualistic reality they perceive outside. They fear this incompleteness will translate into boredom and pain.

In response, Sevens develop the compulsive habit of always making contingency plans to avert any possible frustrations and disappointments that might arise in the future.[27] In their particular efforts to escape the pain stemming from perceived emptiness, Sevens resort to *gluttony*, which is the shadow that follows and haunts them. Gluttony is " the emotional response of wanting to stuff themself with external gratifications in response to the experience of feeling frustrated, empty and needy."[28]

Sadly, we now see how the "neediness" they despise in others becomes in effect an attack on the Seven's projected self. To trivialize the pain of another or to cavalierly dismiss it, is to do psychological and emotional damage to oneself. The Sevens' disgust of others' neediness is reflective of the Seven's own self-disgust.

The idea of gluttony should be understood in this context to go beyond the mere appetite for food. Gluttons can distract themselves with mental pleasures as well as with pleasures of the flesh. One could broaden the notion of gluttony to say that glutton-Sevens want to indulge in any desire or faculty that produces pleasure.

Whatever the indulgence, it's the passion for pleasure which underlies it. This passion is not one which takes kindly to delays. The unhealthy Eternal Youth is like the spoiled child who screams: *"I want it, and I want it now!"* Sevens are not good at delayed gratification and personal sacrifice. For instance, if they cannot afford to get what they want, there's usually little hesitation to buy it on credit. If one credit card is up to the limit, since the credit limit has been reached, no problem, just get another credit card account and use *it* to pay the minimum monthly installment on the first, while heading off to the store to buy another toy. If both cards are maxed-out, no problem; get a consolidating loan. This desperate and self-indulgent strategy cannot continue forever, of course, but it will be tried and reused as long as it works. Clearly, unhealthy gluttonous Sevens can be reckless and uncontrolled with their resources. Worrying about debt is not fun, so why worry? *"The debt will get paid off sooner or later; so what's your problem? Besides, the relative size of the debt will decrease in time with inflation and higher wages! I'll just wait until then to pay off what will be in effect a smaller debt."*

As you can clearly see, there's a lot of rationalizing mental gymnastics going on here diverting attention away from the fact that the individual is up to his or her eyeballs in debt. Without immediate action, restraint on future spending, and personal sacrifice, the problem, acknowledged or not, will never go away on its own, not even in the Seven's dreams of *Never Never Land*.

There's no way to eat, drink, please, or charm your way out of this one. Sevens beware: Gluttony exacts a toll and the toll bell announcing the time for repayment is now ringing!

Goethe's Faust isn't the only one who has to pay up for his worldly follies.

What's important to recognize about the Seven's pursuit of pleasure is that it's not as free and spontaneous as they believe. *"They may blindly and impulsively pursue whatever promises immediate satisfaction, not considering the costs of their impulses. Their philosophy is* 'Enjoy now, pay later.*"*[29]

There are several other features worth noting about the Seven's gluttony. First, there's an insatiability built into this passion. The glutton wants to consume, but is never entirely filled up. This is because consuming rather than digesting is the focus.[30] The Seven cannot be satisfied by one treat and savour the experience. The gluttonous Seven does not wish to immerse themselves in any one kind of experience; rather, their desire is to taste and sample the many varieties of pleasure life has to offer.

Sandra Maitri describes the Seven's mind-set as a shopping mentality. The thrill is in the shopping experience itself, not the items purchased, or the thrill of the items does not last for very long at least. This sampling, tasting, and shopping-experience mentality is what characterizes the Seven's overall superficiality.

The insatiability also points to the addictive nature of their pleasurable pursuits. Some people self-medicate with alcohol and drugs to get through the day or fall asleep. Others uncontrollably seek pleasure as a way to avoid the trials and tribulations of life. Of course, if Sevens find drugs and alcohol pleasurable, they can indulge in both, why limit your options!

The important point is that the pursuit of pleasure is serious business for Sevens. Their lives depend upon it. There's actually a panicky desperation or mania about it in the case of unhealthy individuals. Without pleasurable pursuits, the harsh realities of life would be too much to bear.

The problem with the pursuit of pleasure as an end in itself is that it is a spiritually and psychologically bankrupt proposition. It just doesn't work. As Riso and Hudson put it: "...*gluttony is self-*

defeating in the long run because the more Sevens 'stuff themselves' indiscriminately in an attempt to find the nurturance they feel they were deprived of in childhood, the more unsatisfied they become."[31]

The Seven's pursuit of gratification takes on an addictive quality. Higher and higher doses of pleasure-producing substances and experiences are required for staying in a constant state of stimulation and euphoria.[32] No amount is ever enough. What it takes to get the desired high keeps escalating, with no end in sight. Behind it all, sadly, there's an unconscious depression, a sort of dry unhappiness and emotional dissatisfaction.[33] A most serious consequence for Sevens in their pursuit of pleasure is captured by Sandra Maitri, who writes:

> In their conscious or unconscious aversion to pain, they limit their direct experience of themselves and, consequently, of life and this is the ultimate source of their suffering. They tend to experience things from the safe remove of their minds, testing life to see whether or not it might be safe to enter into it completely. When they want to fully dive into things, they find that they can't completely, since they are trapped in their personality's defenses against direct engagement. They can only exaggerate their experience without fully being inside of it.[34]

Later on, Maitri goes on to say:

> ...if our orientation is toward pleasure, we will orient toward *enjoyable* experiences rather than toward the *truth* of our experience. When we do this, we are perpetuating the gluttony of the personality, rather than aligning ourselves with the attitude of the soul informed by Being. We are relating to spiritual experience as though it were something yummy to consume, and in so doing, preserve our sense of self as empty and in need of being filled.[35]

This is what the ego doesn't want the Seven to recognize.

Therapeutic Recommendations for Promoting Psychological Hygiene and Finding Inner Peace:

As I think about all the things Sevens can do to heal themselves and find inner peace, I'm reminded of Simon and Garfunkel's *59th Bridge Street* song lyric. If you know the tune, feel free to sing along in your mind:

"Slow down, you move too fast. You've got to make the morning last! ... I've got no deeds to do, No promises to keep. I'm dappled and drowsy and ready to sleep. Let the morning time drop all its petals on me. Life, I love you, All is groovy."[36]

Well, if this isn't a song for a stroll in the park, then I don't know what is. It might also serve as some sort of anthem for Sevens wishing to find a better way. What Sevens need to experience is the "joy" of going nowhere fast. They need to stop and smell the roses. As the mystic teaches us, the longest journey is from here to here. This is what the Seven needs to appreciate, not just intellectually, but in a deep heart-felt way, in a transformational way that promotes change. Going nowhere and staying still can be profoundly moving. Sevens need to give this particular option a try, but not while imagining other things to do, or dreaming of other places to go.

The commitment here is to do nothing and watch what happens... if the Seven thinks the outside world is a cornucopia of pleasurable delights, just wait until they see what the inside world is like! Heavenly bliss trumps worldly pleasure every time.

In this journey without distance, whereby aspiring Sevens can hope to reach the still waters of their mind, it will be necessary, unfortunately, to first pass through the rapids of unpleasant thoughts – those that have been repressed and denied over the years. It will be necessary to keep the 'character kayak' afloat through all the turbulent waters of painful memory. No detours are possible; portaging to bypass the unpleasant stream is not an option. Attention will have to be greatly focused.

Though the following recommendation is given in the context of work, I think it applies to attentional practice more generally. The recommendation is that the Seven: "*Keep attention stabilized in the exact present moment and be able to accept exactly what comes up, whether it be joyous or saddening, whether it makes you feel great or it makes you feel bad.*"[37]

The problem is that narcissistic Sevens find the task of keeping attention single-pointedly focused on an inner object of contemplation boring work. Not only that, revelations that emerge may indicate to Sevens that they are less evolved than what their egos have led them to believe[38] which is not so fun to find out. As Helen Palmer puts it: "It takes fortitude and courage for narcissistically inclined meditators, who may be sincerely convinced that they have already evolved past any personal shortcomings, to pay attention to the aspects of themselves that are really not okay."[39]

Finding out about what's not okay is part of what it means to confront one's personal shadow.

On the subject of meditation and attentional focus, it is a good spiritual practice for Sevens to notice more generally how the velocity of their thoughts throughout the day leads them away from any feelings of fear or upset. Whenever Sevens feel a bout of boredom coming on, they should stop and see what's bothering them or what they're avoiding.[40] This is not to suggest that they should wallow in negativity, only that they should not repress or deny it. If mental and emotional pain are the enemy, Sevens are best advised to understand them before defeating them. It's hard to beat an opponent if you can't see him or don't understand his tactics. The first pre-requisite is to notice and focus on the enemy when it presents itself. Authentically experiencing the unpleasant and understanding to eliminate is not wallowing in the negative. It's the way out of the darkness.

Of course, the ego would have you ignore all that bad, unpleasant stuff. It would rather seek another fun-diversion. Nice try, but sorry ego. No addressing of psychological pain, no existential gain. We're building character here, not carnival carousels. Sevens are thus well advised to engage in forms of guided meditation which confront their darker sides.[41]

Here's another therapeutic option for Sevens. They should make efforts to damp down sources of stimulation which often serve as little more than a distraction from the present. If you're a Seven, from time to time, try putting away the cell phones, the BlackBerries, the laptops, the iPods, the DVDs, the newspapers, and the books. Don't be afraid of the anticipated boredom. Are you afraid of boring yourself, of being alone with yourself? But why? Everybody else seems to love and adore you. Don't you love yourself? Aren't you interesting enough?

For present purposes, you need to spend some time alone, undistracted, focused entirely on your own immediate experience. There's no real need for constant hyper-stimulation. Not allowing yourself time for rest and honest self-reflection is largely responsible for your unhappiness now.

By the way, being alone is not about marathon training or training for the *Tour de France*, for example. In both cases, there's still an excessive expenditure of energy and almost an addictive quality to the activity. Both contribute to endorphin highs and continued feelings of superiority – problematic matters for the manic and narcissistic Seven.

On the subject of hyper-activity, Sevens should try to become aware of their mental evasions.[42] By constantly planning, over-scheduling, exploring new options, and working on projects,

Sevens are often on the run, trying to avoid something emotionally upsetting or difficult. The "busy-business" makes it look like life is filled and *"I am important."* The truth often is: *"I am scared, in denial, and looking for escapes."*

Being so busy makes Sevens moving targets, difficult to pin-down with commitments and responsibilities. Indirectly, it can also feed the Seven's attitude of superiority and specialness. Important people are always on the go - or so we're led to think. *"How can I commit when there are so many other important things to do? I'll try to fit you in – if you're lucky!"*

Riso and Hudson make the point that the movement to essence does not actually require the Seven to do anything or to acquire or "get" anything. Rather, to experience essence Sevens simply need the richness of the present moment to touch them, as we all do. Being, in itself, is pleasurable. As Riso and Hudson explain: *"Joy is a natural experience that arises spontaneously when we experience ourselves as Being – when we are free of the endless chatter, planning, and projects of our ego minds."*[43]

Sevens would do well to pay attention not only to their endless planning, but also to their hasty rationalizations designed for pain avoidance. Rationalizing is a way of diverting attention from the real or painful issues of life.

Sevens might also think about their cutting and dismissive remarks directed toward others. Occasions when these arise probably need some further examination and reconsideration, perhaps in a personal journal. The ego has a heavy psychological agenda when it leads people to attack others. The goal is to find out what that agenda is. Once it's discovered, Sevens will be surprised how much more "worthwhile" others will appear. They might even be able to show genuine compassion toward them.

Finally, a major goal for spiritual growth in the Seven is to develop the virtue of *sobriety*.[44]

Sandra Maitri writes:

"Sobriety, then, is not being intoxicated and swept away by our emotions or our minds. It means not becoming drunk with our experience, no matter how lofty and transcendent it is. It also means not indulging and exaggerating our pain but rather experiencing both extremes directly, fully, in a balanced way. It means not getting swept away by an emotional current, pulled out to sea by its undertow, and drowning in it. It means ceasing to relate to ourselves as though we were empty vessels needing to be filled, consumers needing to consume. It means ceasing to move only toward what feels good or familiar, and instead opening to the unbelievably interesting mystery that we are.[45]

For Maitri, sobriety is about being present in the here and now, not lost in our thoughts, dreams and fantasies. Sobriety is what allows us to behave as responsible adults – often a challenge for The Eternal Youth.

CHAPTER ELEVEN

EGO DYNAMICS IN CHARACTER TYPE EIGHT: *THE POWERFUL MAVERICK*

When I dare to be powerful, to use my strength in the service of my vision, then it becomes less and less important whether I am afraid.
Audre Lorde

What this power is I cannot say; all I know is that it exists and it becomes available only when a man is in that state of mind in which he knows exactly what he wants and is fully determined not to quit until he finds it.
Alexander Graham Bell

Lost Essence:

Recently, while at a restaurant, a very young toddler came running out of the main dining room and into the waiting area where I was standing in line. At my age, I've noticed that I can unintentionally frighten slightly older children because of all my silver hair, glasses, and beard – heck, I sometimes frighten myself looking in the mirror!

Seriously though, it was interesting to observe when this little child suddenly realized that it was "lost in space." Looking around, the child fixated on me for a moment and that's when I suspected it would start to cry looking for mamma. Much to my surprise, however, the child approached me, raised both arms above its head, looked up imploringly, and uttered the sounds: *"uh...uh...uh!"*

For never before parents, let me explain that this is 'child-speak' for *"Please pick me up."*

At the risk of appearing like some sort of child abductor, I did indeed pick up the toddler, thinking I would return it to its parents. Well, the mother finally discovered us both and what followed was a noticeable moment of indecision on her part in this age of distrust – at least judging by the expression on her face. I'm not a mind reader, but I sensed she was asking herself: *"Is this some kind of pervert holding my child, or just a kind man who rescued my baby before any danger presented itself? Should I thank him or warn my child never to walk up to strangers?"*

The point of the story is that young children, like the toddler who wanted "up," are essentially innocent. They come to experience with no preconceived notions, no history. They are completely naive. They have no psychological defenses. They are not trying to trick anyone into anything. They have no secret ambitions or hidden agendas. There is no guile, deceit or manipulation. They don't even know such things exist. Hence, they don't fear the intentions of others. They don't impute to others any potential evil-doing, danger or threat. They have no expectations, positive or negative; nor do they have any conditioned fears.

The very young have not lived long enough to develop them. Innocent acceptance is their essential state of being. Translucency is what they're all about. Complete trust is their psychological posture toward the world.

The sublime beauty of childhood innocence is what warms the hearts of adults. Young children approach life with their arms wide open, receptive to whatever experience has to offer. Children are able to see things freshly, without prejudice or memories to drive a wedge into present experience. The child is essentially embodied innocence. That is what it is; that is what we all are, though most of us have forgotten this essential quality of our true Higher Self.

There is something delectable about youthful innocence. The toddler is like a sugared muffin or donut-on-legs. Rather than being comfort food, however, it's more like 'comfort presence.'

Being around the young child makes one feel open, joyful, and spiritually uplifted. The child is able to make magic in the air without effort. In the child, others can see its luminous purity and are then emotionally and psychologically disarmed in the process. Such is the magnificent power of Essential Innocence.

Fortunately, for me, I live near a day-care and so am able to delight in the innocence of children almost on a daily basis as a line of "walking donuts," holding hands, often parades by my house on the way to the park with nurturing child care workers serving as their protective guides. In the winter, when everyone is bundled up in their puffy snow suits, like little Michelin men, the baby donuts turn into walking marshmallows.

Now there's magic again! I'm warmed inside just thinking about the image. Apparently the mere presence of innocence can change hearts in a way that language, force, and logic frequently fail to do.

In every real man a child is hidden that wants to play.
Friedrich Nietzsche

With Eight children, the soft innocent sweetness sadly does not last. We can see why by delving into their early childhood experiences. For example, let's say little Johnny is playing on the Jungle Jim in the local playground. Another child pushes Johnny off the apparatus, at which time our little bundle of joy begins to cry. Mom and dad angrily grab Johnny by the arm, brush him off rather roughly and begin to yell: "Don't take that! Push the other kid back, you sissy! What's wrong with you? Stop your crying! Don't be such a wimp!"

Now imagine this scenario re-enacted time and time again during the child's psychologically most formative years. Or, imagine a child growing up in tough neighborhood where there are drug dealers and gang members on every corner. To appear weak or afraid in such circumstances is surely going to get one into trouble. In the *'hood,* only the strong survive. To be gentle and giving is to invite rejection, betrayal and pain.[1] Weakness can always be sensed for those looking to attack, so you don't want to make yourself a target.

In circumstances such as these, some children get the impression that the world punishes soft tendencies and so they opt for hardness.[2] *"In the harsh realities of life you can't trust anybody but yourself,"* or so thinks the budding Eight.

On this note, Helen Palmer writes:

> Eights commonly describe themselves as having tried to be good when they were young. They say that they initially wanted to please others, but that their innocence was taken advantage of, and that they were hurt when they showed their vulnerable side. They believe that they began to push back in self-defense and quickly found that it was more fun to break the rules than it was to try to keep them.[3]

The aggression witnessed by our young Eight needn't necessarily have occurred on the streets or at the local park. It may have occurred right at home. Often it's the case that the exercise of parental power was grossly unfair or abusive and so the child learns not to expect anything good from parental authority figures.

Implicitly, the child might even decide that parental power is illegitimate.[4] *"Who the hell do they think they are treating me that way?"*

Out of mistreatment, then, can come rebellion against authority. The seeds of a fighting character are sewn early in the Eight's growing season. What ultimately results is a rebel, a maverick, or what some might dub the 'Lone Ranger.' Survival suddenly becomes paramount to our little donut (remember how sweet?).

Now the child is forced always to be on its guard. For many Eights, parental mistreatment and betrayal, or betrayal on the part of other significant persons in their lives, leads them to the conclusion that one must never allow oneself to be left vulnerable or innocent again.[5] *"If no one else can be trusted to look after me, then I'll look after myself."*

With Eights, 'betrayal' takes on an importance far greater than for any other character type. It is their primal spiritual wound. The resulting emotional calluses are what harden them to the world and other people. The original softness of their psychological skin is replaced by tough scar tissue, something which covers the Eight's Essential Innocence. Early betrayal is what prompts the Eight to continually ask: "What do they *really* want?" "What do they *really* mean? "What threat do they *really* pose?"

That which does not kill us makes us stronger.
Friedrich Nietzsche

Some adult Eights also report that they felt like they were required to grow up far too fast, far too soon.[6] They might have been the oldest sibling in a family, for example, asked to become a child caretaker or substitute parent for younger brothers and sisters raised in a single parent home. Perhaps, the young person had to quit school and get a job to financially support the family. This necessity is perhaps less common in North America or the United Kingdom today as compared with the post-World War II era in the late 1940s and 1950s. Nonetheless, being forced to work at a very young age is still a very harsh reality for many people today.

Psychological Worldview and Compensating Strategies:
Now, whether disadvantaged financially, or mistreated, abused

and betrayed at home, or intimidated and pushed around on the streets, Eights draw the conclusion: *"Only the strong survive. You've got to be tough to make it in this world."*

Existentially, personal security thus becomes a focal pre-occupation.[7] Perceptions of others often come down to this: "Is the person a challenge to me or a source of gratification, a way of getting what I want?"[8] Another way to put this is: "Who's an obstacle and who's an object of pleasure?"

You see, the Eight is at war with the world and doesn't believe that one can look to others for support without losing autonomy or position in the pecking order of life.[9] Because a good number of the people Eights encounter belong to "challenge and threat" category, the attentional focus is on the weaknesses of others. "What is their Achilles heel? How can I get at their jugular? What's my best angle of attack? What can I use or do to my advantage?"

On the other hand, those who are perceived as weak and non-threatening, or let's say not a significant source of pleasure for the Eight, are simply dismissed as unworthy of equal treatment, or of garnering any attention at all. Such people are ignored, by-passed or, if absolutely necessary, treated with perfunctory inauthentic courtesy. The dismissive indifference or conde-scending disdain behind the polite smile is often palpable.

Related to the business of security is control. When Eights enter into a new situation, they want to know who has the power and whether that person will be fair.[10] Unconsciously, Eights fear that authority will abuse power in the way it was abused during childhood.

Still feeling like an innocent victim, the Eight needs assur-ances to feel safe. To ask for assurances feels weak, however. To test authority on the other hand is empowering, but we'll talk about compensating psychological strategies in a moment.

Given the Eight's preoccupation with control, less than fully functioning Eights can be quite impatient with "underlings," dismissing them as irrelevant or merely a waste of time.

On this note, I remember an Eight once giving me a word of advice on how to complain properly: *"Never speak to the secretary or any other subordinate for that matter. Personally, I only speak to the president of the company. That's how you get what you want!"*

People without power are barely perceptible in the visual field of the Eight. After all, what do they have to offer except delay, waste, stupidity, and inconvenience? And further, they're about as important as a blip on the radar screen! As insulting and insensitive as this perception may seem, it's how many less than fully-developed Eights view the world, and they don't apologize for it. To do so is for the weak and being 'weak' is not part of their self-concept. *"So what are you suggesting?"* asks the Eight. *"You think we ought to waste our time speaking to stupid insignificant people who can't give us what we want? Are you stupid? Maybe I ought to quit wasting my time with you!"*

These are typical in-your-face type questions that would be likely to be posed by the aggressive Eight, responding to your challenge about human worth. In the questions just raised, we clearly sense the abrasive and arrogant tone which, by the way, a great many Eights take pride in. They regard it as a mark of their inherent superiority.

Another feature of the Eight's worldview is the proclivity to oversimplify matters and to see situations in black-and-white terms. They have an all-or-nothing style of attention.[11] This attentional orientation leads to dichotomous thinking and an existential distortion of others who are perceived and judged to be either weak or strong, fair or unfair, smart or stupid, warrior or wimp, with no middle ground. People are seen in two-dimensional terms, almost as cardboard figures.

This gross oversimplification and narrow focus is further

highlighted when Eights are psychologically threatened or under pressure; then their attention narrows to a measuring of one's own power against the strength or weakness of an opponent. It's then that they're looking for the other's Achilles heel or jugular.

Eights deny complexity. These are not people who dance the dance of ambiguity. Their world is black or white, you're either friend or foe, strong or weak, likeable or not.
　　Michael Goldberg

Eights are practical people who focus on the here-and-now. Usually, awareness of the present is a good thing, but for Eights their attentional focus becomes limiting, not illuminating.

Eights are what Enneagram theorists describe as instinctive or body-based types. Their interaction with reality comes from the "gut," as compared with the heart or the head. Eights are looking for gut-level reactions to what's graspable and concrete, here and now.

There's only agitated impatience when it comes to memories, abstractions, and anticipations. This is all about what isn't, what was, and what might be; not what actually is. To have control requires that one address the situation as it presents itself in the moment.

Unfortunately, the steely determination to do just this leaves the Eight often desensitized to the subtleties of aesthetic and spiritual experience.[12] Thus, for Eights, "Concentration on the present is not simply a manifestation of mental health as it could be in other character dispositions, but the consequence of not deeming anything real that is not tangible and an immediate stimulus to the senses."[13]

My own experience is that most male Eights I know don't bow down to a higher religious authority; nor are they inclined to enjoy the delicacies of ballet or figure skating.

I've also noticed, along with Claudio Naranjo, that Eights tend to scorn the values of traditional education where abstraction, complexity, ambiguity, and uncertainty are firmly planted in the inquiring mind. Education allows for profound theoretical discussion and debate – not things appreciated by the outward looking, action-oriented Eight. Uncertainty and doubt are sources of insecurity. As for principals, administrators, teachers, and other people in control, *"blunt invalidation of authority is the way to be"* for the Eight.[14] Fighting authority, being a nay-sayer, is a way for Eights to wage war against the world. Everyday is a fight.

You talk too much for a fightin' man.
   Wyatt Earp (The Movie)

Your gut tells you what's best.
   Mike Harris, Former Canadian Conservative Premier

The point was made earlier that many Eights perceive themselves to be the victims of abuse and unfairness at the hands of authority figures or those who bullied them. Others relate how they suffered the indignities of constant humiliation throughout their childhood. One Eight, coming from a fairly impoverished background, once told me the story of how, as a young boy, he used to caddy at a local golf course, carrying the golf-bags of the "fat cats" and "high-rollers," as he dubbed them. He recalled dreaming of the day when someone else would be doing the carrying for him. Judging from his tone, he apparently found something demeaning about working as a caddy. He must have thought that a poor boy "begging" (in his mind) for tips from the fat cats was undignified, somehow placing him in a diminished, inferior position.

Whatever his thinking, generally speaking, it's in response to real or perceived humiliations, that the Eight's psychological ego devises an ingenious long-term scheme, namely to take revenge. This revenge is not typically in response to a single episode of injustice, though it could be, I suppose, but in reaction to a generalized perception of injustice and harm done to oneself.

Also, given that Eights have felt the indignity of being demeaned, used and abused, their ego strategy is to turn the tables on the world.[15] After having suffered frustrations and humiliation for the pleasure of others, it is now the Eight's turn to have pleasure, even at the expense of others' pain - or especially then, for thereby one might also enjoy revenge.[16] Those who don't understand Eight psychology might have wondered in the past why there was always a hint of spiteful, aggressive bitterness accompanying some people's successes. Now you know. The wish for some people to shove their success down your throat is a testament to their own feelings of inferiority.

Success is the best revenge.
French Proverb

Another strategy used by the ego to deflect attention away from the internal dynamics of the mind is to engage in bombast and bravado. The Eight ego convinces the individual how important they are, how they are larger than life.[17] The way to do this is through being loud and full of bluster. Eights don't whisper and they don't apologize easily. They fill space and they take up room. Eights often engage in dominance displays like lesser primates and other lower creatures in the animal kingdom. There's a kind of narcissistic exhibitionism to this. It's imperative for Eights that you and I to know they are important. Often these ego displays are sexualized, reinforcing the self-concept that: *"Not only am I powerful, I'm also sexy!"*

When others find their narcissistic displays immature or unbecoming, aggressive Eights are likely to up the ante or challenge their critics with some form of verbal or physical confrontation. Also, if raw primate displays are not enough to impress, then material possessions and status objects might be used. *"Let's compare the relatives sizes of our homes."*

If Eights own a house, you can bet it will be a big house – the biggest they can afford. If they drive a car, it's not likely to be a sub-compact. Eights tend to identify with their possessions as extensions of themselves.[18] Some materially successful Eights are so impressed with themselves that they see no need to wait in lines, either in traffic or at the restaurant. They are the ones who often cut in, leaving it for wimps and suckers to stay politely in place. *"You gotta a problem with that!"*

One Eight I know uses the strategy of slipping money to the *maitre d'* at restaurants to avoid the line and get the best table, even if already seated patrons have to be moved. Moments like these can be simply orgasmic for the Eight. The unfortunate truth, however, is that the special treatment has to be bought. The sense of self-importance comes with a price, the indignity of having to buy it. How paradoxical and sad.

In all of their pursuits and interests, you'll find a high degree of intensity. Eights' body language will make it clear when they're doing something important and when they're not interested in talking to you. They can be entirely absorbed by whatever activity they're engaged in. Of course, intense absorption creates the conditions for disciplined and focused action, something Eights are good at. To those more easy going, there's almost something frightening about the intensity, and Eights would like to know that. No doubt this intensity contributes to their intimidating presence. Who doesn't like to feel powerful?

Because Eights distrust individuals, fearing others are masking their real intentions, the ego's strategy is actually quite clever in provoking others and getting them angry. Eights believe that the truth comes out in confrontation. As the poet Irving Layton (an Eight) once said: *"Never trust a man until you've seen him angry."*

At that point, all defenses are down and you can see the individual in his or her naked honesty. Once people are seen at their "worst" and we know what they're capable of and how they will respond, we can decide whether or not to trust them.

Again, this is a way for Eights to size other people up. Sizing up, as well as challenging, attacking, drawing lines in the sand, and being-in-your-face capture very much the Eight ego's preferred strategies. These strategies would appear to capture the personality preferences of archetypal Eights such as Donald Trump, Judge Judy (Judith Scheindlin), Barbara Streisand, Dr. Phil (TV talk show host), Ernest Hemingway, Rosie O'Donnell, Pierre Elliot Trudeau, Saddam Hussein, Friedrich Nietzsche, Martin Luther King Jr. Henry VIII, and Fidel Castro.

You may notice that none of these individuals like to be told what to do or how to do it. Eights don't take orders from others very well. They prefer to impose their own wills instead.

I go by instinct – I don't worry about experience.
  Barbara Streisand

...the question arises whether it is better to be loved rather than feared, or feared rather than loved. It might perhaps be answered that we should wish to be both: but since love and fear can hardly exist together, if we must choose between them, it is far safer to be feared than loved.
  Machiavelli, *The Prince*

Healthy and Unhealthy Expressions of the Powerful Maverick
I don't think it's any coincidence that Friedrich Nietzsche, an Eight, regarded the "will to power" as the ultimate motivating force in life – not libido (Freud) or the will to meaning (Viktor Frankl). *"What is good?"* he asked. *"All that heightens the feeling of power, the will to power, power itself in man."*[19]

Not just for Eights, but for all of us who experience this will within ourselves, there's the associated feeling of expansive energy. We feel tall, solid, strong, and alive. There's a natural vitality which expands, enlarges, and feels downright primitive. It is boundless and instinctual. We've all felt *"la force"* from time to time.

For the healthy Eight, its occurrence is more frequent and robust. There's no need for ginseng supplements and caffeine to feel alive. In the Eight, the primal and physical are part and parcel of daily experience. There's a great passion for living. Instinct and drive are not suppressed as they are with many pious religious people who consider such things dangerous if not sinful; rather they are acknowledged and celebrated.

Fully functioning Eights are self-confident and self-assured. At their best, they are magnanimous, using personal power to contribute to and build up the community.[20] Others, who are witness to their strength, are inspired to accomplish great things. It's as if the power, courage and determination of the Eight rub off on others who look up to them for confidence and strength. Others find themselves taking risks and doing things which they wouldn't otherwise do.

As leaders, Eights display a can-do attitude and possess the inner drive, determination, and initiative to make things happen.[21] You can imagine what it means to tell an Eight that something can't be done. More often than not, such a statement is little more than a challenging invitation to do exactly what others say is impossible. Rather than shy away, Eights are more likely to confront the situation as something that needs to be overcome. *"Why climb the mountain? Because it's there!"* Challenge is motivation enough.

With respect to leadership, healthy Eights are honorable and authoritative, traits reflecting the importance placed on trust and power. They have a rock-solid commanding presence. They look after people without playing favorites.

When necessary, under adverse conditions, they are able to take the heat, as it were, appreciating the fact that you can't please all of the people all of the time.[22]

It's important to be just, even if one is sometimes forced to hurt the feelings of others. It is in the interests of justice, in fact, that Eights make excellent protectors of the weak and innocent.[23]

Wholesome Eights are typically concerned for the welfare of the underdog and the disadvantaged. It's great to champion and defend those who cannot defend themselves. Using personal power in service to justice or for the benefit of those who have been unfairly treated in life can be enormously rewarding for Eights. They can do much good in the world as a result.

For many introverted toned-down eights, who are not so openly aggressive and extraverted, leadership and protectiveness are frequently displayed in parental behavior and by looking after family members.[24]

As with any character, personal traits taken to an extreme cause problems. For the Eight, "overdoing it" can be so overdone, over stimulation can be so extreme, that it has the effect of deadening the awareness of feelings, especially those of the tender variety.[25]

Such feelings reflect emotional dimensions of life of which the Eight is almost totally unaware. In other words, the Eight can lose touch with an important part of themselves, with how they truly feel inside. Their "gut instincts" may wrongly be taken for feelings, when of course they're really not quite the same thing.

Not everything which energizes from within is related to affect and emotion; here is where Eights are often mistaken, sometimes believing they're people with deep feeling when it's really passionate drive to which they refer. Insofar as self-knowledge requires awareness of the full array of one's feelings, unhealthy Eights suffer from ignorance about themselves. They are not whole, but "weak" in some areas of self-development.

Discovering too much, too late, can have emotionally devastating consequences.

On the subject of feelings, it's not as if unhealthy Eights don't have any. Indeed they do, only some are exaggerated, inflated or more openly expressed, while others are repressed and denied. For instance, Eights clearly have no problem openly expressing their anger. Variations of this include rage and fury. Combine these with the Eight's physicality, and you get a potentially lethal combination. Eights are often oblivious, however, to the fact that they are angry or enraged say, in an argument, and blind to the fact that their actions and words are alienating others around them. Those who leave in disagreement are simply dismissed as stupid or gutless. The Lone Ranger is alone for a reason.

While anger is the Eight's trusted friend, a kind of link to the real world, denial kicks in when unpleasant feelings arise. So does an outwardly focused passion. As Audre Lorde suggests in the opening quotation of this chapter, using personal strength to realize one's goals obliterates any feelings of fear. For the Eight, it's better to be angry than afraid, passionately driven rather than insecure.

Such feelings are denied; but as Freud pointed out, what's denied doesn't magically disappear. It takes up space in the individual's unconscious mind where it assumes power and takes control in ways the person doing the denying can't consciously appreciate or understand.

Paradoxically, the very same anger which is used to get at the real truth in others is what blocks the Eight's own awareness of the truth in themselves. Fear and insecurity are threatening emotions blocked from the Eight's conscious psyche.

So, it's not that Eights are never afraid, insecure or anxious; they just don't pay attention when they are, thus believing they're not. Perhaps the Eight's belief that others are untrustworthy, often lying and deceiving, is little more than a unconscious projection of the Eight's own self-deceptions. If Eights can't trust themselves to be honest with themselves, how can they trust others? The untrustworthy opponent is not somebody else, but me, myself and I! Eights should recognize that the lack of honesty they perceive in others is in many instances just a projection of what is true about them.

The Eight's attention is not only directed away from unpleasant emotions, but also turned almost exclusively toward the physical dimension of reality – the here and now. There's some benefit in focusing on this for some character types, but for Eights, this focus produces a limited perspective on life. The Eight's emphasis on the immediate causes them to see reality through a distorted lens.[26] The problem is that they believe that their "distortion" represents the truth. They created it after all.

Other interpretations are simply signs of weakness or deception – notwithstanding, some non-Eights I know would beg to differ, pointing out that the Eight's belief is likely a part of the Eight's own self-deception designed to protect the precious ego that has been so largely inflated.

Whenever I climb, I am followed by a dog called 'Ego.'
Friedrich Nietzsche

I know my fate. One day my name will be associated with the memory of something tremendous – a crisis without equal on earth, the most profound collision of conscience, a decision that was conjured up against everything that had been believed, demanded, hallowed so far. I am no man, I am dynamite.
Friedrich Nietzsche

Unhealthy Eights can often have an obsession with power. Exerting this power or control can lead Eights to regard other people in their lives as possessions.[27] Those who depend on them for support may be perceived as weak or unable and thus not deserving of respect. Requests turn into commands; suggestions become orders. Further, "dependents" start to be treated in an undignified fashion, in a way that Eights themselves would never wish to be treated themselves.

Dysfunctional Eights start taking delight in belittling and humiliating others in ways painfully reminiscent of their own childhoods. The humiliation drama is played out again, only now it's time for payback and revenge. The tables have turned and the shoe is on the other foot. The sad reality, however, is that every controlling action, or indignity and degradation perpetrated against others is just an unconscious pathetic effort to re-establish a sense of unconditional self-worth that was somehow lost in childhood. Somebody has to pay for the Eight's early pain. It might as well be you. Let justice be done!

If and when the troubled Eight gets to this point, they have evolved into a ruthless and dictatorial person, highly destructive and bordering on the sociopathic.[28] Remember, the Eight is at war with the world and it doesn't plan to lose the fight. I guess we shouldn't take the Eight's controlling anger personally, we're just obstacles or victims of collateral damage in the Eight's battle against reality.

When at their most unhealthy, Eights can suffer from serious paranoia.[29] They fear being betrayed and so often withdraw from others in bitter isolation. Fearing humilating defeats, things like open criticism, being fired, or being divorced by one's spouse, the troubled Eight may engage in a kind of pre-emptive strike, angrily rejecting others first before they themselves can be rejected.

A combination of paranoia and pre-emptive psychological warfare does not make for a pretty scene in interpersonal relations, as you can well imagine. In worst case scenarios it makes for an anti-social personality disorder. Sick Eights take sadistic pleasure in being vindictive. They think getting revenge will make them happy, that hurting people and humiliating them is the best way to nirvana – surely a perverted distortion of the truth, something the Eight both craves and obfuscates at the same time.

Unless some sort of emotional rescue takes place, Eights can drive themselves into a very deep black hole. The more they try to avoid their inner emptiness with ever increasing intensity, anger, attack, heightened passion, and physicality, the more desperate they become.[30] The last act of revenge against the world could be suicide – *"That'll show them who has control,"* says the Eight. *"I even have power over life itself!"*

Personal Shadow:

In order to emerge out of the darkness and into the light, Eights must come to terms with their greatest vice, namely *lust*. This word can be used to denote "...a passion for excess, a passion that seeks intensity, not only through sex, but in all manner of stimulation: activity, anxiety, spices, high speed, the pleasure of loud music, and so on."[31]

On the surface and from the perspective of others, the Eight's lifestyle appears to be one of exciting abundance. There's always lots to be had, whether possessions, fun, food, or merriment. Eights can look like larger-than-life individuals with all of their self-confidence, not to understate their charm and humor.

What undeveloped Eights don't realize, however, is that their greed for increased stimulation is little more than an unconscious attempt to compensate for a hidden lack of aliveness - that black hole of emptiness. A couple of Eights I know personally, like to introduce controversial topics into conversations to initiate heated arguments and debates. Eights display a propensity for boredom when they are not adequately stimulated; they enjoy confrontation. They constantly crave intense excitement and act impulsively toward that end.[32] Starting a "fight" is one good way.

The frenzied, intense stimulation is not just something enjoyed, it's an addiction. Without constant stimulation the "shadow" appears without having lost a single "Chuang Tzu" step.

The irony is that the Powerful Maverick is, like a small helpless child, afraid of their own shadow. Fear is that which *really* motivates them.

The lust for power is not rooted in strength, but in weakness.
    Erich Fromm

The masking feature of lust is what detracts from interiority and psychological depth in the lives of Eights. Exclusive focus on the "now" for Eights – meaning what is present to the senses – precludes insight into the psychodyamics of their ego.

There's a lot more going on inside than Eights want to admit either to themselves or others. What's inside is scary and Eights aren't going there. Recognition and admission of their true motivations would be horribly neutering to the highly sexualized, physically intimidating Maverick.

You see, as with any ego strategy, it's all just an act, an illusion to hide the nature of one's true identity. In this case, think of the Eight's true identity in terms of Essential Innocence as embodied in our little "walking donut" portrayed earlier. One devastating consequence of this lack of self-insight is the failure to recognize that the strong and tough-minded character is actually exhibiting counter-dependency.[33]

The obsessive need to achieve self-sufficiency is grounded in fear of weakness and becoming dependent on others. Were there no fear, there would be no need to look and act tough. There would be no need to prove to the world that *"I did it MY way!"*

The tougher the façade, the greater the fear. People with true authority don't need to exert it. People with real power don't need to flaunt it. If anyone has betrayed the Eight, the ego certainly has.

The ego speaks with forked-tongue, to use a Native expression. On one side of its mouth, it whispers to the Eight, *"You're a little chicken-shit"*. On the other side, it suggests ways to prevent anyone from ever finding out. Now some might argue that such psychological duplicity and betrayal on the part of the ego presents a real cause to be angry – that is, insofar as one can justify being upset at an illusion!

Another problem with the Eight's lust stems from what I'll call the "naughty factor." Given the choice, Eights would prefer "stolen cookies" over those purchased in the store. Somehow, stolen cookies always taste better. It's quite exhilarating for the Eight to experience pleasure through illicit means or through a disordered appetite for carnal pleasures.[34]

Both involve the violation of rules and boundaries, those set by others. Of course, Eights don't handle limitations set by others very well. Usually, they present occasion to prove who's really more powerful or who's really in control. Eights take risks when seeking to satisfy themselves by illicit and excessive means. When we ask ourselves why so many of the beautiful people, the rich and famous and powerful become architects of their own demise, we often have to answer that it's through their attraction to illicit pleasures, things like infidelity, affairs with married people, and illegal drug use. Sure beats yoga... in the mind of the Eight.

There is commonly an exploitive, competitive component to lust. In matters of sex, Eights can become much like predators – polite and charming perhaps – but predators nonetheless. Remember, that in the black-and-white worldview of Eights, others are often regarded as *objects of threat* or *objects of pleasure*. With respect to the latter, there's extreme satisfaction to be had in the struggle and conquest over someone else, to treat them as objects or to have your way with them, as it were.

Triumphing over someone is terrific. Seduction is as much fun as the sex. Sex is like the cookie insofar as it tastes good, but sex after triumphant seduction is like eating a stolen cookie – always better, remember. Here, domination and power combine to make another an object of one's own pleasure.

Over-sexed Eights who have been guilty of such pleasure should note the elements of deception and humiliation involved. One person is objectified, dehumanized, exploited, and degraded in submission to someone's else desire for pleasure.

Sounds like the Eight's childhood re-enacted. The real motivation for sex here is for domination and revenge. It's all about power and it's really fueled by fears of inadequacy. Once the objectified person has been used and abused, that person can be cast aside like a lemon sucked dry. On to the next conquest... You won't find much guilt or internal questioning here, further evidence of Eights' superficiality. Eights find it natural to follow through on sexual attraction and they're not embarrassed by doing so.[35] Limits are for the lame. In the same way that they don't limit their anger, unhealthy Eights don't limit their sexuality out of a moral sense of respect for anyone. Others are shamelessly used without regret.

Still another problem with the shadow of the Eight revolves around their inability to get in touch with the feminine and softer side of life.[36]

People who are always lusting, grabbing, wanting more and all full of themselves with self-inflationary bombast are typically not very sensitive to the tender side of life. They'll exhibit generosity on their own terms. Not to be confused with kindness. Things like compassion and random kindness feel weak somehow, unbecoming for those wielding power and control. How can you exploit someone as a sexual object if you feel sorry for them or identify with their painful degradation?

The Eight is too preoccupied with denying any weakness. Pride may be taken when continuing on while physically injured, for example. In addition, delight could be taken in being the aggressive black sheep or the in-your-face dominatrix. *"I'm not sentimental... I don't give a damn what others think and I certainly don't need you of all people! Hey...I didn't notice you were such a cutie... want to have sex bad-boy?"*

Finally, it's paradoxical that lust, a defining characteristic of the Powerful Maverick's ego dynamic, is the antithesis of control.[37] In lusting after someone or something, power is placed outside.

One is forced to bow down in idol worship to that which is desired, indeed required, for personal happiness. Believing that happiness must be found *out there* somewhere, immediately relinquishes personal authority and self-determination. What is lost is the nobility of self-possession. What replaces it is the undignified scrambling for external sources of satisfaction. No longer self-possessed, the Eight is possessed by lust.

Insecurities arise as the contingencies of life provide no one with guarantees. Anything can happen at any time. Temptations and insatiable appetites can also take over without limit, leading to such things as addiction to alcohol and tobacco. Even when appetites are momentarily satisfied, boredom is just around the corner waiting, and Eights know it at a subconscious level. Without another desperate attempt to forestall conscious recognition of their morbid existential vacuum, without some new ingestion of intensity and drama or conflict, one is surely to fall into the abyss of nothingness.

On the subject of lust and its irony in the context of Eight psychodynamics, Riso and Hudson point out the following:

A further irony arises with lust in relation to control. As we have seen, Eights want to feel that they are in control of their situation. But being in the grip of lust is the antithesis of control: lust is a reaction to something outside the self that inspires it. To lust after a person or an object is to be under its power, whether it is lust for money, a sexual partner or power. As with all the types, the Passion [vice or shadow] is a distortion that ultimately brings the opposite of what the type truly wants.[38]

Therapeutic Recommendations for Promoting Psychological Hygiene and Finding Inner Peace:

While few people like to admit openly that they need help, this is probably never more true than for Eights. To need help or seek it from others is to be placed in a diminished inferior position, not something Eights are comfortable with. By nature – actually, by developed ego strategy – Eights resist ever being placed in such a position, believing that such placement is a reflection on their position in life, and even their self-worth as a human being. Whenever the possibility of such a diminished inferior placement occurs, confrontation becomes the chosen strategy for emotional rescue. Anger leads the charge. Triumph over others is what places one back on top. Anything which exposes the Eight's insecurity is *bullshit*.

By now, we all understand the *psycho-logic* of this strategy. The time has come, however, for Eights to admit to their secret "game." Not to do so would be undignified! To explain why, please excuse me while I use some confrontative "Eight-talk."

Nobody uncovers their ego without some embarrassment. Nonetheless, to continue siding with the ego's maladaptive scheme is to perpetuate a gross form of self-imposed indignity. The ego's deceit has been devastating, and unhealthy Eights have bought into its lies, hook, line and sinker.

No other betrayal has been greater. No deception more egregious. And hence, no humiliation more public or more profound!

A lot of time has been spent inflating, exerting, and imposing an ego which was just a deceptive enemy all along – and you the powerful Eight, were stupid enough to be duped. You were the victim who was conned, yet blind and fearful enough to go along with the ego's plan.

This realization shouldn't make you angry with others; you're the one who fashioned your ego-identity in the first place. You're the one who started the war with the world. Instead of trying to defeat others in your fight against a fabricated reality, you should vanquish your greatest enemy – the ego that dominates you inside. Usurp its power and take it for yourself.

This is the ultimate victory. Isn't regaining honest control of your own life motivating enough? Or do you still want to bash someone else's head in, seduce the next victim or wantonly satisfy an illicit craving, thinking that doing so will buy you peace of mind? This strategy hasn't worked so far, has it? Oh, by the way, watch yourself... there's a big black hole just ahead. You're about to fall into it if you don't change direction – or are you still so stupid that you wish stay the course no matter what?

Where love rules, there is no will to power; and where power predominates, there love is lacking. The one is the shadow of the other.
   Carl Jung

We look forward to the time when power of love will replace love of power. Then will our world know the blessings of peace.
   William Gladstone

Now that the *jig is up* for you if you're an Eight, it's finally possible to start over again. One suggestion for all Eights is to recoup Essential Innocence by working on eliminating pre-emptive strikes against the world. Rather than irrationally and fearfully expecting that others are out to control them and treat them unfairly, Eights should try to walk into new situations without any prior expectations as to what they're going to find.[39] All too often, Eights prepare for warfare by anticipating confrontations; they start sizing up 'opponents' even before they arrive at social gatherings. Decisions are made in advance as to what needs to be proven; what scores need to be settled, and what aggressive strategies will be employed. Walking into situations psychologically prepared and fully armed for a fight is not healthy.

Perceptions are likely to be highly skewed and selective. Fear-based self-fulfilling prophecies are likely to come true. In addition, humiliating lower primate displays, and sexualized narcissistic attention-getting ploys, will be acted out *yet again* to retain one's place in the dominance hierarchy – all in the vain attempt not to play and be victimized by someone else's game of life, one which feels alien and one in which the Eight feels weak and inferior.

The neurotic need to play the Eight's game by the Eight's rules is testament to the weakness of their ego-personality, though the Eight thinks just the opposite. With respect to their narcissistic exhibitionism, Claudio Naranjo explains:

> [Eights]...are entertaining, witty, and often charming, yet not vain in the sense of being concerned with how they appear. Their seductiveness, bragging, and arrogant claims are consciously manipulative; they are geared to gaining influence and elevation in the power and dominance hierarchy. They also constitute a compensation for exploitiveness and insensitivity, a way of buying out others or making themselves acceptable despite traits of unaccountability, violence, invasiveness, and so on.[40]

So we see, that there's a dark underbelly to all their exhibitionism, charm and wit. It's a deceptive ploy to gain place through manipulation of others.

And Eights are worried about others' intentions and whether they can be trusted. It would appear that this deep distrust of others is largely a projection of personal guilt.

The good news is that the psychological disturbances arising from all this guilt and distrust can be ameliorated. To fix the problem, Eights must recognize that their perception of reality is indeed a projection of their fearful minds. If Eights choose to see others as equals, worthy of dignity and respect, and then decide to treat them accordingly, regardless of their relative strength or power, they can then look at themselves in the psychological mirror with less insecurity, knowing that, like everybody else, they have unconditional worth and there's no need to prove it to the world.

The fight against the world can stop now. Peace of mind is but a moment away. To continue the fight is to choose relinquishing the power to take control of one's psychological well-being.

But it will mean finding a new self-definition, one that does not revolve around the questionable use of force, manipulative dishonesty, and physical or emotional violence against others. This is your ego's definition of your false identity. Face it, pounding your chest in front of the world in a sexualized and narcissistic display of power is downright humiliating.

Those who understand the truth of what you're doing aren't impressed, and they aren't laughing with you, they're embarrassed for you. It's time for the Lone Ranger to remove the ego's mask. On the next occasion when you're about to commence another display of your ego's narcissistic exhibitionism, know that there's someone watching who's got your whole game figured out. This should prove to be tremendously embarrassing. If you learn the lesson here, you won't talk so loud and walk so proud. Experiment with respect and humility for a change. It's actually quite liberating. See for yourself.

Eights also need to take into account that their point of view is not the only correct point of view. If nothing else, this book demonstrates that people have many different worldviews, each with its own internal logic and meaningful connections. No one worldview can justifiably be considered to be better than any other. Each captures a partial truth, but no one perspective contains the entire truth about life and human existence. Eights would do well to bear this in mind. Also, they should note that alternative viewpoints need not be considered threatening, but rather interesting and illuminating. Respecting others' viewpoints and taking time to understand them could have some positive effect in terms of producing some depth and substance, which can be lacking in the unhealthy Eight's superficial psyche.

If and when Eights find themselves getting angry at alternative viewpoints, it's good occasion for them to pause and ask themselves what it is that's causing them fear. Remember anger always represents identification with a defensive ego.

Self-observation is powerfully beneficial for all character types. Though it's often embarrassing, it is profoundly liberating in the long run.

What Eights also need to pay attention to is their immense intensity. It wouldn't be a bad thing for them to lighten up once and a while, and not just when prancing and dancing in narcissistic exhibitionism, but at work, the convenience store, at home, and so on. Their intensity is usually accompanied by a single-minded forceful dismissiveness toward those people (objects) who don't promote their interests or who are lesser in their estimation.

In short, the intensity is sometimes condescending and given what we now know about their ego's strategies, quite frankly, Eights have nothing to be condescending about.

A very important insight for Eights to understand and appreciate comes from the notion that Essential Being (e.g., Innocence, Love,

Truth) can only be known in a *receptive attitude*.[41]

The problem is that Eights are seeking to find Being in pleasure and in the power to find this pleasure. Their lustful orientation and insistence on overpowering others makes Eights incapable of receiving – they do not open themselves up to receive what can only be received, like the grace of God.

Eights can't buy Essential Being or God's grace *on demand*. They can't take it from someone else. One does not overpower Being. Humiliation as a strategy won't work; neither will fighting against the world.

As long as Eights stick with their ego's program, they will perpetuate an ontic deficiency.[42] Being will foolishly be sought in vain through lusty pursuits of triumph and other Being substitutes.

Such seeking will always end in bitter disappointment. Such efforts would be laughable if they weren't so sad and misguided. It's time for Eights to unclench their fists and open their hands in welcoming celebration to a new life. Only when the lust for power subsides, can Essential Strength emerge.

It's not suggested here that Eights should relinquish their power. Instead, what they need to do is use it to build others up instead of tearing them down.[43]

There's genuine pleasure to be had in knowing that you have the power and can use it to assist others in making things happen for themselves. It's like being a powerful life-coach, mentor, advisor or guru. Such applications of power are less self-centered and truly do raise one's worth in the estimation of others. One can feel enormously powerful knowing that others can be helped by one's own strength and experience when it overflows in abundance, gratitude, and respect for other persons.

Instead of moving aggressively against others, it would be helpful to move toward them making honest human connections, without all the bombast and narcissism.

As part of the new receptiveness of healthy developing Eights, they would be well advised to speak less and listen more. When the attention is on oneself, there's a lot to defend, and if one chooses to present oneself as "larger than life," then defensiveness of biblical proportions will be required.

It's psychologically soothing just to sit back and hear what others have to say, without simultaneously judging whether or not what's said is *bullshit*, i.e., threatening to the ego. When there's nothing to prove and nobody to attack, it's possible to be more laid back and relaxed.

Only Eights themselves have the power to decide when the war in their minds will end. Whether or not they chose to exercise this power is up to them. Nobody can make them do it – certainly a refreshing empowering thought in all this psychological unmasking.

CHAPTER TWELVE

EGO DYNAMICS IN CHARACTER TYPE NINE: *THE DETACHED PEACEMAKER*

Standing on the bare ground – my head bathed by the blithe air, and uplifted into infinite space – all mean egotism vanishes. I become a transparent eye-ball; I am nothing; I see all; the currents of the Universal Being circulate through me; I am part or particle of God.
Ralf Waldo Emerson

The perfect man has no self; the spiritual man has no achievement, the sage has no name.
Chuang Tzu

Lost Essence:
The element of *Essential Being* highlighted by character type Nine is the sense of *Wholeness, Unity* or *Oneness* with the universe. As Ralph Waldo Emerson (a Nine) so eloquently expresses it in the quotation above, this unity entails that *all mean egotism vanishes*.

When they are aware of their Essential Nature, individuals do not experience themselves as separate objects in a dualistic universe. Rather, they encounter what Oscar Ichazo calls 'Holy Love'.[1]

For Ichazo, Ultimate Being has a dynamic quality of Oneness that flows, transforms and breaks down all barriers, thereby overcoming feelings of separation and isolation – those usually experienced within the boundaries of the ego.[2]

While losing one's ego-identity can be a frightening prospect for some, it allows us to *reconnect with the ocean of Being and realize that at our core, we are this Love.*[3]

Religious people might try to understand the Oneness of Holy Love as: God is everything, and everything that is represents an extension of God's love. Since we are part of everything, it follows that we are extensions of God – that we are one with God and in unity with God. Indeed, like God, our true identity is Love.

God is love and love is essentially what we are. This is what most of us have forgotten and need to remember. All other self-concepts which oppose love or are contrary to love are illusory. So, if you're not seeing yourself as the embodiment of *Holy Love*, to use Ichazo's terminology, then you're not looking at the real you, only a figment of the ego's imagination. You're opting for the ego's illusion of a psychological self over the truth of your Higher Reality – your oneness with your Source. Addressing what's at issue here with respect to Holy Love, Riso and Hudson say:

From point Nine, we experience a sense of Unity or Wholeness. We know that we are not only connected with everything else, but that we are not a 'separate object'. We directly experience the oneness of reality, and our essential union with all creation. Further, we understand that this unity is dynamic, alive, and ever-changing. We know love as the force that breaks through all false boundaries and identities to restore this experience of wholeness. The realization of this state brings a deep satisfaction and contentment – a profound sense of well-being. We feel at peace with reality and with our place in it. We are able to function effectively in the world while knowing that what we are is 'beyond' the world.[4]

Holy Love produces a deep abiding tranquility. It is not heated and lustful, but gentle and serene. It is warm in its comfort, inviting in its stance, compassionate as it reaches out, and without limit in terms of its overflowing abundance. *Holy Love* radiates joyful kindness. It opens our eyes to beauty and dissolves superficial differences.

Love is One. We are One. The universe is One. In this *Oneness* is found peace of mind – our ultimate goal as we try to understand the psychodynamics of all nine character types.

You see, the sense of loving *Oneness* is not strictly for the Nine, but for all of us.

Like for all Essential Qualities, we are limited in our understanding of them by our words because language is predicated on features of *Lower Reality* like space-time dualism, causality, and so on. *Universal Love* exists above and beyond such categories.

St Thomas Aquinas understood this when he deemed his writing nothing but 'straw' after experiencing the divine revelation of God (see Chapter Two).

Making efforts to capture *Essential Unity*, or the *Oneness of God* if you'd prefer, through language, science or logic is like trying to make God in our own image. Unfortunately, our imperfect psychological egos cannot grasp *Divine Perfection*. Be that as it may, our Higher Mind can sometimes catch glimpses of that which 'the eyes do not see'.

Spiritual discernment reveals the reality constructions of our egos for what they truly are – defensive projections and distortions designed to keep us fearful, anxious, and shame-based.

Sadly, like every other character type identified with the ego, Nines lose touch with their Higher Essential Self. As we've seen before, the reasons are largely located in personal developmental history. While parent-child relations alone don't necessarily determine any particular psychological outcomes, they do help to explain how the ego-personality began to form in its earliest days. Our past can help us to understand ourselves without suggesting that it necessarily makes us into who we are in any direct or inescapable cause-and-effect fashion.

As explained at the outset of the book, we are not simply products of conditioning, nor balls of clay shaped by our experiences. Our past presented occasions for experience, but as psycho-spiritual beings, we brought something to that experience as well – a soul essence.

What ultimately resulted from our childhoods was a product of *interaction*. We had a hand in how we chose to interpret and respond to life's events. Thus, even though our pasts influence and perhaps set the initial directions our lives will take, we still remain ultimately responsible for who we are and what we do.

It's clearly misguided, then, to speak with absolute certainty about how people's developmental histories, in and of themselves, form the personality of any given individual. Nonetheless, in view of what has just been said, and at the risk of sounding like a misguided fool, let me suggest that one thing that's *almost for certain* is that Nines were not raised as 'trophy children' to be paraded around and displayed by parents wishing to impress others and thereby vicariously raise their own self-esteem.

Unlike some Three-children, they were not very likely to have been the center of attention in the family. Nines are not people who remember garnering praise for being stars; nor was too much made of the fact when they achieved their goals early in life. Being placed on the pedestal of admiration is not something familiar to the Nine. Indeed the opposite was usually true.

It's more often the case than not that Nines weren't paid enough attention to while growing up. Personal accounts reveal that they typically felt that they were neglected in early life and that this parental neglect turned into self-neglect.[5] "*Heck, if they don't think I'm worthy of care and attention, then why should I think any differently?*" (Whether such 'negligence' or oversight was through parental priorities being elsewhere or circumstances outside their control such as the harsh realities of wartime, which may have prevented parental doting, the effect was that the child felt their parents' attention was elsewhere.) Surely, it's extremely painful for anyone to be ignored, especially a young child. And for the Nine, this early neglect or unavailability constituted the spiritual wound which the ego promised to heal with some ingenious strategies, as we shall soon discover.

In addition to being ignored, many Nines from troubled families have related how they dissociated themselves from the threatening and traumatic events occurring around them.[6] This could have been done by zoning out or withdrawing themselves from the situation, either physically, psychologically or both.

In other instances, Nine children discovered that if they were not demanding and presented few expectations to parents and caretakers, they could protect themselves by staying out of sight. Low maintenance children don't cause problems, nor do they create any waves. Their invisible presence could even have served to calm things down for those who were fighting and stressed over other matters.

With respect to their calming influence, some Nines even remember having accepted the role of peacemaker in the family, whose task it was to mediate interpersonal conflicts.[7] In such cases, Nines became conflict-resolution specialists before they even fully appreciated what they were doing.

I suspect many of these young child mediators now work as professional counselors, and negotiators in their adult lives. This speculation may not be as hasty as one might think. I once gave an enneagram workshop to a sizable group of college counselors and discovered that 81 percent of that particular group were Nines. Possibly only a coincidence... but then again, maybe not. (Unfortunately, I never got a chance to learn about participants' early childhoods. As for any significant correlations between career choice and character type, empirical studies still need to be done.)

Worldview and Compensating Strategies:

Like Fours and Fives, Nines are withdrawn character types. Just as for those other two types, autonomy is extremely important. Rather than adopt an aggressive stance toward the world, like Threes, Sevens, and Eights, or a compliant one like Ones, Twos and Sixes, Nines move away and disengage with others to get what they want.[8]

Nines are not afraid of solitude – indeed they cherish it. They certainly do not adopt an Eight's 'in-your-face' posture or the Three's 'look-at-me' behavior. Invisibility is their preferred stance, *movement away* is their first inclination.

Nines are typically the ones you see meditating at the seashore, on the hillside, or alone in a house of religious worship. They are spiritually nourished by such things as solitude and nature. A well-known nature loving Nine is Henry David Thoreau. You can include Ralph Waldo Emerson in this category. They were both architects of the American transcendentalist movement. Other prominent Nines, not so much nature-oriented perhaps, are the Dalai Lama, Lao Tzu, Carl Jung, Joseph Campbell, Norman Rockwell, Queen Elizabeth II, Whoopi Goldberg, Client-Centered therapist Carl Rogers, Thomas à Kempis, and 'Edith Bunker'(the character from the classic TV series *All in the Family*).

If a man walks in the woods for love of them half of each day, he is in danger of being regarded as a loafer. But if he spends his days as a specu-lator, shearing off those woods and making the earth bald before her time, he is deemed an industrious and enterprising citizen.
Henry David Thoreau

A man is related to all nature.
Ralph Waldo Emerson

As often as I have been among worldly company, I have left it with less fervor of spirit than I had when I came.

Thomas à Kempis

Just like their instinctive, gut-type brothers and sisters – Eights and Ones – Nines have boundary issues. Eights like to defiantly push the boundaries, focusing outwardly. There's always somebody or something to push against, rail against, to beat and defeat.

Ones, by contrast, are more interested in maintaining their internal boundaries. Ones are often found trying to repress temptations or unconscious instinctive impulses like sexuality and aggression from entering their conscious awareness. Such things would violate important principles with which Ones feel obliged to comply.

Nines, by comparison, are left trying to defend both internal and external boundaries. They do not want unpleasant feelings, thoughts, or states to disturb their inner equilibrium, so they construct defensive psychological walls, just like Ones. In their dealings with the external world, Nines protect their ego boundaries by simply turning their attention away from those things that might also disturb their peace of mind.[9] Thus, their boundary issues in life occur on two fronts, as it were, both inside *and* outside.

Regardless of all this internal and external boundary defense, Nines generally seem to be able to maintain a positive outlook on life. Their overarching belief is that everything will work out in the end if we all just stay calm, connected, and friendly with one another.[10]

Nines place great value on peace and tranquility. They display an intuitive sense and appreciation for harmony, for how and when things fit together.[11]

Unlike counter-phobic Sixes and aggressive dismissive Eights who oversimplify things with dichotomous black-and-white thinking, Nines can be quite tolerant of ambiguity, paradox, and contradiction, recognizing them as often little more than differences of perspective.[12]

A Nine psychologist once explained how for his doctoral dissertation he didn't want to do the typical 'critical analysis', by picking one theory and then criticizing it from the perspective of another. Instead he chose to examine how one theory could complement the insights of the other. He wanted to explore synergies and points of agreement and overlap, rather than issues over which there would be irreconcilable differences and disagreement. This respect for differing perspectives, as well as the search for agreement, commonality, and harmony capture something very basic about Nine psychology.

Generally patient people, the typical Nine adopts a *laissez-faire* approach to life which has the effect of encouraging people and events to unfold in their own way at their own pace.[13] As individuals, Nines tend to be non-judgmental and accepting. They are open to alternative possibilities and viewpoints and adopt an impartial perspective, seeing the value in each.

One rarely feels judged in the presence of a Nine. Seldom is someone placed on the defensive. This is not the Nine's style, that is, to confront, evaluate, and get in your face.

The patient attitude of Nines is complemented by their humility. Unlike Eights, they don't need to take control and show the world who's boss. Unlike Threes, they don't need others to be impressed by them. Nines are quite happy to blend into the woodwork. They are unassuming, modest, with no need to show off.[14] There's a kind of soft energy surrounding Nines that's different from the sticky, syrupy Two's energy or the bubbly and fizzy Seven's brightness. Rather than sweet, sensuous or effervescent, Nine energy is calming and re-assuring somehow.

Nines can often be spiritually uplifting to others. There's something airy and light about them, yet paradoxically deep and solid. Our hearts and minds are made tranquil and soothed in their presence. Nines don't generally exhibit the frightening intensity or serious, single-minded focus of some other types. The energy of the Nine is much more diffuse and ethereal. The Nine is a spiritual seeker yearning for connection with others and the cosmos.[15]

I think Lao-Tzu beautifully captures the psychological orientation and outlook of the enlightened Nine in the following words:

> ... the sage holds in his embrace the One, and manifests it to all the world. He is free from self-display, and therefore he shines; from self-assertion, and therefore he is distinguished; from self-boasting, and therefore his merit is acknowledged; from self-complacency, and therefore he acquires superiority. It is because he is thus free from striving that therefore no one in the world is able to strive with him.[16]

With respect to less-than-enlightened Nines, in order to maintain their peace of mind – which is really a *pseudo-peace* for reasons we'll come to appreciate – Nines are forced to come up with a number of compensating strategies in their lives. Since they avoid conflict and confrontation like the plague and because such things are so upsetting to their psychological equilibrium, Nines are forced into self-denial. To begin with, they frequently can't get what they want, for to do so would entail confronting another individual or competing with that person over scarce resources. Easier to deny oneself and say, "*you have it.*" Nines have probably noticed that others appreciate it very much when they show deference. Nines pose no threat or obstacle to others and so they're very much liked. Nines aren't pushy; they're pushovers, and it appears they wouldn't hurt a flea.

Peace does have a price, however. For Nines it costs them the satisfaction of their wants. What Nines don't always realize is that their non-confrontative peaceful demeanor simply buries the anger and bitter resentment they feel below the level of conscious awareness. This too is a dear price to pay for peace, especially since what was purchased by self-denial is only a semblance of peace, not the real thing.

Deference to others also points to another kind of denial for Nines, namely, abnegation of the sense of 'self.' What's at issue here is a form of *self-forgetting*. Nines feel ordinary, like nobody special. Rarely do they feel entitled to privileged treatment – compare this attitude with charming and talented Sevens or self-promoting Threes or belligerantly powerful Eights. By considering themselves very ordinary and by always deferring to others' wants and needs, Nines forget in the end what *they* really want and what *they* really need themselves. They are usually so busy trying to maintain the peace and please others that they lose sight of themselves, putting more attention on other people's agendas, requests, and demands than on their own.[17]

After a while, Nines don't even know what their true desires are. The result is that they find it easier to merge with others. The Nine's lost identity becomes an identity by symbiosis with family, nation, party, club, team, or some idealized other.[18] In this self-forgetting, Nines over-adapt to others and neglect themselves. Sometimes the only way for them to get what they need, is to be ill, at which point they have some respite from their constant mission of looking after others' needs.

In less than healthy Nines, then, the generosity and deference they display is based on discounting the self. Likewise is the case with respect to their humility. So, while generosity and humility are generally thought to be good things, when they are based on unconscious insecurities and habits formed to maintain one's internal psychological equilibrium, such things become inauthentic, self-deceptive, self-defeating, as well as morally and motivationally tainted.

The ego, of course, hides from Nines the true basis of their false modesty and neurotic giving, and it does so using clever means of self-deception. Nines come to regard themselves as *selfless*, believing they don't have any overriding personal needs or goals worthy of upsetting things or causing conflict. Hence, they are quite willing to merge and go along with the agendas of others. Of course, they do have needs and goals; but Nines deceive themselves into thinking none of them really matter, when indeed they do. Merging with the agendas of others is not becoming one with others or with the universe. Humility really becomes pseudo-humility; generosity little more than self-abnegation, and peace of mind under these conditions is little more than an uneasy truce based on repression and bitter resignation.

If you're a Nine, you may have noticed that you've just stepped into the darkness; Please don't run! Oh sorry... don't fall asleep! Help is soon on the way.

Those who are free of resentments surely find peace.
The Buddha

Nothing can bring you peace but yourself.
Ralph Waldo Emerson

To cope with the unpleasantness arising from frustrated needs, Nines protect themselves by retreating, dissociating or by completely shutting down.[19] They often become lost in a fantasy world of their own making or else they focus almost exclusively on those positive things happening in their surroundings. The spaced-out fantasizing by Nines in my college classes, for instance, often makes me think of the expression: "*The lights are on, but nobody's home!*"

Nines are present, but often not there. They hear no evil and see no evil.

This gives new meaning to the biblical expression, *"Seek and ye shall find."* As *A Course in Miracles* teaches, we see what we look for. Some things just happen to be overlooked, while others become the focal point of our attention. In the Preface to *A Course in Miracles* it is written: *"What perception sees and hears appears to be real because it permits into awareness only what conforms to the wishes of the perceiver."* Selective perception is one of the Nine's preferred ego strategies.

Remaining distracted is still another compensating strategy Nines use to deal with the demands and unpleasantries of life.[20] The distractions may come in the form of watching TV, reading, doing crossword puzzles, sleeping, eating, drinking, computer-game playing, and so on. All such distractions appear to be driven by the desire *not* to experience and *not* to see. They all aim to help the Nine *numb-out*. By engaging in these distractions or by getting involved in daily routines – which can be adhered to almost religiously – Nines try to handle the anxiety which inevitably accompanies avoidance of bigger projects and respon-sibilities in their lives.[21] Just thinking about all that has to be done would be mentally disquieting. *"I better clean my desk before I start to work... you can't be productive surrounded by a mess! First, though, I'll make myself a coffee and return a friend's phone call. Then I'll get started... but it'll be dinner by that time... oh well.. .I'll wake up early tomorrow and begin my work then. I'll have a full day to get the job done."* As you can plainly see, diversions and distractions play into the Nines tendency to procrastinate. They also enable Nines to rationalize their lack of momentum and productivity.

While Nines are not volatile and reactive like counter-phobic Sixes or aggressive Eights, that is not to suggest that they never get angry at all by the continuing frustration of their personal wants. Since Nines don't like to consciously deal with anger and upset, the Nine's ego has an adaptive strategy to cope, specifically through passive-aggression.

Sometimes no action can be a response, that is, the action of doing nothing. We can insult others, for example, by not paying attention to what they're saying or by not shaking their hand, or by not showing up at their party. The ego knows there are many creative and ingenious ways to fight back without doing a thing, as it were. For Nines, one of the favorite techniques is using stubbornness.[22] The more others pressure Nines to wake up, get going, or respond, the more they impassively withdraw into the inner sanctums of their minds – which to them is a happy and peaceful place.[23]

"I just won't say what's on my mind and nothing you do can make me!" says the Nine.

"You're in control now," whispers the ego!

I have never found a companion that was so companionable as solitude. We are for the most part more lonely when we go abroad among men than when we stay in our chambers. A man thinking or working is always alone, let him be where he will.

Henry David Thoreau

Finally, one other compensating strategy for the Nine entails living by some sort of formula or adopted philosophy of life.[24] Living by the teachings or having a useful quotation for any difficult occasion helps Nines to deal with troubling situations.[25]

By memorizing and reciting to themselves feel-good principles of successful living as articulated by self-help gurus, they can find comfort by withdrawing into the inner sanctum again. Stoicism, for instance, would likely be a very appealing philosophy of life for many Nines. By means of it they could (questionably) try to justify and rationalize just about anything, believing that it's all for the best according to the Divine *Logos*, what some would call Destiny or Fate, or others would call God.

If all is determined, then there's no sense worrying about things over which we have no control. So again, the Nine needs to do nothing – which is a comforting thought! Basically, all they need to do is accept advice and direction from others. Following someone else's agenda is easier than producing one's own. Everything will work out in the end.

We should have much more peace if we would not busy ourselves with the sayings and doings of others.

Thomas à Kempis

Healthy and Unhealthy Expressions of the Detached Peacemaker:

Healthy Nines are the *bone fide* alchemists of all the character types.[26] For this reason they make good counselors and mediators. Given their outward focus and identification with the needs of others, they are extraordinarily empathic and able to intuit other people's wants and concerns. Add to this the fact that they are open-minded and non-judgmental listeners and you can understand how Nines make wonderful soothers as well as change-agents in people's lives.

They often have incredible transformative powers, helping others to make the most out of their talents and gifts. They can turn the psychological base metal (of hardship and pain) in people's lives into valuable gold (insight and motivation). Their calm disposition can present healing relief to those stressed by the vicissitudes of life. They can provide a safe harbor to people searching for shelter from the storm. Their unflappable and stoic demeanor is wonderfully reassuring to those in need of emotional and psychological assistance.

Another admirable quality about Detached Peacemakers is their unpretentious quality. Nines display a simplicity and earth-iness which is diametrically opposite to the slick Madison Avenue advertising agent, the affected aesthete, or the belligerent legal advocate of the corporate interest.

Nines usually feel more at home in nature than when trying to impress others. There's always danger when trying to sell yourself or wow other people. As Henry David Thoreau warned: *"...beware of all enterprises that require new clothes."* Putting oneself on display is not something Nines like to do.

It is their simplicity, innocence, and guilelessness that puts people at ease and leads others to trust them.[27]

Incidentally, I once gave a personal development workshop for people employed by a natural conservation authority and discovered that about 30 of 50 participants were Nines. This over-representation by one type was clearly beyond statistical probability. The numbers suggest something about how career selection could possibly correlate with character type. I might add that these "tree huggers" didn't come to the workshop dressed in Gucci and Prada. I did see a lot of comfortable flannel, plaid, and Birkenstock sandals, however.

When healthy Nines are in touch with their instincts and when they have moved beyond psychologically defensive self-abnegation in deference to others, they regain their psychological balance. They become aware of what they actually want and what they need. Their own personal goals become important too and they gain a source of motivation and direction.

In pursuit of their goals, Nines become powerful, yet gentle at the same time. To use a natural metaphor, *"...When Nines are in balance with their Instinctive Center and its energy... they are like a great river, carrying everything along with it effortlessly."*[28] We're impressed by the immensity and the calm and how such things combine with the power of this natural flow. By not trying to impress, the Nine impresses. By not trying to overpower, the Nine has power to move others.

Healthy Nines can be extremely imaginative individuals,

enjoying the world of dreams and symbols.[29] Carl Jung comes to mind here. He studied the human psyche by exploring the dream-world, art, mythology, world religions, and philosophy, both eastern and western. In his grand theoretical synthesis, which ultimately gave form to his analytical psychology, Jung included elements of alchemy, astrology, sociology, in addition to classical literature and the arts. Like healthy Nines generally, Jung was able to synthesize many different schools of thought and alternative points of view into one vision.[30]

If patience is a virtue, then it could easily be said of healthy Nines that they are extremely virtuous. Unlike Fives who are always racing against the clock and displaying stinginess with respect to how much time they're willing to share with others, healthy nines are more relaxed, "going with the flow." There's no rush, no urgency. As the French say, *"Que sera, sera,"* whatever will be, will be... (Sing along now: ...the future's not our's to see, *que sera, sera!).* Nines are probably the most patient of all character types. They are also one of the more accepting.

With respect to the unhealthy expressions of the Nine, some have already been mentioned or alluded to under the section dealing with compensating strategies. Their incredible patience can turn into inertia if Nines are not careful. A *wait-and-see attitude* coupled with *going-with-the-flow* can turn into a whole lot of inaction, whereby nothing important gets done.

In addition, we've already seen how easily distracted Nines can become by the minutiae of daily routines. When not properly balanced, they can fail to distinguish between true priorities and trivial pursuits. This gives others the impression that they're scatter-brained. So, combine general inertia with trivial pursuits and we have very little of any significance going on.

Unhealthy Nines' apparent stoic serenity can be largely a manifestation of a rationalized justification for doing nothing.

Further, there is the danger that this self-deception could lead to a fatalistic attitude, an acceptance of negative or even damaging situations as if there were nothing that could be done about them.[31]

The Nine is not worried; but they should be. They do have influence and some control over what happens in life. To think otherwise is again an attempt to escape from personal responsibility. The point is that a forced inner peace based on inertia, reluctance to take on responsibility, and irrational fatalism, is no real inner peace at all. It's merely self-deception.

The false inner peace of the unhealthy Nine also shows up in their relatively flattened affect, say compared with bubbly Sevens and intellectually high-strung Fives. Often wandering aimlessly through life, they come to expect little of themselves and others. It's just easier that way; it causes less psychological and emotional disturbance.

It would seem that many unhealthy Nines have forfeited their highs and lows as a result of their false compromise with the world.[32] To reduce their frustration, they have deadened their desires. To maintain their emotional equilibrium, they have given up their anger. To preclude the possibility of disappointment, they have given up their goals and expectations. So as not to be rejected, Nines say to themselves, *"I'll give up my self."*

So, the price for tranquility is self-abnegation and the denial of one's wants, feelings, desires, goals, and expectations – quite a hefty price to pay for false inner peace!

Of course, the irony here is that Nines require themselves to be the most sacrificing and patiently long-suffering in order to achieve what they think is their inner peace. Suffering in order not to suffer just doesn't make sense. It's impossible to take stoic possession of yourself when you've given yourself away.

Blessed is he who expects nothing, for he shall never be disappointed.
    Alexander Pope

Though it often appears to others that Nines have a deep Buddha-like quality about them, perhaps stemming from their apparent inner peace, it's again ironic that unhealthy Nines are rather simple-minded and superficial.[33] In efforts to maintain their false inner peace, they lose awareness of themselves through self-denial and self-abnegation.

Supportive of others, attentive to others, and intuitively sensitive to others' needs, Nines are left with a rather unexplored superficial self-identity. There's a lack of self-insight with respect to their own feelings, desires, and goals, for instance, and hence an associated lack of vitality that goes with them.

If Nines don't know what they want, what's important to them, or who they are, then there's not a lot of reason for waking up in the morning. Life loses it meaning and Nines lose themselves.

Without a strong sense of identity, what's the point of anything? *There's nobody to be affected, at least nobody important.*

Given this sort of thinking, we can all understand why unhealthy Nines lack fire and passion and why they appear so phlegmatic to others. Nines have forgotten who they really are. Every once and a while, when Nines can no longer take the frustration and deference that they have imposed upon themselves, they become uncharacteristically angry. They may "lose it," as the expression goes.

Much to their surprise, those who become the brunt of their anger often welcome such true expression of emotion. Of course, insecure Eights only trust people when they're angry anyway, believing that's when the truth comes out. With respect to Nines, there's something to this belief.

Personal Shadow:

Detached Peacemakers have paid a large price for their psychological serenity. Not only did they have to disengage and remove themselves from others, they also inadvertently detached from themselves in the process of trying to keep the peace. Peace at any price meant denials of one's wants, desires, goals and ambitions, as well as a kind of self-forgetting based on distorted perceptions of one's self-worth.

Because Nines perceive themselves as just ordinary people, having no special place or significance in the world, they're always ready to follow others' agendas. In fact, they're willing to merge with those agendas. Never mind that less than healthy Nines are lost in space as they do so. Now, all of this self-effacement and deference to others sounds really nice, doesn't it? – especially if you're not a Nine.

However, accompanying this deferential, self-effacing humility is the Nines' personal shadow: *sloth*.

The sloth at issue here has two basic dimensions. The first pertains to common understandings of the term.

When we think of sloth, we tend to associate it with slow movement and laziness. Even in their gait, Nines tend to amble slowly. Nines are the people who dare to dillydally just ahead us as we try to rush to catch a streetcar or run down a narrow staircase. *"Don't these people have a life?"* asks the stressed-out Type A personality Three.

Of course, there's no rush from the vantage point of the Nine. *"What's all the hurry about? Life's only a rat-race if you sign up for the competition. No hurry, no worry!"*

Nines can think this way because they're virtually impervious to those things that ordinarily motivate others: discomfort and hope.[34] Usually, people behave when they have a hope of getting what they want. One could be motivated to finish school, for instance, hoping that an education will help one to find a better job. This discomfort of having nowhere to live because one has no money for rent is usually enough incentive for people to look for work.

It's not to suggest that discomfort and hope never motivate Nines, but because of all their self-denial and self-forgetting, Nines often don't know what their goals and ambitions are. As a consequence of not knowing what they want or need, they frequently don't know what's lacking in their lives and what they could or should do to alleviate that deficiency. *"What's wrong with you? Ah... I don't know."* Easiest to do nothing.

Thus just behind all their "wonderful" humility and deference, then, is the Nine's inertia. Any movement laboriously arising out of it is generally slow or slothful.

A second type of sloth, related to the first, is more subtle. Some have called it "spiritual laziness."[35] Here, we're talking about a loss of inwardness, an aversion to psychological exploration. It was mentioned earlier that Nines project a peaceful Buddha-like presence to the world, looking emotionally stable and deep. However, if one is always staring at the horizon or gazing down from the mountain top, there's not a lot of introspection going on. One doesn't need to dwell on the ego or make the ego one's fetish (a danger for students of personality), but one does need to uncover the obstacles to discovering one's essential nature – obstacles created by the ego.

As Lama Surya Das reminds us, *awareness is curative.* The problem is that Nines do not want to see or be in touch with their inner experience. Confronting one's shadow side is very likely to create negative vibes. Uncovering all of the psychological defensiveness in one's life is likely to disturb one's peace of mind – which would actually be a good thing for the Nine insofar as their's is a fake-peace anyway.

The reluctance to engage in self-exploration is something akin to cognitive indolence, then, based on fear. To maintain an artificial peace of mind, Nines often resort to living life on automatic pilot, engaging in habitual routines.[36] There can also form an excessive attachment to the familiar, to more powerful or idealized others, to group norms, or to how things are customarily done.[37] *"Don't rock the boat....Go with the flow"* could be mottos which capture the Nine's general orientation toward life.

A preoccupation with excessive stability has negative consequences, however. The 'inner witness' or 'witnessing presence' which more truly captures our higher reality is eclipsed. The third eye of spiritual discernment (Emerson's "transparent eyeball") is blinded or at least the eyelid is left shut for fear of being blinded by the light.

The unhealthy Nine is too spiritually lazy to wake up. For Nines, there's a unconscious motivation to stay on the surface of things, primarily oneself.[38] The Buddha-like peaceful demeanor of the unhealthy Nine, when the surface is scratched, is little more than impassive and zoned-out inertia.

What Nines don't want to recognize is that much of the world they, and all of us, inhabit is their own self-imposed reality. The notion that life is what you make it is indeed no less true for Nines than for the rest of us. Whether we're special or ordinary, whether our goals are worth pursuing or not and whether or not life has meaning are all matters of personal choice – a disturbing thought requiring decision and action. *I think I'll sleep on it*, responds the Nine.

Therapeutic Recommendations for Promoting Psychological Hygiene and Finding Inner Peace:

In light of the preceding discussion, it's clear that unhealthy Nines must accept the fact that their current "inner peace" is inauthentic, based on a number of questionable assumptions about themselves. Nines must come to see that they are not just ordinary and unimportant. God's workmanship is not shoddy and He doesn't make mistakes!

As extensions of *Holy Love*, unified with their Source, Nines do have a special destiny, as we all do. Marianne Williamson puts it eloquently when she writes:

> Our deepest fear is not that we are inadequate. Our deepest fear is that we are powerful beyond measure. It is our Light, not our Darkness, that most frightens us. We ask ourselves, who am I to be brilliant, gorgeous, talented, fabulous? Actually, who are you NOT to be? You are a child of God. Your playing small does not serve the world. There is nothing enlightening about shrinking so that other people won't feel unsure around you. We were born to make manifest the glory of God that is within us. It is not just in some of us; it is in everyone. As we let our own Light shine, we unconsciously give other people permission to do the same. As we are liberated from our own fear, our presence automatically liberates others.[39]

She says:

> To remember that you are part of God, that you are loved and loveable, is not arrogant. It's humble. To think you are anything else is arrogant, because it implies you're something other than a creation of God.[40]

Ironically, then, the Nine's humility based on self-abnegation is actually an expression of arrogance. *I know better than God who I am and what my value is. I'm a worthless nobody.*

Such thinking is not meant to elicit pity, for the "worthless" Nine thinks they don't deserve attention.

Only a person unaware and unconscious of their Essential Being could think this in this insane way. The ego has tricked the Nine into believing that deferential self-abnegation is humility, when in fact it's just the opposite.

So, after admitting to the inauthenticity of their inner peace, a second recommendation for Nines is to recognize their inherent worth as extensions of their Divine Source.

"The Thought God holds of you is like a star, unchangeable in an eternal sky." [41]

Such recognition must be heart-felt and internalized. If you're a Nine looking for routine, then make it a daily habit to repeat this message to yourself. The hope is that repeating this and like affirmations will eventually make it so in your mind. To discount yourself is tantamount to discounting your Divine Source from Whom you extend. Do you want to follow somebody else's agenda? Then follow the one your Divine Source has set for you. Be the luminous star that your are! Turn to your Source and say: *Let Thy Will be done.*

We have learned how Nines are prone to self-forgetting because of their deference and merging strategies used to compensate for their own perceived deficiencies. We also learned how such things contribute to sloth and inertia. Self-remembrance will prove therapeutic but require that Nines develop the virtue of action.[42] This involves more than just busy-work and routines. What's involved here is that of overcoming the inertia of personality to remain asleep.

As Sandra Maitri puts it: "Real action ... is a matter of shifting the habitual orientation of our own consciousness." [43]

She goes on to say:

Effort... is required since outer-directedness is one of the primary characteristics of our personality structure – it cannot exist without it, and we have to exert ourselves to overcome the inertia of this tendency.

This inertial pull to maintain our status quo with it outer orientation is one of the deepest and most insidious barriers in spiritual work, and is laziness in action once we are aware that we are asleep. It is the reason that deep and profound experiences of True Nature do not instantly change most people, despite all the stories we read about such occurrences... One of the major characteristics of our personality structure is its tendency to hang on to and quickly reassert the familiar, despite it being an unsatisfying or even a miserable one... Effort is needed if we are to overcome the undertow of the personality, lulling us back into the sleep of our conditioning... Our self-remembering cannot be sporadic or practiced only when we feel like it. To truly have a lasting effect on our consciousness, we must work with it continuously.[44]

One way to start becoming more inner directed is by becoming present to our bodies. Nines, like all of us, need to feel their bodies, not just to occupy them absent-mindedly. They need to turn their attention to physical sensations both at the edges, as well as to the interior regions of the body.[45]

If we continue doing this diligently, "In time, our awareness deepens so that it includes the fabric of our whole field of consciousness – our soul, in other words."[46]

At that point, we will come to apprehend that we are something beyond the physical body, that the soul animates the body and is its vehicle. Once consciousness deepens to the non-physical dimensions of things, we begin to get closer to our Essential Being, what Sandra Maitri calls our True Nature.[47]

This is what I have labeled the Higher Self, the One without a history and without mental constructs defining and structuring the experience of ourselves, others, and the world. This Higher Self is our Higher Reality, our Essential Being.

Being present to our bodies and souls in the moment also entails that Nines must begin to catch themselves in the act of zoning-out or retreating into their imaginations. Finding Essence requires that one be fully engaged in the present moment, even if that means reclaiming one's anger and rage.[48]

No longer should such things be repressed or denied. Such repression and denial of "true feelings" are what has caused the Nine to lose touch with themselves, to forget how they really feel about things which frustrate the achievement of their wants and goals. To gain control over the ego in conscious awareness will require the Nine to reduce psychological defensiveness.

The Nine's 'silent observer' must catch the ego when it tries to bury unpleasant feelings or thoughts which might disturb the Nine's peace of mind. Repression and denial are two of the ego's ploys which constitute obstacles to the awareness of Love's presence, which is everyone's natural inheritance.[49]

In addition to all this heavy spiritual and psychological lifting, there are still some other work recommendations for Nines. For instance, it would be good for Nines to start learning to voice their own opinions in public, without apologizing for them or minimizing their worth.

Starting up a new relationship or a new project could prove to be energizing. Nines need to get excited about something to overcome their inertia. They need to commit to finishing one task, before thinking about or starting another. Nines should try not to become scattered and diverted by trivialities. Produce schedules and then stick to them. And finally, Nines should surround themselves with supportive people. They can thereby receive validation, support, and positive regard for taking personal positions. Such external affirmations and validations can build self-confidence and feelings of self-worth.[50]

Part Three

CHAPTER THIRTEEN

GENERAL THERAPEUTIC RECOMMENDATIONS FOR ACHIEVING INNER PEACE

We shall not cease from exploration / And the end of all our exploring / Will be to arrive where we started / And know the place for the first time.
T. S. Eliot

In the beginning of our life we all came into this world with no sense of self. At birth, there was no ego-identity for any of us. Gradually, as we physically matured, we started to form psychological boundaries of separation between our perceived selves and the external world. Suddenly there was 'me' and 'not-me.' Gone was the complete merging between ourselves and our mother, complete oneness with her and with everything else for that matter. There dawned the perception of our 'mother-as-other'.

Out of the undifferentiated Oneness of Being, the ego also began to establish perceptual boundaries causing us to see separate and distinct objects and persons in relation to us. Thus, the creation of our ego-identity entailed separation from others, our Source, and our Essential Self.

Our central nervous systems and perceptual mechanisms fashioned their own reality in terms of space, time, object, cause-and-effect, and so on. Spiritual realities which could not be perceived by the senses or understood in terms of rational, scientific categories of the mind did not exist – or so our egos had some of us believe.

There's a problem here however. We can understand how by using the ego's logic, the color-blind person could argue that 'color' does not exist in reality because his or her visual apparatus is not equipped to perceive it. Of course, the person would be deceived. So too we are deceived into thinking that Ultimate Reality must be limited and defined by our perceptual mechanisms.

The suggestion here is that another Higher Reality exists beyond the space-time continuum, a reality which can only be known through direct and immediate apprehension, not through science, logic, or sensory experience. This is what the mystics, philosophers, saints, and the spiritually enlightened have taught us for centuries. It is at this higher plane of existence that true healing occurs.

Another thing we learned earlier is that physical, personal, and social reality, as we perceive it at least, is not objectively 'out there', but really a cognitive construction, a product of our mind. The sometimes 'horrible world' that victimizes us and treats us unfairly is actually a projection of the defensive ego. For example, when we are slighted, it's our ego that takes offence. Were someone free of the ego's vanities, no offence would be taken. Whether there was or was not anything offensive that occurred depends on the interpretation of the ego – an interpretation which uses the ego's filter of values and beliefs. Likewise, when we're criticized, it is the voice of the angry ego that attacks back.

In terms of our previous character studies, we found that that so-called horrible world comes in nine different varieties or is seen from nine alternative perspectives or worldviews. Each worldview derives from ego projections, distortions and illusions which result from losing touch with one's Essential

Being, the Oneness and Unity with our Source alluded to earlier.

The ego comes to our 'emotional rescue', helping us to devise ways of compensating for our perceived inadequacies, however deceptive and dishonest its efforts. Following the ego's instructions, some would have to find fault with the world and lay blame on others in order to feel good about themselves. Others would see an uncaring world and have to manipulate others into liking them. Still others would have to impress us, defeat us, or withdraw from us to get what they wanted. By now, we've uncovered most of the ego's tricks and its ingenious strategies.

One general recommendation for spiritual self-healing involves a return to our right-mind which is tantamount to regaining awareness of our Higher Self. We must disengage and dis-identify with the ego. As counter-intuitive as it may seem in this world of branding and self-promotion, we need to forget about developing a positive self-concept or doing things to enhance our self-esteem; such things only inflate the ego.

As *A Course in Miracles* teaches, no self-concept or image of yourself can replace the truth of who you really are. If our true Higher Reality involves Unity and Oneness with God, then there's no need to feel good about yourself. Does God need to work on His self-image? How about His confidence and self-esteem? It sounds foolish and irreverent even to ask the questions. So too with us. Feeling the need to do something about one's image or self-esteem is already to presuppose deficiency, imperfection, inadequacy, moral blemish, and so on. Such things also presuppose difference and separation from our Perfect and Unblemished Source.

Our orientation should not be to compensate for our perceived lacks and grievous faults, but to serve as extensions of God in the world. We need to become instruments of His infinite Peace and Love. The miracle here is that giving is receiving. As we join with others, acting as messengers and extending God's gifts of Peace and Love to them, those gifts are returned to us in kind. In other words, if you want peace, give it. If you hunger for love, share it. Be the love you want to see in the world.

No need to prove the positive effects logically or by scientific study; just try doing what's suggested here and see what happens yourself. It could be a miracle! Let your own experience be the proof.

What we truly were essentially, (and always continued to be, in fact), before the ego took over, was somehow lost or buried in the deep recesses of our unconscious mind. When we lost awareness of our True Self – that which existed before the ego emerged – we lost sight of who we really were.

Forget the fascination with out-of-body experiences; we had an 'out-of-our-right-mind' experience. We became insane, developing the problem of mistaken identity. We all decided to identify with ego-personality and forgot who we really are in Essence. We became our ego and forgot about our Essential Nature. We fell into some sort of dream-like fugue state, choosing to side with our empirical self.

Alas, some still think that's all there is to us: flesh and bones, brains, neurons, and synaptic transmissions. The fundamental error in such thinking comes in not recognizing the fact that the physical packaging is not the same thing as the spiritual inner contents.

There really is a 'ghost in the machine', to use a philosophical expression. We call this ghost *spirit*. Some may try to reduce spiritual experience to some kind of mental disturbance, psychosis, or neuro-biological process, but in the last case at least, that would be like trying to reduce the experience of love to increased heartbeats, elevated hormones, and particular brain-wave patterns – all of which can be measured during an intense feeling of love.

If we could, then we should be able to make somebody love

287

us by simply injecting them with adrenalin, increasing their hormonal oxytocin levels, and teaching them to alter brain-wave patterns through focused attention in ways that match those of others in love. Do you really think that once all the physiological, neurological and bio-chemical requirements were met, the person would suddenly fall in love with us? *If you believe that, I know someone named Ego, who's certainly willing to sell you some fantasy land in Florida!*

When we are in touch with our Essence, which means to be in unity with our Source, we experience the pristine and unblemished Perfection so sought by the One. From the perspective of the Two, we recognize that we are an extension of our Source's Love, that indeed we are Love, for Love is all there is, for God is all there is. This is what the Two is and needs to remember. It's what we all need to remember. From the vantage point of the Three, we appreciate the fact that we all have Unconditional Value that nobody can take away. No conditions can be placed on our self-worth; it is inviolate. No longer do we feel deficient or lacking. From the Four's viewpoint, we recognize that we are entirely Whole and Complete. We are already infinitely more than what our vain egos would have us become. We already have far in excess of everything our pathetic dreams and fantasies would have us yearn for.

When experiencing our Essence, no longer do we dream of being somewhere else, or of being with someone else. We find equanimity here and now.

Like the Five, when we are in touch with Essence, we go beyond mere sensory-based knowledge and purely intellectual pursuits to Platonic *Gnosis*, the direct knowing of the Divine Mind, what Plato would call the realm of forms. With *Gnosis* we exhibit Buddha Consciousness or what some might describe as the Christ-Mind. We experience our own life in ways reminiscent of the thoughts and feelings of these spiritual masters. We also feel secure and safely grounded in Being like the enlightened Six. We are solidly supported by Divine Providence. This in turn allows us to experience openness and exquisite Joy like the Seven. As with the eternal youth, we worry not about the future; nor do we fret about the past. When we experience Essence, we are present to the moment, to all that is now. Now is all there is. Presence is Essence. When living out our self-transcendence, we also feel the Eight's Vitality and Essential Strength. Possessing and experiencing all of these Essential Qualities exhibited by the types mentioned so far, what else could follow but the Nine's Peace of Mind. Of course, this Peace does not just belong to the Nine, just as all the other Essential Qualities just mentioned don't just belong to any singular personality type. The Nine is simply the character type that has the most issues with this element of Essential Being. In fact, any of us, who have identified with the ego as well, have seemingly lost what the Nine thinks they've lost. Inner Peace is the opposite of the troubled mind. Where there is anxiety, depression, anger or fear, there is no experience of Inner Peace. Inner Peace has its own symptoms captured below in a somewhat humorous tongue-in-cheek fashion. Each so-called symptom really contains a prescription. Read on and see.

Symptoms of Inner Peace

Be on the lookout for symptoms of inner peace. The hearts of a great many have already been exposed to inner peace and it is possible that people everywhere could come down with it in epidemic proportions. This could pose a serious threat to what has, up to now, been a fairly stable condition of conflict in the world.

Some Signs and Symptoms of Inner Peace
- A tendency to think and act spontaneously rather than dwell on fears based upon past experiences [read: we

should think and act spontaneously]
- An unmistakable ability to enjoy each moment
- A loss of interest in judging other people
- A loss of interest in judging one's self
- A loss of interest in interpreting the actions of others
- A loss of interest in conflict
- A loss of worry (a very serious symptom!)
- Frequent, overwhelming episodes of appreciation
- Contented feelings of connectedness with others and nature
- Frequent attacks of smiling
- An increased tendency to let things happen rather than make them happen
- An increased susceptibility to the love extended by others as well as the uncontrollable urge to extend love to others.

Caution
If you have some or all of the above symptoms, please be advised that your condition of inner peace may be so far advanced as to not be curable. If you are exposed to anyone exhibiting these symptoms, remain exposed only at your own risk.

In our efforts to achieve Inner Peace, it is important to remember that there are actually nine different paths, depending on one's character type. Recommendations and directions on how to get there are type-specific, in ways we've already covered.

Shockingly, when we finally arrive at our final destination, we will see that our long spiritual journey was never very long at all, actually only from 'here to here'. We never really left our True Selves; for that was and continues to be an impossibility. We couldn't have been anybody other than who we truly were in the first place.

The ego-personality was just a bad dream, a dream from which hopefully we have all been awakened. To quote T.S. Eliot, we now *arrive where we started and know the place for the first time.* We are finally home, home at last! From Essence we departed and to Essence, we now have returned.

The learning of the world is built upon a concept of the self adjusted to the world's reality. It fits it well. For this an image is that suits a world of shadows and illusions. Here it walks at home, where what it sees is one with it. The building of a concept of the self is what the learning of the world is for. This is its purpose; that you come without a self, and make one as you go along. And by the time you reach maturity you have perfected it, to meet the world on equal terms, at one with its demands. A concept of the self is made by you. It bears no likeness to yourself at all... Now must the Holy Spirit find a way to help you see this concept of the self must be undone, if any peace of mind is to be given you.

A Course in Miracles

If we 'get it' that reality is all made up in our minds, this has enormous implications for how we see and judge others. The reality we see is just a worldview created by the ego to handle fear and compensate for separation from our Source. We're desperately deceiving ourselves to relieve pain and to get what we want. In our efforts to do so, we often feel threatened and so must protect ourselves with rationalizations, denials, and other defensive self-deceptions. Sometimes, offence and attack on others is the best ego strategy to employ. If I feel inadequate, I can criticize my neighbor for being a braggart. If I'm insecure about my self-worth, I can attack my colleague's vain ambitious. If I don't know, I can judge somebody as stupid or arrogant. The list goes on.

The point is that all this judgment, criticism, self-deception and attack precludes the possibility of finding Inner Peace. At some level, we know the venom we spew at others is undeserved and more a product of our own insecurities. For this we feel guilty and ashamed. Of course, the ego comes to our emotional rescue and has us project such things onto others. We feel better that way, at least for a moment – until the guilt and shame of doing this unfair and undeserved projecting return in even greater amounts. The spiral downward from attack and blame to guilt and shame, and then from guilt and shame to attack and blame, can only come to an end when we look upon others with forgiveness.

The problem was never with 'them', but always with us. By forgiving others and understanding how others can also fall prey to their own ego illusions, greater peace of mind is possible. Their mis-behaviors and indiscretions and vain pursuits are nothing more than our's, that is, our defensive ego strategies used to cope with psychological and emotional pain. Those who hurt us, annoy us, and irritate us are desperately calling out for love; this is what spiritual discernment reveals.

This is how Jesus of Nazareth could teach us to love our enemies. And when we overlook the seemingly apparent deficiencies of others with respect to their lower ego-identities, using Divine Love and spiritual discernment as our guides, we are able to do the same for ourselves. The loving acceptance we give to others is a wonderful gift we offer to ourselves. By forgiving our brothers and sisters in life, we make it easier for us to forgive ourselves.

Speaking of others, it is important that we recognize our true intentions in our relationships and interactions with them. If, for example, the real reason one is social and gregarious is to receive self-validation, then the person is just fishing for compliments as a way of compensating for their own feelings of insecurity. If, say, you go out of your way to help others just so they'll invite you back, then you're just manipulating them to help you feel good about yourself. If you contact people and do things together for purposes of networking and furthering your career, this is tantamount to emotional dishonesty. Some people develop intimate and long-term relationships to compensate for what they lack, whether it be confidence, looks, or wealth. In this case, our special love relationship is little more than using another for one's own selfish egoistic purposes.

As soon as the partner fails to deliver on the desired goods, the relationship is over. With respect to marriages, the ones I have in mind here are not made in Heaven, but made by the deceptive ego getting people into something that is doomed from the start. Not to worry, the ego will find you your next better half as soon as the divorce is complete, if not before.

When the partners we've selected stop satisfying our wants, remember they have not necessarily done anything wrong. It is *our* demands, needs, wants, and expectations that cause us frustrations. By failing to live up to our ideal pictures of what they should become, others are not guilty or deserving of attack. We see in others what we choose to see. If we changed our expectations, we would alter our perceptions.

Whether a person or situation is met with welcome or disinvitation, assistance or avoidance, love or hate, all depends on the state of one's mind. As we say: *It's all in your head.* To put it bluntly, give others a break and forgive them when they don't live up to your personal designs for them. Their values, beliefs, and worldviews may not match yours and there's nothing inherently bad about that.

Our perverse egos not only interfere with our special love relationships, but also with what *The Course* calls our *special hate relationships*. Understood is the fact that all of us know people we love to hate. We save our most poisonous venom for these individuals.

We're reminded here of an insight offered earlier in the book: *What you can't stand about others is precisely what you don't like about yourself.* Mamma taught us this a long time ago.

So the next time you spend time getting angry over somebody you can't stand or contemplate getting back at someone; stop and reflect. Ask yourself what is going on inside. Clearly, your ego is enraged on behalf of your Lower Self (the Higher Self can't be touched). Remember, your enemy is your teacher; if not that, then the psychological mirror you look into as you see the things you hate about yourself. Since it's self-destructive to hate oneself, blame and attack must be directed outwardly, according to the ego that is. This provides a temporary sense of power, superiority, self-righteousness, pride, importance, and security, which will not result in lasting peace of mind. Feelings and perceptions related to someone's being better or worse, more or less important, and more or less powerful, all hinge on matters of separation and difference, not Essential Being, the only place true Peace of Mind can be found.

In closing, I'd like to finish with the prayer of St. Francis of Assisi. It is teaches us that forgiveness is our function and suggests that by *dying* (to the false ego Self), we are reborn into eternity, what we've been calling Essential Being. The prayer also underscores the universal spiritual teaching that to give is to receive. With devotion and reverence, let us commit ourselves to finding a better way to live as we say in our minds or out loud to ourselves:

> Lord, make me an instrument of Your peace,
> Where there is hatred, let me sow love;
> where there is injury, pardon;
> where there is doubt, faith;
> where there is despair, hope;
> where there is darkness, light;
> where there is sadness, joy;

O Divine Master, grant that I may not so much seek to be
consoled as to console;
to be understood as to understand;
to be loved as to love.
For it is in giving that we receive;
it is in pardoning that we are pardoned;
and it is in dying that we are born to eternal life.

Part Four

CHAPTER FOURTEEN

IMPLICATIONS FOR CONVENTIONAL REALITY THERAPY

The ego.. .keeps its primary motivation from your awareness and raises control rather than sanity to predominance.

There is choice that you have power to make when you have seen the real alternatives. Until that point is reached you have no choice, and you can but decide how you would choose the better to deceive yourself again. This course attempts to teach no more than that the power of decision cannot be in choosing different forms of what is still the same illusion and the same mistake.
Selections from *A Course in Miracles*

In the Introduction I mentioned that this work was in no way intended as just some sort of ancillary or further development of conventional Reality Therapy. Indeed, preceding discussions of character type psychodynamics indirectly constitute a devastating critique of William Glasser's basic notions of motivation, perception, the role of one's past in human behavior, and one's sense of self, insofar as he even acknowledges that people have one as choosing agents.

The idea that ego identity might be relevant to any person's choices or how they choose to control reality is not actually considered.

To help us clearly distinguish between conventional Reality Therapy and what I have in mind with respect to my own kind of spiritual psychotherapy, I will draw upon a number of insights regarding character type ego dynamics already discussed in the book and demonstrate their negative implications for Glasser's theory. As part of this critique, I will also uncover empirical deficiencies and inconsistencies in this thinking.

Before we get started with the critical analysis, however, a very quick outline of his position is helpful. For those having little or no familiarity with Glasser's work, but would like to learn more, a reading list is provided.[1]

What is Conventional Reality Therapy?

Reality Therapy is a method of counseling and psychotherapy based on a notion of brain functioning understood as a control system. The idea is that the human brain works like the regulator found in a thermostat. To anthropomorphize this little device for a moment, let's say that a thermostat seeks to regulate its own behavior by getting what it "wants" as a result of changing and controlling the world around it.[2] If the thermostat is set at 72 degrees Fahrenheit and the temperature dips below that, then the thermostat signals the furnace to start working, or "behaving," as it were. Once the "desired" temperature is reached, that is, once the thermostat gets what it "wants," it shuts off and stops "behaving." In the event that one has central air conditioning and the temperature rises significantly above 72, then different "behaviors" are called for; the air conditioning unit turns on instead and similarly turns off again as soon as it "gets what it wants." In effect, the thermostat "acts upon," "effects change," and hence "controls" the external environment in a want-satisfying fashion. It "chooses" to "behave" in alternative ways to get warmer or cooler, depending on what it "desires" at any given time.

For Glasser, human behavior functions much like the thermostat.

When we perceive a discrepancy between what we want and what we currently have or are getting, then we're motivated to behave in some fashion. Like the thermostat, we engage in regulatory control of our environments. According to Glasser, anyone's particular wants, which are virtually infinite in possibility, are ultimately based on five basic needs which he regards as genetically encoded in our DNA.[3]

Wants, then, serve an instrumental purpose and are designed to satisfy one or more of these needs which include:

1. the need to survive and reproduce
2. the need to belong
3. the need for power
4. the need for freedom and finally,
5. the need for fun.

Regarding the first need, Glasser says, "*What the genes do is best understood if we think of them as providing us with a series of biologic instructions that we must carry out if we are to exist, survive and prosper*".[4] With respect to the other needs, he writes: "*We are at our core biologic beings; that we satisfy some of our genetic instructions psychologically rather than physically makes neither the instructions less urgent nor the source less biologic.*"[5] In other words, these "basic psychological needs" are biologically and genetically programmed into us as well.

According to Glasser, when a child is born, the child has no idea of what satisfies its basic needs. In time, however, it begins to develop mental "pictures" of need-satisfying persons and objects in the environment. These pictures are then placed in what he calls a "mental picture album," speaking metaphorically. For instance, a hungry child might be fed a chocolate chip cookie by grandma, the babysitter. Subsequently, the image of a chocolate chip cookie may be filed away in the child's mind and called up the next time a bout of hunger arises. The hungry child "needs" to satisfy its hunger and has a picture in its mind as to how this can be accomplished. The child now "wants" a chocolate chip cookie to satisfy the basic need of survival, insofar as it involves hunger and food in this instance.

The cookie example is a good illustration of what Glasser claims we all do over an entire lifetime, namely, store pictures of need-satisfying things, people, events, situations, and experiences in our "picture albums" or what is called our "Quality World", an internal place in our mind which contains all the need-satisfying pictures of things we want.[6]

When we feel a basic need, we go to that world of stored pictures and choose what will be most need-satisfying in that moment. If we experience a need to belong, for example, we might picture a friend or some sort of group with which we associate. We might telephone that friend or get the group together. Behaving in this way gets us what we want and thereby satisfies a basic need which motivates us all. Since we all have different friends and belong to different groups, however, collections of pictures in the quality world will necessarily differ from individual to individual. We all have different ideas or pictured ideals of a what is satisfying to us. Though what we want may differ from one individual to another, it still remains that we all have the same five basic needs.

The internal quality world of mental pictures is important with respect to our perceptions and reactions to the external world. For example, if a parent has a picture of the kind of person they would like their son to be – say mature and responsible – and the parent sees the son misbehaving and acting in an immature fashion, then there arises a discrepancy between what is wanted and what the parent is getting. Just as the thermostat turns on the furnace or the air conditioner when there is a discrepancy, any discrepancy between the parent's perception of reality and the picture of what they want in their ideal Quality World will start the "behavioral system" into action. The greater the discrepancy between the perception and the want or need-satisfying picture, the greater the urgency to act, the more motivated one becomes. In this case, the motivation may translate into giving a stern lecture, administering some sort of punishment, making a polite request, or launching a threat perhaps. It is hoped that one, any, or all such behaviors would have a positive moderating impact on the conduct of the son. If the son changes his behavior and acts more maturely and responsibly, then the parent gets what they want.

Experience teaches us, unfortunately, that the behaviors chosen to "control reality" may not necessarily be successful in the long run. The son may buckle down and straighten up, but maybe not. The alternatives presented to the son may not be need-satisfying *for him* and consequently, he may choose to ignore all of the behavioral strategies used to try to change what he's doing. In this case, in order to get what the parent wants, they will have to come up with a behavioral strategy that is more satisfying to the son and allows both of them to get more of what they desire.

Insofar as people's chosen behaviors successfully get them what they want, they are in more effective control of their lives. To the extent that their chosen behaviors do not get people what they want or need, they are in less effective control of their lives. Either way, people are always "controlling"- that is to say, acting upon, arranging, organizing, and trying to effect change in their environments in order to satisfy their basic needs.

In therapeutic situations, individuals often seek help because they are largely unable to satisfy their desires. As already illustrated, parents often lament the behavior of their children. When our existing behavioral repertoire comes up empty in terms of getting us what we want, then new behaviors must be organized. With respect to our immature and irresponsible son, if threats and punishment don't work in "controlling" him, then other behavioral alternatives like "honest talk" or "sharing of feelings" might have to be considered and discussed with a counselor.

What is ultimately done to satisfy one's wants is ultimately the individual's choice. Of course, continuing to choose what does not work is counter-productive to living a need-satisfying life.

On this note, it might be worth pointing out that Glasser changed the name of his theoretical paradigm from "control theory" to "choice theory" in 1996 to reflect its clinical and educational use. Glasser wanted to emphasize the idea that human behavior is a choice.[7] Clearly, there are also some unfortunate negative conno- tations associated with the notion of 'control.' But by 'control', Glasser certainly does not mean coercing others to do as one wishes, although of course, it is possible that some people may try doing this in an effort to get what they want.

What Glasser generally means is that people try to regulate their behavior in need-satisfying ways and do the best they can to get what they want, however productive or unproductive, crazy or useless, that behavior may seem to others at any given time.

As psycho-biological organisms, we are always genetically instructed to satisfy our basic needs. We must behave or act upon the world to accomplish this task. It is in this respect that we are either in less or more effective control. For Glasser, we are constantly trying control reality to get what we want.

While there's much more to "control theory" or "choice theory" than I've discussed here, enough has been covered to explain some of its practical therapeutic applications.

Robert Wubbolding, an associate and long time colleague of

Glasser, gives a particularly clear account of the reality therapy counseling technique captured in the acronym: WDEP. (In actual practice, the process would not be as regimented and clearly sequential as presented here for explanatory purposes.)

Understanding that, the elements are as follows: First, the "W" stands for "want or wants." In counseling, the client often presents problems and complaints about others in their life. There often seems to be much blame to cast and many dissatisfactions to be raised.

Appreciating that blaming, criticizing, and complaining do not usually lead to need-satisfaction, the reality therapist eventually asks in response: *What do you want?*

This can come as a shock to someone who thinks that others are the source of their problem and that changes *in them* will solve it. Appreciating the fact that one person cannot "control" the life of another, the reality therapist likes to bring things back to the client. Of course the therapist helps the client to articulate particular wants so that they have a clearer "picture" of what they're looking for.

Once wants are established, the client is asked to identify what it is that they're actually doing to get what they want. Plainly, the "D" stands for "doing."

Now, after the client or patient becomes self-aware in terms of their chosen behaviors, the therapist asks: *Is what you're currently doing helping you or hindering you from getting what you want?* This is the evaluation component captured by the "E."

Finally, if it's the case that current behaviors are not working, then the client is encouraged to *plan* new behaviors for successful achievement of stated wants – "P."

If it's the case that getting what one wants is impossible (e.g., finding love and belonging with deceased family members), then new possibilities for love and belonging must be explored. New "pictures" of what would satisfy that basic need have to be developed.

In short, the client needs a new plan of action. The basic need itself doesn't disappear. The problem is that some people get stuck in their lives because they keep trying to go back to old ways of satisfying their basic needs.

When this is impossible, like in the example just given, severe depression and hopelessness can result because no alternatives seem to be available to get one's basic needs met. This fact brings to mind a couple of other important elements of choice theory and its applications to Reality Therapy.

First, reality therapy focuses on the present and to a lesser extent, the future. People either are, or are not, getting their basic needs met *now*. If they are, no problem; then they are in greater or more effective control of their lives. If they are not, however, they must examine what they're presently doing and figure out why what they're doing isn't working. Perhaps it will be necessary to do the same things a little bit differently in the future; or, it may be necessary to find better and completely different alternative behaviors to take more effective control. Whatever the case, this is all a matter of personal choice. Whether their behavioral strategies are effective or not, people are always "controlling" the present reality they create.

Still another important component of choice-theory or control theory involves its rejection of stimulus-response behavioral psychology (see "Chapter One: Mistakes of Common-Sense Psychology").

Like myself, Glasser does not accept the notion that stimulus events necessarily determine behavior in any cause-and-effect fashion. He believes that we all have choices about how to act or respond in any given situation. He very much advocates personal responsibility and refuses to let people dwell in the past or use the past as a defensive rationalization for what they're doing right now in their lives. What has happened is over. The past cannot be changed. So, Glasser advocates that we move forward focusing on the present, something over which we do have greater control. Even if one was mistreated and didn't get what one wanted or needed in the past, one still has the free "choice" to live a need-satisfying life now. Appropriate action can be taken. Planning new actions, engaging in them, and evaluating their outcomes in terms of personal wants is what conventional reality therapy is all about. Putting people in effective control of their lives is the ultimate end.

Criticisms of Conventional Reality Therapy

The first serious problem with William Glasser's choice theory deals with its notion of 'basic needs.' The criticism I wish to make is that his list is arbitrary, incomplete, and reductionistic, and that furthermore, it is essentially reflective of 'Eight' psychology – very likely Glasser's own (For a description of the Eight, see Chapter Eleven). On top of all this, Glasser is inconsistent with respect to how he conceptualizes basic needs in the first place.

In what follows, we'll first examine the arbitrary nature of Glasser's list. Then we'll criticize his limited conception of basic needs in terms of character type psychodynamics – those already discussed in previous chapters in this book.

In this section of our critique, we'll also expose his inconsistencies and tendency to be reductionistic. As for the latter part of this critique, we'll pay attention to how Glasser's understanding of 'perception' is problematic and how his failure to take people's personal histories and existential psychodynamics into account can very likely cause reality therapists to send their clients down self-defeating paths of behavioral change.

Oftentimes, all that is really accomplished by helping people get their 'basic needs' met is a perpetuation of their own wrongly perceived deficiencies and inadequacies. As we'll see, a program like Glasser's, which ignores spiritual matters of Essence and focuses entirely on satisfying the biologically-based needs of the Lower Self or psychological ego, is ultimately doomed to fail.

Anyone interested in matters of psychology and human motivation might be intrigued by the list of basic needs produced by Glasser, but still be curious as to exactly how he arrived at it. The needs, as listed, present a certain face validity, but one would nonetheless expect some sort of empirical support or rational justification for them, that is, if one were going to build an entire system of counseling and psychotherapy using them as a theoretical foundation, as Glasser has done. A careful reading of Glasser's works, including his seminal book entitled, *Control Theory: A New Explanation of How We Control Our Lives*, reveals that no adequate scientific or rational support is provided. In one place, he writes:

> Through a careful examination of my life, I have come to believe that I am driven by five needs that together make up the forces that drive me. While lecturing, I have discussed these with thousands of people, and almost all agree that they are driven by the same needs. As I describe them, examine your own life and see if you are driven by these needs. I believe you will find that you are, because it is likely that all creatures of the same species are driven by similar forces.[8]

From the quotation above, we see that Glasser is certainly guilty of fallacious reasoning. He uses his own personal experience of what "motivates *him*" or "drives *him*" as evidence that others are likewise motivated. A sample of one does not permit empirical generalization. Admittedly, this hasty conclusion does not go entirely unsupported. Personal anecdotal evidence, stemming from conversations with members of his own lecture audiences, is also used to support his position. However, such evidence is clearly unacceptable again. Even if the overwhelming majority of lecture participants did agree with Glasser, majority opinion is still insufficient to prove his point. One simple reason is because the majority is often wrong. Something is not necessarily true or justified simply because most people share the same beliefs. For instance, the majority once believed that the sun revolved around the earth until the Polish astronomer Nikolas Kopernik (better known as Copernicus) proved otherwise. In addition, it's quite possible that those attending Glasser's lectures – often paying customers – were drawn to him for whatever personal reasons and were thus more inclined to agree with Glasser at the outset. In this case, Glasser's informal survey would suffer from a skewed sample. Perhaps it was their like-mindedness which drew audience members to his lectures in the first place and gave rise to their agreement about basic needs. The point is that Glasser's beliefs and his personal anecdotal evidence are neither rationally justifiable, nor scientifically, empirically or statistically acceptable to prove his case. His list constitutes little more than a personal and arbitrary selection.

In claiming that Glasser's basic needs' list is arbitrary, I don't wish to suggest that humans are not ever driven or motivated by the things he says. Common experience informs us that normally functioning individuals need care, love, and a sense of belonging in their lives. We all seek our own survival and like to enjoy freedom and fun. Some of us might even be inclined to accept such things as central, or at least highly important, to our lives.

As for power, while not everyone wants to be the boss, exert control over others, or take charge, it probably goes without saying that personal empowerment is a good thing. Virtually everyone likes to feel in charge of their own lives and not submit to the will of others who would have their way with us.

So, my second criticism is not that Glasser is entirely wrong about his list of basic needs; the problem is that his list is incomplete. What's meant by 'basic' is also a little troubling, as we soon shall see.

The incomplete nature of Glasser's list can be illustrated if we go back to our discussion of character type psychodynamics. Take Character Type One, for instance. As we learned, Ones put a high premium on integrity and moral perfection. They have a deep psychological need to do things right. Their *raison d'être* is to reform the world and make it a better place. Ones have a thirst for moral righteousness and wisdom in action.

Curious Fives, by contrast, are greatly motivated by a desire to know and understand the world or how things work. They *need* to know the truth and to apprehend ultimate realities by getting past mere superficial appearances. Again, this is not an option for Fives. This yearning is deep-rooted. The search for truth and understanding is part of the fiber of their being.

As for Nines: they, like all of us, have a basic desire for *peace of mind*. Given their existential psychodynamics, this desire is likely greater for them than for other character types. To achieve peace of mind, they seek out solitude and rest. They are not adrenalin junkies looking for fun and excitement. Alone in the woods, they are not out to conquer the world, establish meaningful relationships with others or develop a sense of belongingness.

Though Glasser could argue that freedom comes with solitude, it should be pointed out that freedom (from work, others, social responsibility, and so on) is sought instrumentally as a means to an end, and not as an end in itself. Freedom to be alone in the woods is a way to cultivate peace of mind. Peace of mind is not sought to find freedom in the woods.

So, for Nines, *peace of mind* is even 'more basic' or funda- mental than freedom. *What good is it to be free to do what you like if you're psychologically tormented at the same time?* asks the Nine. The Nine's entire psychodynamic is geared around achieving inner peace. This is what the Nine needs to live a satisfying life and much of what the Nine desires or wants (e.g., the freedom to be left alone) is directed toward that end.

That being said, Nines don't put the same value on freedom as Eights might. Freedom might help create the conditions for peace of mind, but it is not necessary. I believe it was a stoic slave who once said: "*I was never freer than when I was on the rack*" (a torture device). What was motivating the stoic even under painful and unfree conditions was attaining a state of mind free of disturbance. For the stoic slave, *lack of freedom touches not the soul, not in the slightest degree.*

In addition to what's been said so far, a Four could take exception to Glasser's list of basic needs insofar as the need for establishing identity or authentic self-expression is not included. Again, Glasser could argue that expressing yourself however you'd like enhances freedom and is fun and that his list is inclusive of the Four's concern. But, as before, freedom and fun are tangential to what's really at issue here. Self-expression may be fun, but one does not try to develop an authentic sense of self for the ultimate purpose of having fun. In fact, honest self expression can sometimes communicate anguish and emotional pain. The need to tell the world that *I am here, I exist, I matter,* and *I am unique* is arguably as basic as the psychological need for fun. The Four would likely suggest, *More basic!*

Glasser could argue that if the Four's need for self-expression does not satisfy the need for fun, perhaps the need at issue could be freedom instead; after all, without freedom, self-expression would be stymied. In response, one could grant that personal freedom creates favorable conditions for self-expression, but again it would be wrong to conclude, therefore, that self-expression is something everybody wants in order to satisfy their need for freedom. Unique and authentic self-expression is not about spreading freedom's wings; it's more about the way one expresses one's identity in original and creative ways. It's about finding and expressing one's inner, subjective truth. In tone and in substance, there is little of such concern in choice theory psychology.

For Glasser, emotional depth is reduced to an observable behavior designed to satisfy one's basic needs – in particular, those identified and defined by him. Surprisingly, Glasser's writings suggest that he might allow for *motivational diversity* and not require that we view everyone's behavior in terms of his arbitrary and limited list of basic needs. In *Control Theory*, he writes:

> It is not important to the thesis of this book that I establish with any certainty what the basic needs are that drive us. To gain effective control of our lives, we have to satisfy what we believe is basic to us and learn to respect and not frustrate others in fulfilling what is basic to them. All you will ever know is what drives *you*, just as I will know only what drives *me*. We cannot look into other people's heads and see what drives them. We can listen to what they tell us and look at what they do, but we should not make the mistake of assuming that we *know* what drives them.[9]

The problem with Glasser's statement above acknowledging "motivational diversity" – something which comes later in *Control Theory* – is that it contradicts what he says earlier in the same book. On the one hand, Glasser quite clearly and explicitly makes the claim that basic needs are all biological and genetically programmed, including psychological needs, while on the other hand, he waffles on about the certainty of *what the basic needs are that drive us.*

As he suggests above, you and I could have different drives. If the need for fun is "genetically programmed," however, it is not optional or a matter of personal choice. We don't need to look into people's heads. If it is "biologic," as he claims, and part of human nature, then it must drive all of us, not just some of us.

Another problem with Glasser's recognition of "motivational diversity" stems from the fact that it makes him guilty of a second inconsistency. On the one hand, his inability to establish "certainty" *vis-à-vis* his list of basic needs leads him to say that we cannot know for sure what drives others; we can only know what drives us. However, notwithstanding his admitted lack of certainty, and his admission that we can't read other people's minds about what motivates or drives them, Glasser writes:

> I hear frequently from people who claim that there is just one universal need: the need to know. They claim that this single need underlies everything: All of our behavior is initiated by this need to find out more and more about the world around us. I don't deny that knowing about the world, and ourselves as part of it, is important, but I don't believe this is a basic need and that we try *to know* just for the sake of knowing any more than I believe that people climb mountains just because they are there... Ask your neighbor if he would like to join you in learning to read Chinese, and if he can't wait to start, I will believe the need to know.[10]

On the subject of religion, Glasser continues:

> Others argue that religion, or the holy spirit inside us all, is the single need from which all others are derived. This may be, but there is no hard evidence that this is the case for many people....The bulk of the evidence is that for many, religion may be a basic need, but it is unlikely that it is any more *the* basic need than the need to survive.[11]

In fairness to Glasser, he's objecting in these passages to the notion that there's only one universal need from which all others are derived. He doesn't believe truth or religion are primary, and in the case of the latter, any more basic than survival. Fair enough. But on the topic of the need to know, Glasser draws an analogy with mountain climbers suggesting the real reason they climb is for power, fun, freedom or companionship, not to find out what's on top.[12]

The corollary is that people don't really pursue knowledge for its own sake, but that there's some further end at stake as with the mountain climber.

Now, the problem for Glasser is that he's reading the minds of people whose minds cannot be read, if we take him at his word, at least.

Remember what he said, *"All you will ever know is what drives you, just as I will know only what drives me"*.

So, on the one hand, Glasser is doing what by his own admission is impossible. Second, he's discounting the need to know and trying to reduce it to his original list of basic needs – the needs for which he has no solid justification or proof. These are the ones which must simply be a reflection of "what drives me," speaking as William Glasser. On top of all of this, he admits that what's 'basic' to one person may not be 'basic' to another person.

In other words, his list of basic needs may be basic *to him*, but not to others. If one accepts this premise, then the need to know may be basic and intrinsically valuable for some people and not reducible to any of Glasser's five basic drives. The fact that your neighbor doesn't wish to learn Chinese with you doesn't mean he or she isn't interested in learning about philosophy or insects or how engines work. At the risk of displaying some bad reasoning myself or committing some sort of an *ad hominem* attack against Glasser, let me suggest his glib and dismissive remarks about studying Chinese are ones typically expected from anti-academic Eights who tend to see things in oversimplified dichotomous terms.

On this note, it's fascinating to observe that Glasser makes so much of power, freedom and fun in his motivational psychology. The need to "control reality" is certainly central to the Character Type Eight. Remember that Eights don't like to be told what to do by others. Eights don't like to play by others' rules and so they always try to make sure they set the ground rules themselves in any interpersonal interactions. Matters of freedom and control are central preoccupations of the Eight overly concerned with boundary issues. Recall too, that Eights are gut-based, instinctive types out to feed their appetites in a big way. They lust (want) for pleasure and all that satisfies them far more than most, if not all, other character types. Getting what they want, when they want it, and having the authority, resources, power or control to do so are extremely important life concerns. For the Eight, it's fun to beat and defeat and compete! Winning, and, if necessary, taking from others or exploiting them are ways in which survival is enhanced. Playing dirty can be fun!

The possibility that Glasser's Control theory (or Choice theory, if you prefer) is largely a reflection of his own Eight psychology is also evidenced in his approach to traditional psychiatry. Glasser is very much a maverick denouncing traditional psychiatry as misguided, claiming that many psychiatrists are little more than pill-pushers. His anti-establishment position is captured in the title of a recent book: *Warning: Psychiatry can be Hazardous to Your Mental Health.*[13]

As a psychiatrist himself, Glasser refuses to prescribe medications to his patients suffering from psychological disturbances.[14] He regards most of such problems as stemming from poor choices and unsatisfying relationships. Of course, troubled relationships often involve "boundary issues" – things near and dear to the heart of any Eight.

One further note: in his writing and in his therapeutic practice, Glasser changes nouns like 'anger,' 'depression,' and 'anxiety' into verbs like "angering," "depressing," and "anxieting."

He does so because he believes that conventional English does not capture the 'fact' (in his mind) that emotions are not "internal states" but actions. When someone looks to 'be' depressed, they are actually *depressing*, according to Glasser, doing the best they can to get what they want.

So, whether Glasser is balking at traditional psychiatry or changing the English language to suit his own needs, it appears quite clear that Glasser "goes his own way." I mention this not as a criticism, but simply as an observation to reinforce the idea that Glasser's own maverick tendencies, coupled with his treatment of instinctive needs like power and freedom make him somewhat of a poster child for Character Type Eight.

For now, we'll dispense with any further psychoanalysis of the man himself. Who he is as a person is not as relevant as the ideas that emerge from his ego-personality. Nonetheless, his motivational theory does appear to be as much a projection of his character type as was Hobbes' political philosophy (see Chapter Nine) or Friedrich Nietzsche's conception of the will-to-power (see Chapter Eleven).

Further insights into the limitations and inadequacies of control theory or choice theory psychology can be revealed by changing linguistic paradigms on Glasser and using the language of psychological pioneer Abraham Maslow. In his now classic book entitled, *The Farther Reaches of Human Nature*, Maslow distinguishes between what he calls deficiency-motivation ("D-motivation") and being-motivation ("B-motivation").[15] The former works like Glasser's thermostat. When the individual detects a "deficiency" of some sort (e.g., dehydration), he or she is "motivated" to act in order to rectify the situation (e.g., by drinking liquids). Something is wrong, as it were, and needs to be fixed. In response to biological and psychological deficiencies, hungry people are motivated to eat and insecure people are motivated to achieve, please, or impress. Generally speaking, people with average to below average mental health are motivated by D-motives. Their behavior aims primarily to gratify lower level requirements.

Musicians must make music, artists must paint, poets must write if they are to be ultimately at peace with themselves. What humans can be, they must be. They must be true to their own nature. This need we may call self-actualization.

Abraham Maslow

By comparison, those who have their "basic needs" met and suffer from no lower-level deficiencies – so called self-actualizing individuals – are moved by "meta-needs" or higher-order needs, ones different than those listed by Glasser.[16]

It might be more accurate to say that meta-motivations are not based on any conception of needs as such, but on "values" instead. For Maslow, highly functioning people don't live their lives preoccupied with reducing tensions or rectifying deficits, as is the case for Glasser. They are not "controlling" the environment around them to satisfy basic needs which at any moment could be frustrated. Rather, they aim to enrich and enlarge their experience of life.[17]

Maslow's Being-motivation is much more closely aligned with the Essential Qualities discussed earlier under each of the character types. Values and ideals can and often do provide the impetus for action. The motivating force could also be spiritual in nature, emanating from our *inner guidance*, something like Socrates' *Daemon*, or the Voice of the Holy Spirit calling out to us. Priests and nuns with religious vocations understand the concept very well. To have a religious vocation is to be called into service by some higher power. Religious or not, Being-motivation contains an element of self-transcendence – going beyond oneself or one's psychological ego.

Our sense of inadequacy, weakness and incompletion comes from the strong investment in the "scarcity principle" that governs the whole world of illusions. From that point of view we seek in others what we feel is wanting in ourselves. We "love" another in order to get something ourselves. That is, in fact, what passes for love in the dream world....The Self That God created needs nothing. It is forever complete, safe, loved and loving. It seeks to share rather than to get; to extend rather than project. It has no needs and wants to join with others out of their mutual awareness of abundance.

A Course in Miracles

A quick look at Maslow's list of meta-motivations reveals that the first three are *Truth*, *Goodness*, and *Beauty*. As suggested before, such things are motivational preoccupations for Fives, Ones, and Fours. Maslow also includes in his own list of B-Values the meta-need of *Unity* or *Wholeness* – a major focus of the Nine.

We also find *Justice* and *Aliveness*, matters of particular concern for Eights and Threes respectively. For Maslow, actions which are motivated by such values reflect the psychology of self-actualizing individuals. They are higher-order in nature or, as Maslow suggests by the title of one of his books, they reflect *the farther reaches of human nature* – not what's primitive, instinctual and basic.

Another thinker whose research points to higher-level motivations is Viktor Frankl. An existential psychiatrist, (and also a One), he argues that the 'will-to-meaning' is *the* basic motivational force in life. For proof, he points out that people who have lost all meaning in their lives are often prepared to commit suicide. A life without meaning is not a life worth living for some individuals.

Thus, Glasser's 'survival' takes a back seat to meaning-fulfillment. The will-to-meaning can be more "basic" than the desire to live. What good is fun, freedom or power, or even life itself, if they all *mean nothing* in the mind of the person who has all such basic needs met? Take many Hollywood celebrities for instance; money and fame can buy them a lot of power (influence), fun (parties), freedom (travel) and friends (belonging), yet it is precisely these self-indulgent super-stars, who are getting their 'basic needs' met, that are ending up in addiction rehabilitation centers. Some of them intentionally commit suicide, while others die accidentally by drug overdose or by excessive efforts to get what they want or think they need. The lesson is that sometimes getting what you want is the worst thing that can happen.

Not only is it serious that Glasser leaves out matters of meaning with respect to human motivation, but it's curious that *happiness* doesn't show up either. Philosophical utilitarians like John Stuart Mill and Jeremy Bentham believe that maximizing happiness is the ultimate goal of living. Sevens would vouch for its impor-tance as well. What good is all the power and freedom in the world if one is still left unhappy? It's possible to have all of Glasser's basic needs met, yet still be miserable and dissatisfied. In this case, the "lack" is not biological, physical or genetically based, but rather spiritual in nature.

Viktor Frankl actually has a term for this spiritual emptiness; he calls it an *existential vacuum*.[18] For Frankl, it is through a process of self-transcendence that one finds meaning in life. Living strictly to satisfy one's own needs is a morally and psycho-logically bankrupt proposition for him. It is when individuals move beyond themselves or when they invest themselves in others or in a cause greater than themselves that they find happiness, meaning and peace. A life solely devoted to getting everything one wants is, for Frankl, a life destined for depression and existential despair.

The works of Frankl and Maslow deserve certainly much greater discussion and critical analysis in the context of conventional reality therapy than I have provided here. It would also be interesting to compare how their theories compare with the insights and observations concerning the notion of character type addressed in this book, but alas, such a discussion would take us too far afield from my primary intentions.

Suffice it to say that meta-motivations dealing with B-values like Truth, Beauty, Goodness, Happiness, Meaning, Justice, Aliveness, and Unity or Wholeness point to many of the Essential Qualities of the character types profiled in this book.

Such values and qualities fall well outside what conventional reality therapy is properly equipped to deal with. Without an inclusion of these value-based being motivations, Glasser's list of basic needs is sorely inadequate to capture the full spectrum of what makes humans behave they way they do. In what might be regarded as typical Eight fashion, Glasser chooses to ignore or diminish the importance of existential, religious, spiritual, and moral values in his motivational scheme.

To acknowledge them would require "interiority," something alien at least to unhealthy and emotionally insensitive, action-oriented Eights. An integration of them would also necessitate the establishment of norms that could place limits on personal want satisfaction – not a desirable thing for mavericks like Glasser seeking to be in control of themselves. In short, his failure to deal with spiritual, moral, and transcendental values limits the scope of his motivational theory. Life is not just about fun, freedom, power, survival or belonging, notwithstanding Glasser's claims to the contrary regarding their 'basic' nature.

When he's not being inconsistent, Glasser takes his 'partial view of motivational reality' and tries to understand everyone else's problems in terms of it. Sadly, this is like trying to fit a square peg into a round hole. People are indeed psychologically different and so are their 'basic' motivations. If Glasser wishes to continue adhering to his one set of 'basic needs,' then I think my criticisms stick, so to speak. If, on the other hand, he continues with his inconsistencies and allows people to be driven by alternative and/or higher-order needs, ones other than *his* basic needs for freedom, fun, and so on, then the entire program of reality therapy is called seriously into question. What was once considered 'basic' is no longer basic. The entire motivational premise of reality therapy collapses. There arise important wants and needs that motivate behavior and yet have nothing to do with those biological and genetically determined ones identified by Glasser.

The will-to-meaning – like happiness, the need to know, or the inner urge toward self-realization or self-transcendence – is not even on Glasser's radar screen. This constitutes a serious psychological oversight. By dwelling on lower reality and on basic need satisfaction, he ignores and misses entirely the higher reality encompassed by spiritual concerns pertaining to matters of essential being and psychological self-transcendence. Getting past the needs of the ego-personality is one of the major goals of Higher Reality Therapy.

It is important to get past the ego-personality's wants and needs, for to cater to them would be to prolong what could be termed the individual's *metaphysical malaise* or what Frankl might term *noögenic neurosis*. If you're a character type Three, for instance, you may want more notice from your fellow workers. You may need their attention to feel good about yourself. When you earn their notice you feel important.

Now, let's suppose you strategized with your therapist as to how you might increase this attention and let's also assume you planned and successfully achieved your goal in this instance. You and your reality therapist might regard the situation as one in which you gained more effective control of your life by fulfilling to a much greater extent your basic need for power. Yet, in this case, you might end up doing yourself more harm than good.

Recall that Threes are insecure about their status and crave the approval of others. They fail to recognize their essential self-worth as human beings. For unhealthy Threes, life is all about performance, production, and presentation. They are always scrambling to prove to the world that they are important by virtue of their successes. The greater the need to provide this proof to the world, the more unhappy the individual. For their own sense of well-being, Threes need to learn that their personal value as human beings does not hinge on their accomplishments. Others don't need to notice them to establish their existential worth. Encouraging individuals to produce plans which feed their own sense of deficiency is self-defeating in the end, certainly unhelpful and more than likely detrimental to their psychological hygiene.

Without an acknowledgment of people's Essential Qualities, those beyond the concerns of the ego-personality, conventional reality therapy risks perpetuating the very distress and dissatisfaction it seeks to alleviate.

However much the Three gets what it wants (e.g., praise, promotion, and pre-eminence), peace of mind will still elude our struggling and insecure star. Power is not what the Three really needs, but healing of their spiritual wound stemming from childhood. Troubled Threes don't understand that their value as human beings is unconditional.

We've seen why Glasser chooses to focus on the present in dealing with clients. As mentioned before, he doesn't want people to wallow in past miseries. He also doesn't want clients to blame people in their past for what they're doing today. The problem with this "present" focus on getting one's needs met in the here and now is that it fails to appreciate the existential psychodynamics which led up to the client's wants and problems in the first place. Such problems cannot simply be ignored or dismissed or casually tossed into the trash bin of one's developmental history.

As our Three example points out, working on promotions or dressing to garner attention may serve to get what the individual wants, but what's wanted is exactly the problem. Since childhood, Threes have irrationally tried to impress significant others to establish their self-worth. Continuing this practice is certainly not advised for them.

By contrast, for withdrawn fear-based Fives, learning to become more visible, noticed and productive may be a good thing – even if that's *not* what they want. Ironically, doing and getting what you don't want may in some instances be healthier than doing what you do want in hopes of getting what you believe you need.

For Threes, allowing others to lead or take center stage is probably an exercise they need to engage in to extricate themselves from the clutches of their vain and insecure egos. Insofar as this is true, the value of satisfying particular wants and needs can only be properly understood in the broader context of one's personality and ego dynamics.

Such things have a developmental history. Without taking this history into account, conventional reality therapists operate in a timeless vacuum and fail to meet the client or patient where they are at in their life. The past needn't serve as an excuse for the present; but it should be understood that the client's perceptions of reality and current needs have been influenced by their past.

To empathize and relate on a deep and intimate level, the therapist cannot just pay lip-service to one's personal history before scurrying off to identify one's wants. To do so would be to dismiss interiority in deference to practical action.

For some types, exploring the inner world is exactly what they need, even if it's not what they want. As a general observation Eights, like Threes, Sevens, and Nines probably have the most 'inner work' to do insofar as their worldviews don't allow much time or inclination for self-reflection. As for Threes, their preoccupation with image and self-improvement, is not what is at issue here. The concerns are much deeper. It's not about getting more notice to gain greater power. Getting what they want really means just choosing different ways and means of perpetuating the same illusions and the same mistakes. From the perspective of Essential Being, there is no deficiency or lack that needs to be rectified. That's the ego's ploy to deceive the lower psychological self. One's Higher Essential Self needs nothing to be complete. This point is underlined in *A Course in Miracles* in a section entitled, "The Illusion of Needs."[19]

> While lack does not exist in the creation of God, it is very apparent in what you have made. It is, in fact, the essential difference between them. Lack implies that you would be better off in a state somehow different from the one you are in. Until the 'separation,' which is the meaning of the 'fall,' nothing was lacking. There were no needs at all. Needs arise only when you deprive yourself. You act according to the particular order of needs you establish. This, in turn, depends on your perception of what you are.

Of course, *your perception of what you are* is actually your ego-identity or sense of psychological self. It is this illusory Lower Self which establishes priorities and determines which needs are "basic" to use Glasser's terminology. Perceived deficiencies and orders of needs are thus different for each of the nine character types we've studied. Each character type is deluded into thinking there's something essentially wrong with their very being as human organisms. Each character type spends an entire lifetime trying to make up for deficiencies that don't exist.

It's like we're going from room to room searching for the key to happiness, when all along it's been in our hand. We've just been unaware of its presence. We've never lost what was always in our possession; we just didn't know it.

Not only is the issue of needs problematic, but in the context of our earlier discussion of character type psychodynamics, we can see that Glasser's understanding of perception is also something deserving criticism. Glasser accepts what might be termed "naive realism" when it comes to perceiving the external world.

This position can be encapsulated by the saying: *What you see is what you get.*

On this view, objects in the world exist independently of the one perceiving them. For Glasser, what one sees is either satisfying or it is not when compared to pictured wants in the individual's Ideal Quality World. The problem with naive realism, however, is that it fails to grasp the fact that perception is a product of an interaction between the subject and stimulus events originating in the environment.

Think back to our example of Becky and Lance in Chapter One. Lance was that good-looking high school football captain who was offended by the new good looking girl in class, Becky. Recall how Lance perceived her as a "stuck up bitch" but that he completely misread her intentions and body language. She was actually fearful and insecure and afraid to speak up or be noticed by others. What Lance saw was an object of scorn, a manifestation of his own insecurities projected onto Becky. Were Lance not insecure about his reputation, Becky's behavior would probably have been perceived neutrally, as nothing necessarily good or bad. Because, however, she posed a threat to Lance's wish to be seen as some sort of sex idol, Lance made her into something she was not, namely a "bitch." True, she was not giving him what he wanted, but this does not make her into some sort of object of scorn, objectively speaking She turns into one as a result of Lance's projected insecurity. Had Becky paid attention to Lance, he probably would have perceived her as a real "hotty" instead. The point is that whether Becky is a "hotty" or a "bitch" is all in the mind of the perceiver - in this case, Lance. In Lance's mind, Becky had been transformed into a threat. And, like most people, Lance responded to the threat with an attack on Becky - a kind of psychological pre-emptive strike to make himself feel better about himself. Lance's experience here goes to show that what we see is always a projection of our wants and fears.

Our minds are not just blank slates. We do not just passively sit back and perceive the world or have it stamp itself on our psyches. Our minds actually have a hand in constructing the reality we perceive. To change one's mind, therefore, is to change one's perception of reality. Focusing exclusively on behavior or on controlling the external environment, rather than on internal psychodynamics is what makes reality therapy psychologically naive and misguided both in its intent and in its process.

The charge here, then, is that reality therapy's emphasis on effectively controlling the environment in need-satisfying ways misses the true source of anyone's psychological and emotional problems.

If, as the stoic reminds us, *external things touch not the soul*, then there's really no need to rearrange the world in order to make up for perceived deficiencies and for what's lacking in ourselves, as we see it.

When we re-arrange what's inside, the outside will look refreshingly different as a result. This rearranging will require that we re-train the mind to perceive reality differently. Effective control of our lives is an inside job.

If Lance no longer feels deficient and no longer needs others' attention, at that point Becky will be perceived much more positively. Re-organizing behaviors to elicit more want-satisfying responses from Becky continues to leaves Lance in trouble.

Therapeutic efforts to assist in that reorganization are again psychologically naive and not very helpful. As long as Lance, like the rest of us, remains a slave to his ego by virtue of his vanity and insecurity he will never have effective control of his life, regardless of those few fleeting moments of ego satisfaction.

This is the lesson taught by Higher Reality Therapy and missed by Glasser's choice theory psychology. We would be well advised, then, to get our "internal world" in order rather than focusing on controlling external reality. *As within, so without.*

Appendix

Character Type Self-Diagnostic

Aim: The purpose of this self-diagnostic is to help you identify your character type. Doing so will enable you to select appropriate psycho-hygienic recommendations provided in the book which are individually suited to you and others sharing your character type's perspective and psychological worldview.

Instructions: Listed below are statements reflecting different psychological attitudes, behaviors and orientations. In the blanks, indicate how well that numbered statement (or statements) reflects what you are really like or what you really believe using the scoring scheme provided below. Honesty in your answers is paramount.

Scoring Number Scheme
   1 = not at all like me
   2 = a little bit like me
   3 = very often like me
   4 = almost always like me

Identifying Statements

_____1. It's extremely important for me to be morally correct. I want to do the right things for the right reasons.
_____2. The impression I make on others is very important. I need people's approval.
_____3. My life is more goal-oriented than relationship-based.
_____4. I want to understand myself and it's important to me that others understand me as well.

_____5. I am very observant. I tend to see things that others overlook.

_____6. I am a traditionalist. I strongly identify with groups, institutions, and friends.

_____7. I am unpredictable, spontaneous, and fun-loving. I often overdo it at parties.

_____8. I am forcefully direct, no-nonsense, able to take charge when necessary.

_____9. I always try to keep the peace. Harmony is very important to me.

_____10. I try to achieve perfection at work. Others should do the same.

_____11. I generally stay away from people who don't appreciate me.

_____12. I make constant efforts to make a success out of myself.

_____13. Beauty and taste are extremely important to me. My physical surroundings affect my mood in a very strong way. I go out of my way to beautify my surroundings.

_____14. I have a strong desire to seek knowledge and to understand the world around me.

_____15. I try never to show disloyalty. It is one of the worst things you can do.

_____16. I encourage people to lighten up and not take things so seriously.

_____17. I don't shy away from conflict, opposition, and confrontation.

_____18. I avoid disagreement and confrontation whenever I can. There's little point in arguing.

_____19. I tend to be formal and idealistic.

_____20. I make people feel comfortable and welcome by catering to their needs.

_____21. I often go out of my way to make good first impressions on people.

_____22. I'm easily bothered or hurt by intrusions.

_____23. I tend to hold on to whatever little or however much I have acquired.

_____24. I hate it when people don't give me clear guidelines and when they don't tell me where I stand.

_____25. I really like and enjoy most people. They tend to like and enjoy me.

_____26. I hate being told what to do.

_____27. I'm usually perceived as friendly and easygoing, though sometimes I can be very stubborn.

_____28. I get upset when people flagrantly break the rules.

_____29. I sometimes annoy people when I'm only trying to help them.

_____30. I can read my audience and adapt to whatever group of people I'm with.

_____31. I am more envious than most people.

_____32. Being alone is no problem for me. I love my privacy.

_____33. I'm more sensitive and aware of dangers and threats than most other people are.

_____34. I simply dread being bored, and having no plans and nothing to do.

_____35. I usually need to be in control of things and to exhibit my strengths.

_____36. I prefer to be optimistic and above the conflict, rather than engaged and fighting.

_____37. You can count on the fact that I'll do what I promise. Integrity is very important to me.

_____38. I easily show my feelings, though I'm shy to express them because they might be offensive to others.

_____39. I like competition. I like to win and achieve.

_____40. I often appear melancholy, sad, and emotionally withdrawn.

_____41. I have a tendency to intellectualize my problems, rather than deal with them from the heart.

_____42. I tend to be highly anxious, worried about all the bad things that could happen.

_____43. I enjoy novel activities and physical sports that provide excitement and fun.

_____44. I emphasize practical results over abstract ideals. Doing is more important to me than planning.

_____45. I often need encouragement to get things started. Once I get going, I'm okay. It's getting started that's the problem.

Scoring: The preceding statements' numbers have been arranged and assembled according to character type. Next to each statement number, place the numerical value you assigned to it reflecting your level of agreement.

1. One: The Perfectionist

    1. _____
    10. _____
    19. _____
    28. _____
    37. _____

    Total: _____ (add values next to 1, 10, 19, 28, and 37 to calculate total)

2. Two: The Selfless Giver

    2. _____
    11. _____
    20. _____
    29. _____
    38. _____

    Total: _____

3. Three: The Performing Star

   3. _____
  12. _____
  21. _____
  30. _____
  39. _____

Total: _____

4. Four: The Deep-Feeling Individualist

   4. _____
  13. _____
  22. _____
  31. _____
  40. _____

Total: _____

5. Five: The Observant Thinker

   5. _____
  14. _____
  23. _____
  32. _____
  41. _____

Total: _____

6. Six: The Committed Loyalist

   6. _____
  15. _____

24. _____
33. _____
42. _____

Total: _____

7. Seven: The Eternal Youth

7. _____
16. _____
25. _____
34. _____
43. _____

Total: _____

8. Eight: The Powerful Maverick

8. _____
17. _____
26. _____
35. _____
44. _____

Total: _____

9. Nine: The Detached Peacemaker

9. _____
18. _____
27. _____
36. _____
45. _____

Total: _____

My highest total is _____ reflecting the _____
character type. (see mini-descriptions below. More detailed
descriptions for each of the character types are found in Part Two
of the book. Read those chapters to help you confirm your type.)

Character Type Mini-Descriptions

Character Type

One: The Perfectionist - Rational, hardworking, ethical, serious,
emotionally rigid or unexpressive; can be wise and discerning;
often impatient, angry and humorless.

Two: The Selfless Giver – Caring and nurturing; friendly, self-sacri-
ficing and altruistic; can also be possessive, proud and manipulative, creating dependency relationships.

Three: The Performing Star – Adaptable and chameleon-like;
motivated by success; ambitious and image conscious; can be
overly competitive, emotionally shallow, driven, opportunistic
and arrogant.

Four: The Deep-Feeling Individualist – Typically shy and introverted; quiet and gentle, inspired and creative; sees themself as
special; introspective; can be moody, melancholic, inhibited, and
self-pitying.

Five: The Observant Thinker – Intelligent, insightful and curious;
independent and innovative; great capacity for knowledge and
system-building; can be emotionally distant, isolated, eccentric,
intellectually intense and awkward with people.

Six: The Committed Loyalist – Dependable and trustworthy; committed, reliable, security-oriented, dependent on others, compliant, endearing; can also be defensive and suspicious, creating "in" and "out" groups; may hide fear by acting tough.

Seven: The Eternal Youth – Usually energetic and enthusiastic; playful and spontaneous, likeable and optimistic; can be infantile, excessive and self-centered or insensitive to others.

Eight: The Powerful Maverick – Powerful, strong, assertive, resourceful, forthright and decisive; Aggressive; can be belligerent and confrontational; overly controlling.

Nine: The Detached Peacemaker – Stable, trusting; blends into their surroundings; at one with the world; accommodating; avoids conflict, minimizes upset; can also be stubborn, inattentive, impenetrable, lazy and neglectful.

Endnotes

Introduction
1 Source: Thomas Merton, *The Way of Chuang Tzu,* Copyright 1965, by The Abbey of Gethsemani. New Directions Publishing Corp.

Chapter 1
1 John Locke, "Introduction", *An Essay concerning Human Understanding,* Vol.1 (New York: Dover Publications, 1959 [original publication 1894]), p.26. Collated and Annotated by Alexander Campbell Fraser
2 Quotation from Leslie Stevenson and David L. Haberman, *Seven Theories of Human Nature,* (New York: Oxford University Press, 1974), p.93
3 Immanuel Kant, *Critique of Pure Reason,* (tr.) Norman Kemp Smith, St. Martin's Press, New York, 1965, p.41
4 Piaget quotation taken from Anthony Falikowski, *Experiencing Philosophy,* Pearson Prentice Hall, Upper Saddle River, NJ, 2004, p.231

Chapter 2
1 See Jean Piaget, *The Construction of Reality in the Child,* Ballantine Books, New York, 1974

Chapter 4
1 Don Richard Riso and Russ Hudson, *The Wisdom of the Enneagram,* Bantam Trade Paperback: New York, 1999, p.101
2 Ibid.,
3 Ibid., p.102
4 Nine Points of View: Enneagram Series, DVD produced and directed by Helen Palmer, Berkeley, California,
5 See Claudio Naranjo, *Character and Neurosis: An Integrative*

View, Gateway Publishers, Nevada City, CA, 1994, p.52

6 Ibid.

7 Ibid., pp.54-55

8 Ibid.,

9 In the *Wisdom of the Enneagram*, Riso and Hudson have done an excellent job of outlining the psychological and spiritual practices that will help Ones develop. The insights expressed in that work will inform the following discussion for the One as well as later discussions dealing with recommendations for the other eight character types.

10 This insight derives from *A Course in Miracles*. For a more accessible discussion of this point, see Gerald Jampolsky, *Love is Letting Go of Fear*, Celestial Arts: Berkeley CA, 1979

11 Riso and Hudson, ibid., p.121

Chapter 5

1 Richard Rohr and Andreas Ebert, *The Enneagram: A Christian Perspective*, The Crossroad Publishing Company: New York, 1999, p. 63

2 Ibid., p.63

3 As reported by a female Two in *Nine Points of View: Women on Relationships. DVD produced by Helen Palmer*

4 Riso and Hudson, ibid., p.55

5 The notion of special relationship is discussed at length in *A Course in Miracles*. In the *Course*, one also finds discussion of special hate relationships. Both serve the purposes of the ego, putting us in a state of wrong-mindedness, one which draws attention away from our essential nature. The discussion here borrows ideas from the *Course*.

6 Claudio Naranjo, ibid., pp.46-48

7 Claudio Naranjo, ibid.

8 Riso and Hudson, ibid., p.149

9 Ibid.

Chapter 6
1 Riso and Hudson, ibid., p.155
2 Claudio Naranjo, ibid., p.52
3 Riso and Hudson, ibid.p.157
4 Ibid., p.158
5 Jerome P. Wagner, *The Enneagram Spectrum*, Workshop Materials, 1998
6 Claudio Naranjo, ibid., p.57
7 Riso and Hudson, ibid., p.154
8 Naranjo, ibid., p.54-55
9 Riso and Hudson, p.169
10 Ibid.
11 This wonderful advice is dispensed by Claudio Naranjo, ibid., p.64
12 ibid., p.65
13 Shakespeare, *Hamlet* II, ii, 115-117
14 Riso and Hudson, ibid., p.172
15 Ibid.,

Chapter 7
1 Riso and Hudson, ibid., pp.182-183
2 Ibid.
3 For a detailed discussion of this lost essential aspect, see Sandra Maitri, *The Enneagram of Passions and Virtues*, Jeremy P. Tarcher/Penguin, New York, 2005, pp. 131-150
4 Riso and Hudson, Understanding the Enneagram, Revised Edition, Houghton Mifflin, Boston, 2000, p. 378. I have capitalized the words identity and self (the authors don't) when referring to essence in order to distinguish the psychological ego-self and identity from one's Higher-Self which is spiritual in nature.
5 Helen Palmer, *The Enneagram*, HarperSanFrancisco: New York, 1988, pp.193-194
6 This expression is borrowed from Sandra Mairtri, *The*

Enneagram of Passions and Virtues, Tarcher/Penguin: New York, New York, 2005, p.138

[7] Riso and Hudson, *The Wisdom of the Enneagram*, p.180

[8] ibid, pp.183-184

[9] This quotation relating to the Four was taken from Michael J. Goldberg, *Getting Your Boss's Number*, Harper Collins, San Francisco, 1996, p.83

[10] Helen Palmer, *The Enneagram*, HarperSanFrancisco: New York, 1988, p.171

[11] Ibid., p.175

[12] Helen Palmer, *The Enneagram*, ibid., p.175

[13] Riso and Hudson, ibid., p.183

[14] Michael J. Goldberg, *Getting Your Boss's Number*, HarperCollins, San Francisco, 1996, p. 86

[15] Helen Palmer, ibid., pp.191-192

[16] Riso and Hudson, ibid., p.201

[17] See Riso and Hudson, for a detailed discussion of unhealthy Fours, ibid., p.188. The discussion here draws heavily from their work.

[18] Sandra Maitri, ibid., p.138

[19] Claudio Naranjo, cited in Maitri, ibid., pp. 138-139

[20] These eloquent and apt descriptors are taken from Maitri, ibid., p.140

[21] Ibid., p.140

[22] Ibid., p.134

[23] Ibid., p.136

[24] Maitri, ibid., p.132

Chapter 8

[1] Riso and Hudson, *Personality Types*, pp.178-179

[2] Don Riso and Russ Hudson, *Understanding the Enneagram*, Revised Edition, 2000, p.378

[3] Helen Palmer, *The Enneagram*, p.231

[4] Helen Palmer, *The Enneagram*, p.204

5   Ibid.,

6   Helen Palmer, ibid., pp.215-216

7   Riso and Hudson, *The Wisdom of the Enneagram*, p.209

8   Claudio Naranjo, *Ennea-Type Structures*, ibid., p.88

9   Ibid., p.88

10 Ibid. p.88

11 Helen Palmer, ibid., pp.212-213

12 Riso and Hudson, *The Wisdom of the Enneagram*, p.216

13 Riso and Hudson, ibid., p.216

14 From Helen Palmer, ibid., p.227

15 Riso and Hudson, *Personality Types*, p.176

16 Helen Palmer, ibid., p.227

17 Riso and Hudson, ibid., p.176

18 Ibid., p.174

19 Claudio Naranjo, *Ennea-Type Structures*, ibid., p.89

20 Helen Palmer, *The Enneagram*, ibid., p.235

Chapter 9

1   A.H. Almaas's point is made in Sandra Maitri, *The Enneagram of Passions and Virtues*, p.155

2   Ibid.

3   Riso and Hudson, *The Wisdom of the Enneagram*, p. 259

4   Ibid., p.259

5   Michael Goldberg, *Getting Your Boss's Number*, HarperSanFrancisco: New York, 1996, pp.132-133

6   Thomas Hobbes, *Leviathan*, Francis B. Randall, ed. (New York: Washington Square Press, 1964), p.84

7   Ibid., p.85

8   When guilty of using a genetic fallacy in reasoning, one criticizes an idea or premise on the basis of its source, and for no other reason. Whether or not an argument in favor or against abortion should be accepted, for example, doesn't hinge on whether the source of the argument is a man or woman. The argument stands on its own, regardless of the gender of the

arguer.

9 Riso and Hudson, *Personality Types*, p.224

10 Riso and Hudson, *The Wisdom of the Enneagram*, p.238

11 Michael Goldberg, *Getting your Boss's Number*, p.138

12 On August 22, 1939 Hitler said the following to his military leaders:"Kill without pity or mercy all men, women or children of Polish descent or language. Only in this way can we obtain the living space (Lebensraum) we need. The destruction of Poland is our primary task. The aim is... annihilation of living forces."

13 Micheal Goldberg, ibid., p.133

14 Claudio Naranjo, ibid., p.102

15 Ibid.

16 Sandra Maitri, ibid., p.158

17 Ibid., p.162

18 Ibid., p.169

19 Michael Goldberg, *Getting Your Boss's Number*, Harper Collins, San Francisco, 1996, p.127

20 Claudio Naranjo, *Ennea-Type Structures*, Gateways Publishers, Nevada City, CA, 1990, p.101

21 Ibid.

22 Riso and Hudson, *The Wisdom of the Enneagram*, p.248

23 Sandra Maitri, ibid.

24 Riso and Hudson, ibid., p.235

25 Sandra Maitri, ibid., p.170

26 Claudio Naranjo, ibid., p.110

27 Ibid. p.105

28 Ibid., p.103

29 Riso and Hudson, *The Wisdom of the Enneagram*, p.244

30 Claudio Naranjo, *Ennea-Type Structures: Self-Analysis for the Seeker*, pp.102-103

31 Claudio Naranjo, ibid., p.106

32 Riso and Hudson, *The Wisdom of the Enneagram*, 253

33 Learn more about Herbert Benson's relaxation response by

going on-line and visiting his website: http://www.tranceso-lutions.com/free-hypnosis-downloads/ts-the-relaxation-response-herbert-benson.pdf The quotation here comes from that site.

34 Ibid., Benson lists a number of positive results associated with the relaxation response on his website.

35 Riso and Hudson, ibid., p.254

36 Quotation was found in Goldberg, ibid.

37 Rohr and Ebert, p.142

38 Ibid., p.142

39 Goldberg, ibid., p.148

40 Rohr and Ebert, *The Enneagram: A Christian Perspective*, p.142

Chapter 10

1 Riso and Hudson, *Understanding the Enneagram*, revised edition, (2000), p.375

2 See Jerry Wagner, *The Enneagram Spectrum of Personality Types*, Metamorphous Press, Portland Oregon, 1996, p.103; also see Helen Palmer, *The Enneagram: Understanding Yourself and Others in Your Life*, HarperSanFrancisco, New York, 1988, p.279.

3 Michael Goldberg, *Getting Your Boss's Number*, p.156

4 Riso and Hudson, *The Wisdom of the Enneagram*, pp.264-265

5 Michael Goldberg, ibid., p.157

6 Claudio Naranjo, *Ennea-Type Structures*, p.117

7 Helen Palmer, *The Enneagram: Understanding Yourself and Others in Your life*, p.277

8 Ibid., p.283

9 ibid., p.294

10 Michael Goldberg, ibid.,

11 Ibid., p.156

12 Michael Goldberg, ibid., p.156

13 Rohr and Ebert, ibid.,p.146

14 Ibid., p.146

[15] Jerome Wagner, ibid., p.103

[16] Riso and Hudson, *The Wisdom of the Enneagram*, p.262

[17] Ibid.

[18] Riso and Hudson, ibid., p.266

[19] Michael Goldberg, ibid., p.156

[20] Ibid.

[21] Ibid., pp.291-292

[22] Helen Palmer, ibid., p.299

[23] Ibid., p.284

[24] Ibid., p.284

[25] Rohr and Ebert, ibid., p.147

[26] Ibid., ibid., p.147

[27] Helen Palmer, *ibid.*, p.277

[28] Riso and Hudson, *The Wisdom of the Enneagram*, p.272

[29] Riso and Hudson, *The Wisdom of the Enneagram*, p.279

[30] Sandra Maitri, *ibid., p.174*

[31] Riso and Hudson, ibid., p.273

[32] Ibid., p.279

[33] Sandra Maitri, ibid., p.176

[34] Ibid., p.176

[35] Sandra Maitri, ibid.,p.184

[36] Song lyrics borrowed from the following on-line site: www.lyrics007.com

[37] Helen Palmer, ibid., p.297

[38] Ibid., p.297

[39] Ibid., pp.297-298

[40] Riso and Hudson, *The Wisdom of the Enneagram*, p. 281

[41] Rohr and Ebert, ibid., p.160

[42] Helen Palmer, ibid., p.303

[43] Riso and Hudson, ibid., p.286

[44] Sandra Maitri, ibid., p186

[45] Sandra Maitri, ibid., pp.187-188

Chapter 11

1 Riso and Hudson, *The Wisdom of the Enneagram*, p.291
2 Michael Goldberg, ibid., p.162
3 Helen Palmer, ibid., p310
4 Claudio Naranjo, ibid., p.132
5 Riso and Hudson, ibid., pp.292-293
6 Ibid., p.291
7 Margaret Frings Keyes, *Emotions and the Enneagram: Working Through Your Shadow Life Script*, Molysdatur Publications, Muir Beach, California, 1992, p.63
8 Sandra Maitri, ibid., p.59
9 Riso and Hudson, ibid. p.297
10 Helen Palmer ibid., pp. 313-314
11 Helen Palmer, ibid., p.309
12 Claudio Naranjo, ibid., p.133
13 Ibid., p.133
14 Claudio Naranjo, ibid., p.132
15 Claudio Naranjo, ibid., p.131
16 Ibid., p.131
17 Riso and Hudson, ibid., p.302
18 Ibid., p.302
19 Friedrich Nietzsche, *The Anti-Christ*, (tr.) R.J. Hollingdale, Penguin Books, Baltimore, Maryland, 1968, p.115
20 Michael Goldberg, ibid., p.110
21 Riso and Hudson, ibid., 290
22 ibid.
23 David Daniels and Virginia Price, *The Essential Enneagram*, p.50
24 Riso and Hudson, ibid., p.293
25 Helen Palmer, ibid., p.330
26 Sandra Maitri, ibid., p.53
27 Riso and Hudson, ibid., p.305
28 Ibid., p.296
29 Riso and Hudson, ibid., p.308

[30] Jerry Wagner, ibid., p.115
[31] Claudio Naranjo, p.127
[32] Ibid., pp.128-129
[33] Ibid., p.128
[34] Ibid., p.129
[35] Helen Palmer, ibid., p.329
[36] Jerry Wagner, ibid., p.113
[37] Riso and Hudson, ibid., p.
[38] Riso and Hudson, ibid., p.300
[39] Helen Palmer, ibid., p.328
[40] Claudio Naranjo, ibid., pp.134-135
[41] Claudio Naranjo, ibid., p.138
[42] Ibid., p.138
[43] Jerry Wagner, ibid., p.116

Chapter 12

[1] Oscar Ichazo, cited in Riso and Hudson, ibid., p.340
[2] Riso and Hudson, ibid., 340
[3] Ibid., p.340
[4] Don Riso and Russ Hudson, *Understanding the Enneagram: The Practical Guide to Personality Types*, revised edition, Houghton Mifflin: Boston, 2000, p. 376
[5] Jerome Wagner, ibid., p.123
[6] Riso and Hudson, *The Wisdom of the Enneagram*, p.317
[7] Ibid., p.317
[8] Riso and Hudson, *The Wisdom of the Enneagram*, p.63
[9] Riso and Hudson, ibid., pp.53-54
[10] Michael Goldberg, ibid., p.200
[11] Jerome Wagner, ibid., p.120
[12] Michael Goldberg, ibid., p.202
[13] Ibid., p.120
[14] Ibid., p.121
[15] Riso and Hudson, ibid., p.316
[16] Tao Te Ching, (tr.) L. Legge, *Sacred Books of the East*, Vol. 39,

1891

[17] David Daniels, ibid., p.54

[18] Claudio Naranjo, ibid., p.147

[19] Riso and Hudson, ibid., p.319

[20] Claudio Naranjo, ibid., p.148

[21] Riso and Hudson, ibid., p.319

[22] Riso and Hudson, ibid., p.331

[23] Ibid., p.331

[24] Ibid., p.330

[25] Ibid., p.330

[26] Michael Goldberg calls them philosopher stones; I prefer to think of Nines as people, rather than things. See Goldberg, ibid., p.200

[27] Riso and Hudson, p.337

[28] Ibid., p.316

[29] Riso and Hudson, ibid., p.337

[30] Ibid., p.320

[31] Riso and Hudson, ibid., p.330

[32] Michael Goldberg, p.201

[33] See Claudio Naranjo, p.143; also see Riso and Hudson, p. 326

[34] Margaret Frings, Keyes, ibid., p.73

[35] Claudio Naranjo, ibid., pp.142-143

[36] Riso and Hudson, ibid., p.326

[37] Claudio Naranjo, ibid., p.143

[38] Sandra Maitri, ibid., p.34

[39] Marianne Williamson, *A Return to Love: Reflections on the Principles of A Course in Miracles*, Harper Collins Publishers, New York, 1992, p.165

[40] Ibid., p.28

[41] A quotation from Marianne Williamson, ibid., p.25

[42] Sandra Maitri, ibid., p.43

[43] Ibid., pp.43-44

[44] Ibid., pp.45-46

[45] Ibid., p.46

46 Ibid., p.46
47 Ibid., p.48
48 Riso and Hudson, ibid., p.338
49 This is a basic teaching of *A Course in Miracles*.
50 Recommendations in this paragraph come from Helen Palmer, ibid., p.376

Chapter 13
1 I discovered this on the web years ago. No source provided at the time.

Chapter 14
1 For anyone wishing to learn more about the theory and practice of Reality Therapy, I suggest you read Glasser's *Control Theory: A New Explanation of How We Control Our Lives*; also have a look at his *Choice Theory: A New Psychology of Personal Freedom*; see also *Counseling with Choice Theory: The New Reality Therapy*. *Reality Therapy for the 21ˢᵗ Century*, written by Robert Wubbolding, is another excellent book which describes and extends Glasser's theory.
2 A good synopsis of Glasser's work is found in Robert E. Wubbolding, *Reality Therapy for the 21ˢᵗ Century*, Routledge: New York, 2000, pp.10-31. I have used it here for purposes of my own descriptive outline.
3 William Glasser, *Choice Theory: A New Psychology of Personal Freedom*, HarperCollins: New York, 1998, p.28
4 William Glasser, *Control Theory: A New Explanation of How We Control Our Lives*, p.7
5 William Glasser, ibid., p.9
6 Robert Wubbolding, ibid., p.18
7 This point is made by Wubbolding, ibid., p.11
8 William Glasser, *Control Theory*, ibid., p.5. In *Choice Theory: A New Psychology of Personal Freedom*, Glasser says: "I believe that some of these...genes provide a basis for our psychology

– how we behave and what we choose to do with our lives....I believe we are genetically programmed to try to satisfy four psychological needs: love and belonging, power, freedom, and fun.....our genes motivate us far beyond survival." (pp. 28-29)

9   Ibid., p.16
10 Glasser, ibid., pp.16-17
11 Ibid.,p.17
12 Ibid., p.17
13 Published by Quill: New York, 2003
14 Glasser, ibid., p.5
15 See Abraham Maslow, *The Farther Reaches of Human Nature*, Penguin: New York, 1976.
16 See Abraham Maslow, ibid., p.22; also see pp. 308-309
17 A good part of the summary description of Maslow's thinking comes from my own *Mastering Human Relations*, Pearson Education Canada: Toronto, 2007, pp.173-181
18 Viktor Frankl, *The Doctor and the Soul*, Vintage Books: New York, 1986,
19 See the hard cover second edition, pp. 13-14

BOOKS

O is a symbol of the world, of oneness and unity. In different cultures it also means the "eye," symbolizing knowledge and insight. We aim to publish books that are accessible, constructive and that challenge accepted opinion, both that of academia and the "moral majority."

Our books are available in all good English language bookstores worldwide. If you don't see the book on the shelves ask the bookstore to order it for you, quoting the ISBN number and title. Alternatively you can order online (all major online retail sites carry our titles) or contact the distributor in the relevant country, listed on the copyright page.

See our website www.o-books.net for a full list of over 500 titles, growing by 100 a year.

And tune in to myspiritradio.com for our book review radio show, hosted by June-Elleni Laine, where you can listen to the authors discussing their books.

MySpiritRadio